Lecture Notes in Computer Science

Commenced Publication in 1973
Founding and Former Series Editors:
Gerhard Goos, Juris Hartmanis, and Jan van Leeuwen

Christoph Bussler   Val Tannen
Irini Fundulaki (Eds.)

Semantic Web and Databases

Second International Workshop, SWDB 2004
Toronto, Canada, August 29-30, 2004
Revised Selected Papers

 Springer

Volume Editors

Christoph Bussler
National University of Ireland
Digital Enterprise Research Institute (DERI)
Galway, Ireland
E-mail: Chris.Bussler@DERI.org

Val Tannen
University of Pennsylvania
Department of Computer and Information Science
200 South 33rd Street, Philadelphia, Pennsylvania 19104-6389, USA
E-mail: val@cis.upenn.edu

Irini Fundulaki
Bell Labs Research, Lucent Technologies
600 Mountain Avenue, Murray Hill, NJ 07974, USA
E-mail: fundulaki@research.bell-labs.com

Library of Congress Control Number: 2005920538

CR Subject Classification (1998): H.2, H.3, H.4, H.5, I.2, C.2.4

ISSN 0302-9743
ISBN 3-540-24576-6 Springer Berlin Heidelberg New York

Springer is a part of Springer Science+Business Media

springeronline.com

© Springer-Verlag Berlin Heidelberg 2005
Printed in Germany

Typesetting: Camera-ready by author, data conversion by Scientific Publishing Services, Chennai, India
Printed on acid-free paper   SPIN: 11390060   06/3142   5 4 3 2 1 0

SWDB 2004 Co-chairs' Message

We would like to welcome you to the Proceedings of the 2nd International Workshop on Semantic Web and Databases (SWDB 2004) that was held in conjunction with the 30th International Conference on Very Large Data Bases in Toronto, Canada.

The Semantic Web is a key initiative being promoted by the World Wide Web Consortium (W3C) as the next generation of the current Web. The objective of this workshop series is to gain insight into the evolution of Semantic Web technologies and their applications to databases and information management. Early commercial applications that make use of machine-understandable metadata range from information retrieval to Web-enabling of old-tech IBM 3270 sessions. Current developments include metadata-based Enterprise Application Integration (EAI) systems, data modelling solutions, and wireless applications. All these different areas utilize databases and therefore the combination of Semantic Web and database technologies is essential.

In total, we received 47 submissions, out of which the program committee selected 14 as full papers for presentation and publication.

SWDB 2004 shared its two very interesting and stimulating keynotes with another one of the VLDB 2004 satellite events, the 5th Workshop on Technologies for E-Services (TES 2004). The first keynote was given by Boualem Benatallah with the title "Service-Oriented Computing: Opportunities and Challenges." The second keynote was given jointly by Alex Borgida and John Mylopoulos with the title "Data Semantics Revisited." The keynote speakers agreed to contribute to these proceedings by providing articles detailing their keynote talks.

We would like to thank all authors who submitted and presented papers at the workshop for their hard work and the keynote speakers for their excellent contributions. We would like to thank the Program Committee members for providing (almost) all reviews in time, and for the quality of their reviews, as it directly reflects the quality of the workshop and of these proceedings. Michal Zaremba did a great job setting up and maintaining the paper management system, we owe him many thanks for making the whole process very smooth. Finally, we would also like to thank all workshop attendees for their active participation, which added the final ingredient to what we believe was a very successful event.

October 2004   Christoph Bussler
                                                            Val Tannen

Workshop Organization

Program Chairs
Chris Bussler (Digital Enterprise Research Institute, Ireland)
Val Tannen (University of Pennsylvania, USA)

Steering Committee
Isabel Cruz (University of Illinois at Chicago, USA)
Vipul Kashyap (National Library of Medicine, USA)
Stefan Decker (Digital Enterprise Research Institute, Ireland)

Program Committee
Karl Aberer (EPFL, Switzerland)
Sibel Adali (Rensselaer Polytechnic Institute, USA)
Gustavo Alonso (ETH Zurich, Switzerland)
Bernd Amann (CNAM and INRIA, France)
Boualem Benatallah (University of New South Wales, Australia)
Sonia Bergamaschi (Università di Modena e Reggio Emilia, Italy)
Alex Borgida (Rutgers University, USA)
Stephane Bressan (National University of Singapore, Singapore)
Fabio Casati (HP Laboratories, USA)
Vassilis Christophides (ICS-FORTH and University of Crete, Greece)
Isabel Cruz (University of Illinois at Chicago, USA)
Umeshwar Dayal (HP Laboratories, USA)
Tim Finin (University of Maryland, Baltimore County, USA)
Irini Fundulaki (Bell Labs, USA)
Zack Ives (University of Pennsylvania, USA)
Vipul Kashyap (National Library of Medicine, USA)
Christoph Koch (Technische Universitaet Wien, Austria)
Harumi Kuno (HP Laboratories, USA)
Maurizio Lenzerini (Università di Roma "La Sapienza," Italy)
Ling Liu (Georgia Tech, USA)
Dennis McLeod (University of Southern California, USA)
Alex Poulovassilis (Birkbeck College, UK)
William Regli (Drexel University, USA)
Jérome Siméôn (IBM T.J. Watson Research Center, USA)
Rudi Studer (Universitaet Karlsruhe, Germany)
Kevin Wilkinson (HP Laboratories, USA)

Publicity and Publications Chair
Irini Fundulaki (Bell Labs, USA)

RoboCup Rescue Robot League
Adam Jacoff, National Institute of Standards and Technology, Intelligent
  Systems Divition, USA
RoboCup Rescue Simulation League
Tomoichi Takahashi, Meijo University, Japan
RoboCup Junior
Luis Almeida, University of Aveiro, Portugal
Jeffrey Johnson, Open University, UK
RoboCup Websites
Ansgar Bredenfeld, AIS, Germany

Table of Contents

Service Oriented Computing: Opportunities and Challenges
Boualem Benatallah, H.R. Motahari Nezhad 1

Data Semantics Revisited
Alexander Borgida, John Mylopoulos 9

Dynamic Agent Composition from Semantic Web Services
Michael Czajkowski, Anna L. Buczak, Martin O. Hofman 27

Ontology-Extended Component-Based Workflows: A Framework for
Constructing Complex Workflows from Semantically Heterogeneous
Software Components
Jyotishman Pathak, Doina Caragea, Vasant G. Honavar 41

Data Procurement for Enabling Scientific Workflows: On Exploring
Inter-ant Parasitism
Shawn Bowers, David Thau, Rich Williams, Bertram Ludäscher 57

XSDL: Making XML Semantics Explicit
Shengping Liu, Jing Mei, Anbu Yue, Zuoquan Lin 64

Refining Semantic Mappings from Relational Tables to Ontologies
Yuan An, Alexander Borgida, John Mylopoulos 84

Triadic Relations: An Algebra for the Semantic Web
Edward L. Robertson 91

Semantically Unlocking Database Content Through Ontology-Based
Mediation
Pieter Verheyden, Jan De Bo, Robert Meersman 109

Representation and Reasoning About Changing Semantics in
Heterogeneous Data Sources
Hongwei Zhu, Stuart E. Madnick, Michael D. Siegel 127

Context Mediation in the Semantic Web: Handling OWL Ontology and
Disparity Through Context Interchange
Philip Tan, Stuart Madnick, Kian-Lee Tan 140

HCOME: A Tool-Supported Methodology for Engineering Living
Ontologies
  Konstantinos Kotis, George A. Vouros, Jerónimo Padilla Alonso   155

Query Answering by Rewriting in GLAV Data Integration Systems
Under Constraints
  Andrea Calì   167

Utilizing Resource Importance for Ranking Semantic Web Query Results
  Bhuvan Bamba, Sougata Mukherjea   185

Querying Faceted Databases
  Kenneth A. Ross, Angel Janevski   199

Constructing and Querying Peer-to-Peer Warehouses of XML Resources
  Serge Abiteboul, Ioana Manolescu, Nicoleta Preda   219

Author Index   227

Service Oriented Computing: Opportunities and Challenges

Boualem Benatallah and H.R. Motahari Nezhad

School of Computer Science and Engineering,
The University of New South Wales,
Sydney, NSW 2052, Australia
{boualem, hamidm}@cse.unsw.edu.au

Abstract. Service oriented architectures (SOAs) are emerging as the technologies and architectures of choice for implementing distributed systems. Recent advances and standardization efforts in SOAs provide necessary building blocks for supporting the automated development and interoperability of services. Although, standardization is crucial by no means is sufficient. Wide spread adoption of service technologies requires high level framework and methodology and identification of appropriate abstractions and notations for specifying service requirements and characteristics to support automated development and interoperability. In this paper, we identify interoperability layers of SOAs, review major approaches for service development and highlight some research directions.

1 Introduction

Service-oriented architectures (SOAs) are emerging as the technologies and architectures of choice for implementing distributed systems and performing application integration within and across companies' boundaries [6][7][8]. The vision of SOAs is to allow autonomous partners to advertise their terms and capabilities, and engage in peer-to-peer interactions with any other partners and enable on demand computing through composition and outsourcing. The foundation of SOAs lies in the modularization and visualization of system functions and exposing them as services that: (i) can be described, advertised, and discovered using (XML-based) standard languages and (ii) interoperate through standard Internet protocols. SOAs are characterized by two trends that were not part of conventional (e.g., CORBA-like) middleware. The first is that, from a technology perspective, all interacting entities are considered to be (Web) services, even when they are in fact requesting and not providing services. This allows uniformity in the specification language and interaction protocols (e.g., the interface of both requestor and providers will be described using the Web Services Description Language -WSDL).

The second trend, that is gathering momentum, is that of including, as part of the service description, not only the service interface but also *the business protocol* supported by the service, i.e., the specification of which message exchange

C. Bussler et al. (Eds.): SWDB 2004, LNCS 3372, pp. 1–8, 2005.

sequences are supported by the service. The interactions between clients and services are always structured in terms of a set of operation invocations, whose order typically has to obey certain constraints for clients to be able to obtain the service they need. In addition to the business protocol, a service may be characterized by other abstractions such as security (e.g., trust negotiation) or transaction policies that also need to be exposed as part of the service description so that clients know how to interact with a service.

While standardization is crucial in making SOA a reality, the effective use and widespread adoption of service technologies and standards requires: (i) high-level frameworks and methodologies for supporting automated development and interoperability (e.g., code generation, protocol compatibility and conformance), and (ii) identification of appropriate abstractions and notations for specifying service requirements and characteristics. These abstractions form the basis of service development frameworks and methodologies.

In this paper, we identify interoperability layers of SOAs and review major approaches for developing service-oriented applications. We also briefly outline some directions.

2   Service Oriented Architectures: Overview and Interoperability Layers

When services are described and interact in a standardized manner, the task of developing complex services by composing other (basic or composite) services is considerably simplified. Indeed, as SOA-related technologies mature, service composition is expected to play a bigger and bigger role in service development. Since Web services will be sought during assembly of composite services, their functionality need to be described such that clients can discover them and evaluate their appropriateness and compositions. The above observations emphasize both opportunities and needs in service development. In fact, they raise the issue of how to support the protocol specification lifecycle, and of how to guide the implementation (especially in the case of composite services) by starting from protocol specifications. Business protocols and compositions are not the only aspects presented in this paper. In addition, one of the major concerns of SOA that is interoperability at various abstraction layers is discussed.

Let us consider a motivating example of B2B integration (B2Bi) where Company A wants to purchase a product from company B. Companies A and B after discovering their match for business (e.g., using a public or private registry), need to agree on the joint business process, i.e., activities, message exchange sequence and interaction contracts, e.g., security, privacy and QoS policies. Companies A and B also need to know and understand the content of exchanged messages. For example, company A needs to know how to send a purchase order to B in terms of product description, order and message structure. Finally, there might be a way to communicate the messages that contain requests and business documents between A and B. In the remainder of this section, we discuss interoperability issues at the following layers: *messaging, content, business protocol* and *policy*.

2.1   The Messaging Layer

This layer provides protocols and adapters for interoperable message exchange among business partners over the network in a reliable and secure manner. A communication protocol consists of a set of rules, which determine message format, transmission and processing for the purpose of exchanging information between two or more services. Software applications usually have a close tie to the syntax of protocol. In addition, it is very often the case that business partners use different platforms, communication protocols or different versions of the same protocol. For example, company A may support SOAP 1.2, while company B supports SOAP 1.1; however, changes in SOAP 1.2 are minor and almost exclusive to additions rather than modifications, e.g., adding HTTP GET method, while SOAP 1.1 only supports HTTP POST method. These are changes in the syntax of the protocol but affect the compatibility of communication protocols of partners so an adapter is required to allow both systems to interoperate successfully.

2.2   The Content Layer

This layer provides protocols, languages and mediators for interoperable and consistent interpretation of the content of exchanged messages by hiding encoding, structure and semantic heterogeneities. Encoding differences arise when two services provide the same functionality using different operation signatures, i.e., different operation names and input/output schemas [11]. Structure heterogeneity happens due to presence of structure differences between the interfaces of two or more partner services, e.g., missing/extra operations or input/output messages in operations of one of the services. Semantic heterogeneity means that services provide overlapping but not the same functionality or when they have different interpretations of the same concept in exchanged business documents. For example, the data item "Price" in an invoice document may mean inclusion or exclusion of tax.

2.3   The Business Protocol Layer

This layer deals with the semantic of interactions between partners. The semantic of interactions must be well defined such that there is no ambiguity as to what a message may mean, what actions are allowed, what responses are expected and in what order messages should be sent. For example, if the protocol of a client requires explicit acknowledgement when sending a purchase order message, the protocol of the provider should support that. Interoperability at this layer is a challenging task since it requires understanding the semantics of external business protocols of partner services. In traditional EAI middleware, e.g., CORBA-based solutions, components interface describes very little semantics and collaborative business processes are usually agreed upon offline. In SOAs, richer descriptions are needed, since services should be self-describing. Automation requires rich description models but a balance between expression power and simplicity is important for the success of the technology.

2.4   The Policy Layer

This layer is concerned with the matching and compliance checking of service policies (e.g, QoS, privacy policies). Policies play a vital role in B2Bi by making the implicit information, as in closed environments, explicit, which is essential in autonomous environments. Policies compatibility checking is essential to find a composition of policy assertions that allow autonomous services to interoperate.

3   State of the Art

In this section we discuss three major approaches in service-oriented architectures: Web services, ebXML, and Semantic Web Services.

3.1   Web Services

Web services are self-described and autonomous software entities that can be published, discovered, and invoked over the Internet (using XML-based standard languages and protocols). The basic technological infrastructure for Web services is today structured around two major standards: SOAP and WSDL (Web Services Description Language). These standards provide the building blocks for service API description and service interoperation, the two basic elements of any programmatic interaction. Web service technologies are evolving toward being able to support more advanced functionalities including discovery, security, transactions, reliability, and collaborative processes management. Several (sometimes overlapping and competing) proposals have been made in this direction, including for example UDDI (Universal Description, Discovery and Integration), WS-Security, WS-Transaction, WS-ReliableMessaging, BPEL4WS (Business Process Execution Language for Web Services), and WSCI (Web Service Choreography Interface). These standards, once they mature and become accepted, will constitute the basis on top of which developers can develop reliable and secure communications among Web services.

At the messaging layer, Web services use SOAP for document exchange and encapsulation of RPC-like interactions. However, the extensibility points provided in the specification are the source of interoperability issues. In addition, incorporation of security and reliability features are still evolving. At the content layer, WSDL describes Web services as collections of endpoints (port types). Port types described the structure of messages the endpoint support. Port types are not enough to define business protocols. Several efforts that recognize the need for extending existing service description languages to cater for constraints such as the valid sequence of service invocations exist [1]. These include work done in standardization efforts such as WSCL (Web Services Conversation Language) and WSCI. However, these protocol languages offer only limited primitives to describe important abstractions such as temporal constraints (e.g., a maximum interval between the invocation of two operations) or the implications and the effects of service invocations from requester perspective (e.g., whether requesters can cancel an operation and what is the cancellation fee) [3].

At the business protocol layer, while proposals like BPEL4WS and WSCI feature some support for defining the conversations that a Web service supports, they are not entirely adequate for specifying business protocols. The conversation functionality provided by BPEL4WS is essentially driven from its composition nature: in other words, BPEL4WS has been primarily designed as a composition language, in which the same formalism used for composition (a process) can also be used for defining conversations. WS-Transaction and the OASIS Business Transaction Protocol (BTP) also deal with conversations and in particular with transactional conversations. However, their goal is that of providing a framework through which services can be coordinated to enforce transactional protocols, rather than providing conversation abstractions and high-level modeling [1].

At the policy layer, WS-Policy defines a base set of extensible constructs for Web services to describe their policies. WS-PolicyAssertions provides an initial set of general message-related assertions such as preferred text encoding. However, neither a high level framework and abstractions for modeling various polices nor a methodology for analyzing relationships between policies (e.g., matching, refinement) is provided.

To summarize, current efforts in Web services area focus on identifying different aspect of services such as interface descriptions, business protocols and policies and propose specifications to cater for such requirements. However, there is no high-level modeling framework and notation for identifying and describing important abstractions such as transactional implications and trust negotiation. Nor is there any framework for helping developers on where and how to apply such abstractions, e.g., security, privacy policies in Web service environment. In addition, the description of policies is mainly characterized by ad-hoc methods that can be time consuming and error prone. Hence, there is a need for high-level frameworks and tools to guide developers on how to use Web service infrastructures (e,g., standards) and provide support for automating the development, enforcement, and evolution of protocols and polices of services.

3.2   ebXML

ebXML (Electronic Business XML) [4] presents a set of specifications and standards for collaborative B2B integration. It takes a top-down approach by allowing partners to define mutually negotiated agreement at a higher level, i.e., business protocols and contracts, and then working down towards all the details of how to exchange concrete messages.

At the messaging layer, partners exchange messages through the messaging service (ebMS). ebMS extends SOAP for secure and reliable payload exchange using existing security infrastructure (e.g., SSL, digital signatures). However, it does not support advanced security features such as federated access control, identity management and trust negotiation. At the content layer, ebXML uses business documents, which consist of a set of fine-grained information items that are interchanged as a part of business process. It allows the use of domain vocabularies derived from standardized core components. However, the shared documents are agreed upon collaboratively.

At the business protocol layer, ebXML defines collaboration protocol agreements (CPAs) using informal descriptions. At the policy layer, ebXML does not explicitly support expression of policies. However, collaboration protocol profiles (CPPs) can be used for this purpose. A CPP defines capabilities of a party to engage in business and so policies can be listed as the capabilities of a company in its CPPs. In addition to the fact that ebXML does not provide for the fragmentation of different policies, the lacks of high level modeling and reasoning about protocols and policies hinders the specification of relevant properties in a way that is useful for activities such as formal analysis, consistency checking of system functionalities, refinement and code generation, etc.

3.3   Semantic Web Services

Semantic Web aims at improving the technology to organise, search, integrate, and evolve Web-accessible resources by using rich and machine-understandable abstractions for the representation of resources semantics. Ontologies are proposed as means to address semantic heterogeneity among Web-accessible information sources and services. Efforts in this area include the development of ontology languages such as RDF, DAML+OIL, and OWL. In the context of Web services, ontologies promise to take interoperability a step further by providing rich description and modelling of services properties, capabilities, and behaviour. OWL-S (formerly called DAML-S) [5] is an ontology for describing Web services.

OWL-S consists of three interrelated subontologies, known as the profile, process model, and grounding. The profile describes the capabilities and parameters of the service. The process model details both the control structure and dataflow structure of the service required to execute a service. The grounding specifies the details of how to access the service, via messages (e.g., communication protocol, message formats, addressing, etc).

At the messaging layer, semantic Web services rely on the efforts in Web services approach. At the content layer, OWL-S uses the profile. At the business protocol layer, OWL-S uses the process model. Although, it does not cater for important abstraction such as transactional implications, temporal constraints.

At the policy layer, OWL-S does not explicitly formalize and specify policies. However, the profile of OWL-S can be used to express policies such as security and privacy as a part of unbounded list of service parameters of the profile. But, there is no consideration for fragmentation of different policie and identification and representation of important service abstractions such as transactional implications and trust negotiation. Although, it should be noted that ontologies provide the basis for defining vocabularies to represent policies (e.g, [10] uses an ontology-based approach for representing security policies).

4   Directions

Recent advances in Web service technologies provide necessary building blocks for supporting the development of integrated applications within and across organizations. A number of XML-based standard languages and protocols exist today (e.g., SOAP, WSDL, BPEL). Service development tools (e.g., BPEL4WJ, Collaxa) that support emerging standards and protocols also started to appear. However, the effective use and widespread adoption of Web service technologies and standards requires: (i) high-level frameworks and methodologies for supporting automated development and interoperability (e.g., code generation, compatibility), and (ii) identification of appropriate abstractions and notations for specifying service requirements and characteristics. These abstractions form the basis of service development frameworks and methodologies [2].

We argue that abstracting Web services protocols will benefit several automation activities in Web services lifecycle. We believe that once the research and development work on the aspects identified above has been completed, this approach will result in a comprehensive methodology and platform that can facilitate large-scale interoperation of Web services and substantially reduce service development effort. This will foster the widespread adoption of Web service technology and of the service-oriented computing paradigm by providing pillars abstractions and mechanisms to effectively discover, integrate, and manage services in large, autonomous, and possibly dynamic environment. It should be noted that model driven development of applications is a well-established practice [9]. However, in terms of managing the Web service development lifecycle and model-driven Web service development, technology is still in the early stages. In particular, with regard to model driven approaches to Web service protocols prior work are either [1]:

- too low-level and consequently not suitable for automating activities such as compatibility checking, code generation, and protocol specification refinement and conformance, or
- do not explicitly take important service abstractions into account, and are consequently ineffective for automating services discovery, interoperation, development, and evolution.

It is worth mentioning that several ongoing efforts in the area of Web services recognize the need for the high-level specification of conversation protocols. These efforts focus on conversation protocols compatibility and composition. Similar approaches for protocols compatibility exist in the area of component-based systems. These efforts provide models (e.g., pi-calculus -based languages for component interface specifications) and algorithms (e.g., compatibility checking) that can be generalized for use in Web service protocol specifications and management. Also, in the area of business process modeling, several approaches based on formal formalisms such as Petri nets, labeled transition graphs, and state charts exist. However, the conversation protocol specification languages used in these approaches do not consider important abstractions such as temporal constraints (e.g., when an operation should occur), the implications and the effects of service invocations from requester perspective (e.g., whether requesters can cancel an operation and what is the cancellation fee).

To summarize, effective abstracting of service protocols and policies can form the basis of the building blocks of a scalable and agile service oriented infrastructure. For example, richer conversation models enable a more effective static and dynamic binding, as clients can be more selective on the behavior properties of the services they bind to. Clients for instance may require that the selected service allow the cancellation of a given operation within a certain time interval from its completion. Other automation that will benefit from service protocols abstraction are compatibility of protocols, validation of service composition models, generation of service composition skeletons, and joint analysis of compositions and protocol specifications [1].

Acknowledgement. Authors would like to thank Fabio Casati, Farouk Toumani and Halvard Skogsrud for their valuable contributions to this work.

References

1. Benatallah, B., Casati, F., Skogsrud, H., and Toumani, F.: Abstracting and Enforcing Web Service Protocols. Int'l Journal of Cooperative Information Systems (IJCIS). World Scientific, December (2004) (To appear).
2. Benatallah, B., Casati, F., Toumani, F.: Analysis and Management of Web Service Protocols. Proceedings of the 23rd International Conference on Conceptual Modeling (ER). Springer-Verlag, Shanghai, China, November 2004 (To appear).
3. Benatallah, B., Casati, F., Toumani, F.: Web Service Conversation Modeling: A Cornerstone for e-Business Automation. IEEE Internet Computing, vol. 8, no. 1, Jan/Feb (2004) 46-54.
4. ebXML: www.ebxml.org.
5. OWL-S: Semantic Markup for Web Services. www.daml.org/services/owl-s/.
6. Alonso, G., Casati, F., Kanu, H., Machiraju. V., Web Services: Concepts, Architectures, and Applications. Springer Verlag, (2004).
7. Papazoglou, M.P., and Georgakopoulos, D.: Special Issue on Service-Oriented Computing. Communiocation of ACM, vol. 46, no. 10, (2003) 24-28.
8. Chung, J.Y., Lin, K.J., Mathieu, R.G.: Special Section on Web Services Computing. IEEE Computer, vol. 36, no. 10, (2003) 35-71.
9. Mellor, S., Clark, A. N., and Futagami, T.: Special issue on Model-Driven Development. IEEE Software, vol. 20, no. 5, (2003).
10. Kagal, L., Paolucci, M., Srinivasan, N., Denker, G., Finin, T., Sycara, K.: Authorization and Privacy inSemantic Web Services. IEEE Intelligent Systems, vol. 19, no. 4, July-Aug (2004) 50-56.
11. Ponnekanti, S., Fox, A., Interoperability Among Independently Evolving Web Services, 5th International Middleware Conference, October, 2004.

Data Semantics Revisited

Alexander Borgida and John Mylopoulos

[1] Dept. of Computer Science, Rutgers University, NJ, USA
borgida@cs.rutgers.edu
[2] Dept. of Computer Science, University of Toronto, Toronto, Canada
jm@cs.toronto.edu

" ...It struck me that it would be good to take one thing in life and regard it from many viewpoints, as a focus for my being, and perhaps as a penance for alternatives missed. ... "
R. Zelazny: *24 Views of Mount Fuji* (1985) [1]

Abstract. The problem of data semantics is establishing and maintaining the correspondence between a data source and its intended subject matter. We review the long history of the problem in Databases, and contrast it with recent research on the Semantic Web. We then propose two new directions for research on the problem and sketch some open research questions.

1 Introduction

Two panels, held at SIGMOD'98 (Seattle, June 4) and CAiSE'98 (Pisa, June 11), discussed the topic of data semantics and its place in Databases research in the next millennium. The first, titled "Next Generation Database Systems Won't Work Without Semantics" included as panelists Philip Bernstein, Umesh Dayal, John Mylopoulos (chair), Sham Navathe and Marek Rusinkiewicz. The second one, titled "Data Semantics Can't Fail This Time!" included as panelists Michael Brodie, Stefano Ceri, John Mylopoulos (chair), and Arne Solvberg.

Atypically for panels, participants to both discussions generally agreed that data semantics will be *the* problem for Databases researchers to tackle in the near future. Stefano Ceri summed up well the sentiments of the discussions by declaring that

"...The three most important research problems in Databases used to be 'Performance', 'Performance', and 'Performance'; in years to come, the three most important and challenging problems will be 'Semantics', 'Semantics', and 'Semantics'... "

What is the data semantic problem? In what sense did it "fail" in the past? ... "And why did the experts agree – unanimously – that the situation was about to change?

We review the data semantics problem and its long history in Databases research, noting the reasons why solutions of the past won't work in the future. We then consider recent work on the Semantic Web and the directions it is taking. Finally, we sketch two new directions for research on data semantics.

C. Bussler et al. (Eds.): SWDB 2004, LNCS 3372, pp. 9–26, 2005.
© Springer-Verlag Berlin Heidelberg 2005

2   The Problem and Its History

A data source is useful because it models some part of the real world, its *subject* (or *application*, or *domain of discourse*). The problem of *data semantics* is establishing and maintaining the correspondence between a data source, hereafter a *model*, and its intended subject. The model may be a database storing data about employees in a company, a database schema describing parts, projects and suppliers, a website presenting information about a university, or a plain text file describing the battle of Waterloo.

2.1   Semantic Data Models

The problem has been with us since the very early days of the Relational Model. Indeed, within four years of the publication of Ted Codd's classic paper [2], there were proposals for semantic data models that were more expressive than the Relational Model and were – therefore – capable of capturing more "world knowledge". Specifically, in 1974 Jean-Raymond Abrial proposed a semantic model that was, in fact, an early object-oriented data model [3]. At the very first Very Large Data Bases conference in 1975, there was a whole session on semantic data models, including Peter Chen's presentation of the Entity-Relationship (hereafter ER) model [4]. Dozens of other proposals followed, and the race was on for ever-more expressive semantic data models that would slay the data semantics dragon.

But how was database practice to be influenced by these proposals? Three basic options were considered:

- Offer semantic data models through DBMS technology; this option implies building DBMSs based on a semantic data model, e.g., an Entity-Relationship DBMS.
- Use semantic data models only during design-time – i.e., while the database is being designed – and factor them out completely during run-time.
- Use semantic models as part of the user interface to make the contents of a database more understandable to the end user.

For performance reasons, option two prevailed. This means that the semantics of the data in a database were factored out from the running database system and were distributed to its operational environment, i.e., its database administrator and its applications programs. If you wanted to know what the data really meant, you'ld have to talk to the administrator of these data and/or check out carefully the applications that accessed and updated these data.

Data Semantics Solution 1 *Data semantics is managed by the operational environment of a database system, i.e., its database administrator(s) and applications programs.*

This is a practical solution that has worked well as long as the operational environment of a database remains closed and relatively stable. In such a setting, the meaning of the data can indeed be factored out from the database proper, and entrusted to the small group of regular users and/or application programs.

Unfortunately, there is a well-known drawback to this solution: *legacy data*. After years of use, organizations have found themselves time after time in a situation where no one knows any more what a particular database and its applications really mean. It has been estimated that legacy data cost organizations around the world billions of euros to maintain and reengineer.

When it comes to building database technology, Solution 1 leaves semantic issues and semantic data models out in the cold. In this respect, research on data semantics has largely been sidelined in database conferences since the early '80s. Instead, semantic data models found a place in database design methodologies. They also influenced in a substantial way software modeling languages proposed more than a decade later, including UML.

As noted, Solution 1 assumes that the environment of a database system remains closed and stable. Throughout the '90s, there was steady progress in making software systems ever-more distributed, open, and dynamically reconfigurable. With the advent of web technologies and standards, e-Business, peer-to-peer systems, Grid computing and more, that trend promised to usher in a new era of computing where computer systems were universally connected, open, dynamic and autonomic. *That* was the change panelists at SIGMOD'98 and CAiSE'98 saw forthcoming. And *that* was the reason for predicting renewed interest in and growing importance for the problem of data semantics.

2.2   The Semantic Web

Unlike database-resident data, Web data have until recently only been intended for human consumption. Rightly so, Tim Berners-Lee realized that Web data can't be made machine-processable unless they come with a formal account of their meaning. Hence his call for the Semantic Web, which has enjoyed considerable interest since it was made in the Spring of 1999 [5].

This call, amplified in [6], and then taken up by many others, envisions technologies and methodologies for attaching semantic annotations to web data, so that they can be interpreted and reasoned about by applications. These annotations can be based on formal ontologies of concepts and relationships that provide a formal – and hopefully widely accepted – vocabulary for a particular domain, be it general (e.g., social actions and interactions), or specific (e.g., manufacturing, genomic biology, or cardiology).

Although there are no generally-accepted detailed proposals of how specifically data semantics should be represented on the semantic web, one approach might be to have an XML document, with annotations to ontologies, as in the following example text, where the word "seminar" is disambiguated by pointing to the concept Course in some ontology, which is further qualified to be offered at UniTN.

> "...The <**concept subClassOf** = x:Course, **hasValue** = [x:offeredAt
> , UniTN], ...> seminar </**concept**> covers a lot of material about
> the Greek philosophers in a short time ..."

Note that this makes it clear that "seminar" does not refer in this case to a one-time lecture presented by a visitor, which is one of its other possible meanings.

There has been considerable effort and progress on formal languages for describing metadata/ontologies. For example, the specification of the Course concept might look as follows in the OWL ontology language [7].

```
<owl:Class rdf:ID="Course"> ...
      <rdfs:subClassOf>
            <owl:Restriction>
                  <owl:onProperty rdf:resource="#offeredAt" />
                  <owl:allValuesFrom rdf:resource="#School" />
            </owl:Restriction>
      </rdfs:subClassOf>
      <owl:disjointWith rdf:resource=" #Student"/>
   ...
</owl:Class>
```

The above then provides a second vision of what constitutes a data semantics solution:

Data Semantics Solution 2 *Annotate data with terms defined in a formal ontology.*

There has been much less effort on the use of ontologies, and serious questions remain concerning the scalability of the approach, i.e., can we build scalable technologies for it? Equally questionable are our technologies/methodologies for aligning and interoperating data sources in the presence of multiple ontologies. As well, it remains an open issue whether "mere mortals" (i.e., your average practitioner) can use expressive formal languages. Indeed, experience with formal, logic-based languages such as SQL, Datalog and Z in other areas of Computer Science suggests otherwise. Making Semantic Web languages widely usable will definitely require tools far beyond the state-of-the-art.

We propose to look next at a more precise variant of Solution 2, taking a careful look at the notions of model and modeling.

3   Models and Mappings

What happens if we take to heart the notion that the data we have is a *model* of some application domain? To do so, let us first take a more general look at the notion of *model*. In an insightful philosophical analysis, Ladkin [8] argues, among others, that

> " ... 'model of' is a ternary relationship, relating the subject S, the model M, and the purpose P for which the model is built ... "

Consider, for example, the case of a geopolitical globe as a model of the Earth. Such a globe shows countries, borders, cities, major rivers and mountains, but not climatic regions. In turn, a model of the Earth for the purpose of studying the motion of planets in the solar system, would likely not be a globe, but instead would reduce our world to a single point, corresponding to its center of gravity.

In the large majority of cases, *the purpose of a model is to answer certain kinds of questions about the subject*. This means that in some ways it is possible to answer these questions more easily/quickly/precisely in the model than in the subject itself. In such cases, in order to describe a modeling situation we need at least the following:

- A set Q_S of *questions* about the subject world that we would like to have answered using the model.
- The *model*, which is an information source, capable of answering certain questions Q_M, after it has been built/evolved.

– *A mapping from questions* in Q_S to one (or more) questions in Q_M, and *an inverse mapping from the answers* in M to answers about the subject S.

In the example above, concerning the globe, the (informal) questions to be asked have to do with the existence and (relative) position of features on the Earth's surface, but not its interior composition. The questions about the model are answered by direct observation of the model by a human, aided perhaps by a string/ruler/compass (something which is not possible for the life-size subject). The mapping of questions and answers is based on the scale reduction of the Earth's spherical surface to that of the globe.

We can apply the above framework to information systems, such as databases. Suppose we have a relational database with a table indicating when courses meet. This can be viewed as a model of the (real-world) university, for purposes of answering (natural language) questions such as "When does a course meet?", "When is a room free?", but not "Is there a projector in the room?". The questions for the model are likely expressed in SQL, and the answers are tables of tuples. The mapping between subject questions and model questions is informal, in the mind of the programmer or database user. On the other hand, if there is a natural language interface to the database, then the mapping is in fact computed (heuristically) by the natural language processing system.

Looking at information systems, one recognizes the additional need for explicit operators that construct and update the model itself, as the subject evolves or more information is discovered about it. For example, in the case of the above database, these are SQL DDL statements for defining the database schema, as well as SQL DML statements for inserting/updating appropriate tuples. Of course, the usefulness of the answers depends on the accuracy of this model-building activity.

To summarize, we have identified the need for the following in the case of information models:

– a subject world, for which *a set of questions* Q_S is of interest, with answers of the form A_S.
– a model, equipped with (i) *Declare* operations for describing generic/schema-like aspects of the model; (ii) *Tell* operations for providing detailed information about the current state of the model; (iii) *Ask* operations which take queries in language(s) Q_M and provide answers in language(s) A_M; (iv) a specification of how query answering depends on the told information, and for practical systems, an implementation thereof[1].
– *a mapping f from a question in* Q_S *to one ore more questions in* Q_M;
– *a mapping ∂ from answers in* A_M *to* A_S.

Data Semantics Solution 3 *The semantics of the data in a model resides in its ability to answer questions about the subject, and is hence captured by Declare/Tell/Ask operations, associated languages, and mappings.*

In order to better understand this approach, let us take a brief look at each of the above components.

---

[1] The core of such a functional view of information sources was first offered by Hector Levesque [9].

3.1   Models

We have found it useful to categorize models according to the way in which query answering is specified. In this paper we consider *intensional models*, consisting of collections of sentences in some formal language $\mathcal{L}$. $\mathcal{L}$ is assumed to be equipped with an entailment relationship $\models$, on which question-answering is based: the answer to a query q is True if the collection of told sentences KB entails q. Information models based on logical theories, such as Description Logics [10], and Ray Reiter's reconstruction of the Relational Data Model in First Order Logic [11] are examples of such models.

Models can also be categorized in regards to their support of partial information (nulls, disjunction, closed/open world assumption), inconsistency, inaccuracy (errors and bounds). Moreover, information models can be distinguished on the basis of efficacy of query answering (formal complexity as well as practical implementation), and how this varies depending on the languages supported by the *Tell* and *Ask* operators. These have been key concerns of Databases and Knowledge Representation research over the past decades.

3.2   Subjects

To begin with, the subject domain is often partitioned into (i) generic, usually time-invariant aspects (so-called *definitional* or *terminological* component) dealing with human conceptualizations of the domain, and (ii) specific facts, describing individuals and their inter-relationships in the current state of the world (*assertional* component). These often give rise to distinct components of information models (schemas vs. tuples/documents/...).

When discussing data semantics, one often hears talk about the information system modeling "*the real world*". Although in some situations data may be obtained from sensors, in most cases the view of the world is mediated by some human being(s), so that the subject is more appropriately viewed as *human beliefs about the world*. Finally, recent developments in information processing have made not uncommon situations such as an XML document representing data from a database, or conversely, a database storing an XML document. In this case, the subject is itself a formal system, which allows us to describe the mapping in a formal fashion.

For example, in a database schema designed from an ER diagram, we can think of the entities as unary predicates, relationships as n-ary predicates, and attributes as binary relations, and then express the mapping between the ER and relational model using predicate logic:

$$\texttt{db:enrolment}(\texttt{sname}, \texttt{crsId}, ...) \leftrightarrow \exists X, Y.\texttt{er:Students}(X) \wedge \texttt{er:Course}(Y) \wedge$$
$$\texttt{er:hasName}(X, \texttt{sname}) \wedge \texttt{er:hasId}(X, \texttt{crsId}) \wedge \texttt{er:EnrolledIn}(X, Y) \wedge ...$$

3.3   Mappings

The sets of questions Q_S and Q_M are usually infinite, and we require some finite means for specifying the mapping from the former to the latter. This can be achieved by making both query languages *compositional*, and then reducing the problem of mapping from Q_S to Q_M to the problem of (i) relating the primitive (non-logical) terms of the two languages, such as their predicate symbols/schemas and constants; and (ii) providing some kind of a homomorphic extension of this mapping to composite formulas.

There are several ways of expressing the base relationships. One approach is a relatively simple specification of correspondences between components of schemas, as used for input in the Clio system [12] or in model management [13].

A more elaborate approach, based on logic, is illustrated in the above example involving the student database and ER schema, where each predicate in the model had associated with it an expression over the subject predicates. This can be seen as an analogue of the Local-as-View (LAV) approach to information integration [14, 15], where the so-called mediated schema is the subject domain. An advantage of this approach is that it provides a way to obtain simple atomic facts that can be told to the system in order to build up the model. Alternatively, in analogy with the Global-as-View (GAV) approach, each predicate of Q_S can be associated with an expression in Q_M e.g.,

$$\texttt{er:Students}(X) \leftrightarrow \exists \texttt{sname.db:enrolment(sname,\ldots)} \land X = f(\texttt{sname})$$
$$\texttt{er:hasName}(Y, N) \leftrightarrow \exists \texttt{sname.db:enrolment(sname,\ldots)} \land Y = f(\texttt{sname})$$
$$\land N = \texttt{sname}$$

where f is some injective function, guaranteed to return a different value for each argument, thereby ensuring a different student individual for each student name in the enrolment database relation. An advantage of this approach is that it facilitates translation of queries from the ER subject world to the database model, in marked contrast to the LAV approach discussed above. The – more general – GLAV approach introduced in [16] and used, among others, in [12, 17], provides for collections of arbitrary query pairs $q_S(x)$ and $q_M(y)$, each of which returns sets of (tuples of) substitutions, and these can then be related in quite general ways (e.g., by set theoretic containment, membership, or numeric comparison). In fact, [18] suggest that a mapping is an arbitrary formula in some logical language, involving elements of the two models.

Note that in view of such options, the directionality implied by the expression "mapping from model M to subject S" is somewhat misleading since there are different ways of expressing the mapping, some of which seem to be from S to M. Moreover, the mapping from M to S is used to translate queries from S to M. Note also that in cases other than the GAV approach, there may be no precise query translation, and one may be reduced to approximations, as with query answering using views.

The formal (query) languages used in specifying mappings can be based on standard First Order Logic, or subsets thereof (e.g., Datalog, SQL, Description Logics) or more complex variants involving structure (e.g., XQuery) or higher-order aspects (e.g., Hylog, Infinitary or Second Order Logics).

For example, suppose that part of the contents of relational tables

```
db:class(cId,cTitle,term)
db:enrolment(cId,sname)
```

concerning course enrolments, is to be published in an XML document with schema described by the DTD[2]

---

[2] We omit PCDATA elements, for brevity.

```
<!ELEMENT catalog (course*) >
<!ELEMENT course (title, students) >
<!ELEMENT students  (student*) >
```

A standard two-step approach is to first map the relations to simple XML trees, where the first level corresponds to relation names, and the second level to tuples

```
<!ELEMENT class (ctuple*)>
<!ELEMENT ctuple (cId,cTitle)>
<!ELEMENT enrolment (etuple*)>
<!ELEMENT etuple (cId,sname)>
```

and then use XQuery to describe the construction of the final desired document:

```
<catalog>
{for $c in $db/class/ctuple
return <course>
                <title> $c/cTitle </title>
                <students>
                    {for $e in $db/enrolment/etuple where $e/cId = $c/(
                    return  $e/sname }
                </students>
            </course>
}
</catalog>
```

This XML document is a model of the relational database for purposes of answering certain questions. Hence *the meaning of the XML model is (should be) defined in terms of the meaning of its predecessor, the relational database, using the mapping and the queries to be supported*. This is in line with our third take on data semantics, based on the notion of model introduced at the beginning of this section.

A final note concerning mappings: while normally these are concerned with the intensional/schema aspects of the models, it is useful to also look at the extensional/individual aspects. In particular, mappings between ontologies, for example, tend to assume that the individuals in the subject and model world are identical. However, we have seen that this is more complex in the case of mappings between object-centered models such as ER, and "flat" data models – such as relational databases – where we have to introduce Skolem functions. In general, things can be even more complex, as in the case of a census database about households that is used as a model for information about individuals. Here, we need to keep a binary relation between each household and the individuals living in it, as envisioned in [19, 20], for example.

Of course, the above framework for data semantics, based on the notions of model and mapping, is just a recasting of voluminous previous work in databases and knowledge representation. In particular, research on *data integration* (e.g., [14, 15, 21]) has developed a rich framework where a mediated schema is inserted between users and the heterogeneous information sources they are trying to access, with the users issuing queries against the mediated schema. These are translated into queries about the original data sources, using mappings.

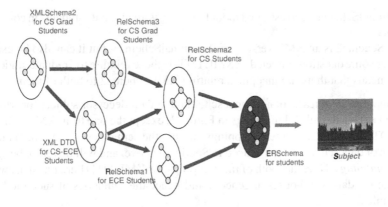

Fig. 1. The mapping continuum

4 The Mapping Continuum

Consider the following examples of modeling:

- A photograph of a landscape is a model of the landscape (its subject matter).
- A photocopy of the photograph is a model of a model of the landscape.
- A digitization of the photocopy is a model of the model of the model of the landscape
- etc.

This kind of situation, first considered by Brian Cantwell Smith [22], shows that meaning is rarely a simple mapping from symbol to object; instead, it often involves *a continuum of (semantic) correspondences* from symbol to (symbol to)* object. Succeeding sections discuss how this paradigm can be applied to information systems. This paradigm constitutes our first attempt at a novel approach to data semantics.

4.1 The Mapping Continuum Hypothesis

Consider the chain of information models illustrated in Figure 1. In this case we have a series of models and mappings supporting the modeling relationship:

- The ER schema is a (conceptual) model of the university domain, or at least the part of it dealing with students. (There can be no formal mapping between the ER schema and the (informal) domain of discourse.)
- RelationalSchema1 is a model of the ER conceptual schema, for the purpose of queries concerning electrical and computer engineering students. (We have illustrated its associated in Section 3.2.)
- RelationalSchema2 is a model of the conceptual schema, for the purpose of queries concerning computer science students.
- XML DTD1 supports queries about either CS or ECE students, and is hence a model of both the previous relational schemas. Therefore we show arrows to both, representing the existence of mappings. (We have given an example of the associated mapping at the end of Section 3.3.)

- RelationalSchema3 is a restricted model, dealing with graduate students in computer science.
- XMLSchema2 is an XML version of RelationalSchema3, but it can also be used to answer some questions directed to XML DTD1 (those relating to graduate students). This means that there are mappings relating XMLSchema2 to both of them.

Some mappings are *lineal*, connecting a schema to the predecessor subject for which it is intended to be a model. All mappings in Figure 1, except the one from XML Schema2 to XML DTD1, are lineal. Lineal mappings capture the semantics of the schema in the third sense of data semantics, introduced in Section 3 above, and will therefore be called *semantic mappings*. Note that both of the mappings for XML DTD1 are lineal, as would be the case for data warehouses in general, and hence the semantics of such models is more complex.

A situation described by a mapping continuum can be represented by a graph, whose nodes are models/schemas, and whose edges are mappings. In order to avoid circularity, the semantic mappings must form an acyclic subgraph, ending at so-called *ground nodes*. Ground nodes will likely be closer to a conceptual/ontological view of the domain of discourse, and in some sense anchor the semantics of other models. Ideally, there would in fact be a single ground node, corresponding to an ontology of the application domain. However, as with the semantic web, we acknowledge that agreeing on a single, universal ontology is likely to be infeasible. We are now in position to offer a fourth version of a solution to the data semantics problem:

Data Semantics Solution 4 *Every (non-leaf) model in the semantic continuum comes with an explicit semantic mapping to some other model, and its meaning is the composition of the mappings relating it to the ground node(s) reachable from it.*

This solution leads to a research program that includes issues such as:

Mapping Composition. Since we are proposing to define the meaning of an information source in terms of the composition of the semantic mappings emanating from it, we must of course clarify the notion of "composition" itself. Fagin et al [18] point to at least two possible interpretations: their own, which is query-independent, and that of [17], which is parameterized by a query language. In our case, this parameter would naturally be determined by the set of queries that the model is intended to answer. Additional questions to be settled include the choice of language to express the composition of two mappings (it may be some variant of infinitary or second order logic), and the computability of the mapping itself, if we are trying to use it to "populate" one model using instance data from another model.

Consistency of Semantics. In the case of graphs where nodes have multiple predecessors, we need to consider the problem of how meaning is defined in the case when there are multiple lineal predecessors. For example, do we want all paths to ground models or just the individual mappings? And in general, we need to consider the issue of consistency when there are multiple paths from a model to some other node in the continuum. In such cases, it isn't clear how consistency is to be defined.

Although we started from an analysis of the notion of modeling, and the correspondence continuum, others have proposed similar frameworks. Research on *peer-to-peer data management* [23, 19, 20] has proposed a framework where queries to each peer may be translated, using mappings, into queries of neighboring peers ("acquaintances"), and this process may be repeated. The connection of peers to each other corresponds to the mapping graph of our mapping continuum, although without a requirement for acyclicity.

Likewise, research on *data provenance* [24] considers the situation where one data source is partially populated with information from one or more antecedents, but there are updates that need to be propagated (both backwards and forwards). Moreover, for an answer to a given query, one wants to know the source(s) of each element of the answer. There is an obvious mapping from a data source to its antecedents, although it is not clear that this mapping is semantic – i.e., to what extent the latest information source's semantics are captured *entirely* by that of its antecedents.

The above areas have tended to study the problem at the same level of "semantic abstraction" (e.g., connecting multiple relational databases). Our research program is distinguished primarily by an emphasis on (directed) semantic mappings, and their path to ground nodes.

4.2   A Detour on Mapping Discovery

The above framework can be interpreted as suggesting that rather than having to re-construct the semantics of a data source every time it is needed, it might be better to maintain/discover mappings between that data source and others. To make this scenario work, we need some evidence that mapping discovery might be easier than semantic reconstruction (e.g., ontology building and alignment), which we have argued is hard.

As intimated above, we believe that *lineal mappings* ought to be codified and pre-served during the development of a new information source. So the ER conceptual model, and the mapping from the relational schema designed from it, ought to be formalized and maintained, so that it can support later data warehousing, for example (e.g., [25]). But what if this did not happen, or if we want to find non-lineal mappings? Experience indicates that most end-users have problems with logical formalisms, even ones as sim-ple as Datalog. To address this problem, we need *tools* that help derive such mappings. A recent successful tool of this sort is Clio [12, 26], which takes as input *correspon-dences* (graphical pairings) between *elements* (usually columns/tags) of relational or XML schemas, and produces a GLAV-style mapping between the two schemas that can be used to transfer data from one information source to the other. To understand better the mapping, examples involving specific data values might also be used as devices for eliciting information from Clio users.

For example, in trying to transfer cs : Teach information, about who teaches whom, from source db, the user might indicate that cs : Teach . student corresponds to db : Enroll . sname, and that cs : Teach . prof corresponds to db : Course . instructor (since db : Enroll does not explicitly list the course instructor). In Figure 2, this is indicated by two correspondence arrows, vc1 and vc2. Although cor-respondences indicate connections between different schemas, it is also necessary to find logical/semantic connections between attributes in a single schema. Clio assumes that these are suggested by co-occurrence of attributes in a single relation, and by foreign keys. So the db schema is augmented by foreign key information, as indicated by the

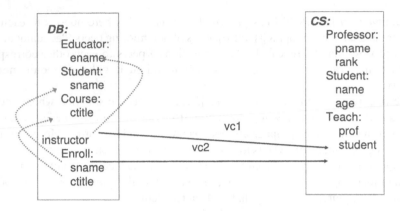

Fig. 2. Schemas and their correspondences

dashed arrows in Figure 2. As a result of these foreign keys, and a chase-like process, the right-hand side of the mapping will be

```
db:enroll(pname,ctitle),db:course(ctitle,instructor),
db:pupil(pname,...), db:educator(instructor,...)
```

while the left-hand side will be

```
cs:teach(prof,studntId)
```

and these will be connected using the equalities

```
instructor=prof, pname=studntId
```

which represent the correspondences, yielding the Horn rule

```
cs:teach(prof,studntId) :-
    instructor=prof, pname=studntId,
    db:enroll(pname,ctitle), db:course(ctitle,instructor),
    db:pupil(pname,...), db:educator(instructor,...).
```

To summarize, the hypothesis underlying Clio is that users will find it is easier to specify simple correspondences, and that the actual mappings desired will be among the ones generated by the tool.

We have recently developed a tool, Maponto [27], for uncovering mappings between relational schemas and ontologies. The tool can be used not just in cases when lineal mappings were not preserved, but also when the ontology was independently developed (e.g., a data warehouse or semantic web scenario). Inspired by Clio, this tool also starts from correspondences of table columns to datatype properties in the ontology. It then finds connections between the concepts bearing these attributes in the ontology, viewed as a graph, and orders these connections according to total length, while keeping in mind semantic information available in the relational schema as foreign keys. One aim of this heuristic algorithm is to derive the "natural" mapping induced by the classical relational schema design process from ER diagrams, in the case when the ontology is exactly the ER schema, and the relational schema has not been de-normalized.

5   Intentional Semantics

Traditionally, the semantics of data deals with the "*what/when*" aspects of a subject: what are the objects, their inter-relationships, their groupings into concepts, and constraints thereof. To achieve a more nuanced understanding of the semantics, it makes sense to consider "*how*" aspects: distinguish (conceptual) objects that represent activities and processes in the domain. In fact, some conceptual modeling languages proposed several decades ago followed this approach, applying the same paradigm to describe both static and dynamic aspects of a domain. For example, Taxis transactions [28] were classified into taxonomies with inheritance; Taxis scripts [29] extended this to workflows, which were Petri nets that used message passing for communication; and RML [30] used class hierarchies to organize objects, events and assertions while specifying requirements for a software system.

To motivate the need for more, consider a university, where an information system maintains, among others, relations

```
Student(st#,nm,addr,advisor,dept,degree)
Course(crs#,crsname,instr,dept,yr,term,size)
```

Suppose that the enrolment process at this university requires students to sign-up for courses at the end of one term (say, May), and pay for each course at the beginning of the next term (say, September), once the official "add/drop" period is over. Consider now a query such as "Find the total size of courses in a specific semester". The meaning, and *proper use*, of the answer depends on the meaning of `size` in table `Course`. If the size was incremented every time a student signed up for a course, then the sum of the sizes may not be an accurate reflection of the total enrolment in courses for that term, since some students may change their mind, not pay for the course, and therefore fail to be officially enrolled. So the sum of sizes is likely to be an *overestimate* of enrolments. This may be satisfactory from the point of view of the university central administration, which would like high enrolment figures to support its request for more Government funding. However, this may be less than satisfactory for the university planning department, which needs the most accurate answer possible.

Such considerations should be part of the data semantics solution because they bring in the dimension of trust in the data we are trying to interpret. This naturally leads to the question of how such information is to be obtained and represented. For this, it is helpful to recall that information systems are software systems, hence subject to the much the same development processes as other kinds of software. Now, the development of software can be viewed as being split into several stages, including:

- *Early requirements*, when analysts are trying to understand an organizational setting; this results in an organizational model.
- *Late requirements*, when analysts formulate (software-based) solutions needed by the organization, resulting in contractual requirements.
- *Design and development* of the software system itself.

The organizational model is concerned mostly with the actors/stakeholders, their goals, and how these are currently met/dependent. Presumably the requirements describe a (software) actor that helps further the goals of (some) organizational stakeholders. We

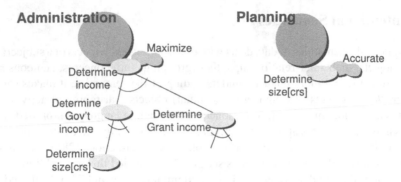

Fig. 3. Actors and their goals

shall use the above university setting to introduce briefly the notions of the *i** notation for capturing early requirements [31], and how this can be applied to capture design decisions during software development, as suggested by the Tropos project [32]. The aim of the presentation – however sketchy and speculative – is to argue for the need to link intentions to data semantics.

To begin with, we model in Figure 3 actors (e.g., Administration) represented by circles. Actor goals (ovals), include determining income for the forthcoming year (for Administration). This goal can be decomposed into a number of subgoals (indicated by edges connected by an arc), such as determining income from the government, and income from grants. In turn, determining government income relies on estimating sizes for courses.

Now we are ready to consider one of the novel features of i*/Tropos: in addition to standard goals, it is possible to also model so-called *softgoals*, which capture general intentions of actors, but which usually don't lead to functional requirements for the new system. Instead, softgoals are used to make choices between alternatives (architectures, designs, implementations).

In the above case, one of the softgoal of the Administration actor (represented as a cloud-like shape) is to *maximize* income, which in this case results in wanting to maximize various subgoals, including course sizes. As shown in Figure 3, the Planning department is also an actor in this setting, and it happens to also have among its subgoals the determination of course sizes. However, its softgoals associated with its wish to know course sizes are different in that it wants information that is as accurate as possible. (Imagine *maximize* and *accurate* as being among a list of possible qualities, for which a "logic" has been established.)

Before we turn to realizing these goals, we need to introduce one more bit of notation, concerning the activities and data that are used in the implementation. Consider, in Figure 4, the student goal of accumulating course credits. Analyzing it, we realize that it *concerns* several objects – a student and some courses, so that these must become "resources" (data objects) in the implementation. (Further implementation decisions will represent these as relational tables such as those diagramed above in rectangles.) At the same time, the hexagonal box, labeled `take[st,crs]`, with an arrow pointing to the goal, shows an activity that can be used to achieve that goal. (There may be

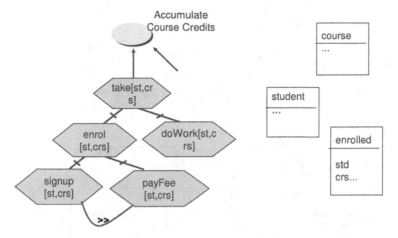

Fig. 4. Goals, tasks and objects

other ways of achieving the goal, such as working or being a teaching assistant.) The diamonds underneath, linked by crossed edges, indicate subactivities, which may be related by double arrows marking temporal precedence. So take[st,crs], involves among others enrol[st,crs], which in turn requires first signup[st,crs] and then payFee[st,crs].

Consider now alternative ways of fulfilling the size[course] goal. One would be to count how many students have signed up for the course – represented as the activity count signups, in the hexagonal box in Figure 5. A different alternative is to count payments. The effect of these alternatives on the two softgoals, Maximize and Accurate, are represented by arrows labeled with + and –, indicating positive and negative contributions towards them. From this representation it is possible to read off that counting signups will tend to maximize course size but decrease accuracy, in contrast to counting payments.

We also have alternative implementations for the count signups process: we can either issue a select count(*) type of query over the enrolment relation, or we can essentially "cache" the size of each course, by incrementing it as part of the signup[st,crs] activity carried out by each student, as diagrammed in Figure 4. The second approach might be more efficient from the point of view of time, and hence contribute positively to the overall non-functional requirement of fast response time.

Data Semantics Solution 5 *Data semantics involves not just the schema and operations but also the intentions behind their design.*

Note that Solution 4 dealt with data semantics by answering the question "Where did the schema of the data come from?" Solution 5, on the other hand, focuses on intentions and accounts for data semantics by offering a framework for answering the question "Why is the design of the schema the way it is? What were the alternatives? Why was it chosen among the alternatives?" This is a radical solution, to be sure. But trust is a major issue for data that are created and used in an open, distributed environment such as the Web. And questions of trust can't be accounted for without bringing into the picture somehow the

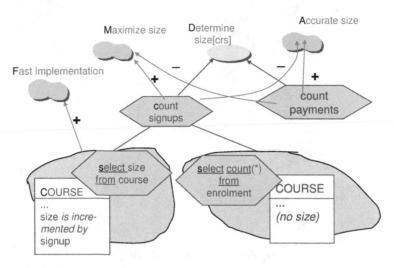

Fig. 5. Different activities for determining course size

intentions of the designers and the managers of an information source. Radical solutions lead to radical research agendas. Here are some issues worth exploring:

- **From goals to schemas.** Traditionally, database design amounts to a series of steps that first construct a conceptual (e.g., ER) schema, and then transform this into a relational one through well-defined transformations. This process needs to be augmented, so that the designer starts with stakeholder goals and softgoals and through goal analysis generates a set of possible schema designs. The output of the design process is now a set of schemas, along with their evaluation with respect to a set of softgoals. Among these schemas, one is chosen for further refinement using existing techniques. The KAOS project [33] offers a glimpse of what this design process might look like, but focuses on the design of software rather than databases.
- **Trusted query processing.** Suppose that along with a query, we also specify desired qualities (e.g., maximum/accurate course size numbers). Given a database and its schema design, we'ld like to be able to tell (i) if the data in the database "match" the desired qualities; (ii) (if not) develop techniques for populating exactly/approximately alternative schema designs with the data that exist. For example, if the Government wants accurate course size counts but is getting instead optimistic ones from University administration, perhaps data from previous years can be used to derive approximate, but more accurate course size counts. Such "data correction" mechanisms are bread-and-butter for economists, journalists and political scientists. In the era of the Semantic Web, such mechanisms can form the basis for dealing with issues of intent and trust.

6 Conclusions

We have briefly reviewed the history of the problem of data semantics, as well as recent research trends towards the vision of the Semantic Web, pointing out solutions that worked in the past, or might work in the future. We conclude from this review that the problem of data semantics would have been with us even without the Web and its semantic extensions. The problem arises from general trends towards open, distributed computing, where it is no longer possible to assume that the operational environment of an information source is closed and stable. Accordingly, we should be looking for solutions that are general, i.e., not Web technology-specific.

We expressed concerns about current research towards ever-more expressive modeling languages, both from the point of view of scalability for relevant technologies, and usability for emerging tools. As an alternative to prevailing research directions, we proposed a framework where the meaning of data is determined by its origin(s) through (design-time) lineal mappings. This solution places an emphasis on schema mappings and traceability techniques. As another alternative, we suggested concepts and design techniques adopted from (software) Requirements Engineering for analyzing stakeholder goals and softgoals to generate and select designs. This – admittedly radical – solution focuses on the intentions behind a database design, as a means for understanding the data in the database. We believe that issues of trust (in the data one is trying to understand) will ultimately have to be dealt with in terms of intentions and stakeholders.

Acknowledgements

We are grateful to Yannis Velegrakis for helpful feedback on an earlier draft of this paper, and to Yijun Yu for his generous efforts in reformatting the presentation.

References

1. Zelazny, R.: 24 views of Mount Fuji. Isaac Asimov's Science Fiction Magazine **7** (1985)
2. Codd, E.: A relational model for large shared data banks. Communications of the ACM **13** (1970) 377–387
3. Abrial, J.R.: Data semantics. In Klimbie, Koffeman, eds.: Data Management Systems, North-Holland (1974)
4. Chen, P.: The entity-relationship model: Towards a unified view of data. In: Proc. International Conference on Very Large Databases (VLDB'75). (1975)
5. Berners-Lee, T., Fischetti, M.: Weaving the Web: The Original Design and Ultimate Destiny of the World Wide Web by Its Inventor. Harper, San Francisco (1999)
6. Berners-Lee, T., Hendler, J., Lassila, O.: The semantic web. Scientific American (2001)
7. W3C: Web ontology language (owl) version 1.0, http://www.w3.org/tr/2003/wd-owl-ref-20030331 (2003)
8. Ladkin, P.: Abstraction and modeling, research report RVS-Occ-97-04, University of Bielefeld, 1997; http://www.rvs.uni-bielefeld.de/publications/abstracts.html#AbsMod. Technical report (1997)
9. Levesque, H.: Foundations of a functional approach to knowledge representation. Artificial Intelligence **23** (1984)
10. Borgida, A.: Description logics in data management. IEEE Transactions on Knowledge and Data Engineering **7** (1995) 671–682
11. Reiter, R.: Towards a logical reconstruction of relational database theory. In M. Brodie, J. Mylopoulos, J.S., ed.: On Conceptual Modelling, Springer-Verlag (1984) 191–233

12. Miller, R., Haas, L., Hernadez, M.: Schema mapping as query discovery. In: Proc. International Conference on Very Large Databases (VLDB'00), Cairo. (2000)
13. Pottinger, R., Bernstein, P.: Merging models based on given correspondences. In: Proc. International Conference on Very Large Databases (VLDB'03), Berlin. (2003) 826–873
14. Levy, A., Rajaraman, A., Ordille, J.: Querying heterogeneous information sources using source descriptions. In: Proc. International Conference on Very Large Databases (VLDB'96), Mumbay,. (1996) 251–262
15. Lenzerini, M.: Data integration: A theoretical perspective. In: Proc. International Conference on Principles of Database Systems (PODS'02). (2002) 233–246
16. Friedman, M., Levy, A., Millstein, T.: Navigational plans for data integration. In: Proc. National Conference on Artificial Intelligence (AAAI'99). (1999) 67–73
17. Madhavan, J., Halevy, A.: Composing mappings among data sources. In: Proc. International Conference on Very Large Databases (VLDB'03), Berlin. (2003) 572–583
18. Fagin, R., Kolaitis, P., Popa, L., Tan, W.C.: Composing schema mappings: Second-order dependencies to the rescue. In: Proc. International Conference on Principles of Database Systems (PODS'04). (2004) 83–94
19. Bernstein, P., Giunchiglia, F., Kementsietsidis, A., Mylopoulos, J., Serafini, L., Zaihrayeu, I.: Data management for peer-to-peer computing: A vision. In: Proc. SIGMOD WebDB Workshop. (2002) 89–94
20. Borgida, A., Serafini, L.: Distributed description logics: Assimilating information from peer sources. Journal of Data Semantics (2003) 153–184
21. Proceeding of semantic integration workshop, at ISWC'03, Sanibel Island, October 2003. http://ceur-ws.org/vol-82 (2003)
22. Smith, B.C.: The correspondence continuum, TR CSLI-87-71, Stanford University. Technical report (1987)
23. Halevy, A., Ives, Z., Suciu, D., Tatarinov, I.: Schema mediation in peer data management systems. In: Proc. International Conference on Data Engineering (ICDE'03). (2003)
24. Buneman, P., Khanna, S., Tan, W.C.: Why and where: A characterization of data provenance. In: Proc. International Conference on Database Theory (ICDT'01). (2001) 316–330
25. Calvanese, D., De Giacomo, G., Lenzerini, M., Nardi, D., Rosati, R.: Data integration in data warehouses. Journal of Cooperative Information Systems 10 (2001) 237–271
26. Velegrakis, Y., Miller, R., Mylopoulos, J.: Representing and querying data transformations. In: Proc. International Conference on Data Engineering (ICDE'05), to appear. (2005)
27. An, Y., Borgida, A., Mylopoulos, J.: Refining mappings from relational tables to ontologies. In: Proc. VLDB Workshop on the Semantic Web and Databases (SWDB'04), Toronto, August 2004. (2004)
28. Mylopoulos, J., Bernstein, P., Wong, H.: A language facility for designing database-intensive applications. ACM Transactions on Database Systems 5 (1980) 185–207
29. Barron, J.: Dialogue and process design for interactive information systems using Taxis. In: Proc. ACM SIGOA Conference on Office Information Systems, Philadelphia. (1982) 12–20
30. Greenspan, S., Mylopoulos, J., Borgida, A.: Capturing more world knowledge in the requirements specification. In: Proc. International Conference on Software Engineering, (ICSE'82), Kyoto. (1982) 225–235
31. Yu, E.: Modeling organizations for information systems requirements engineering. In: Proc. IEEE International Symposium on Requirements Engineering (RE'93), San Diego, IEEE Computer Society Press. (1993) 34–41
32. Castro, J., Kolp, M., Mylopoulos, J.: Towards requirements-driven software development methodology: The tropos project. Information Systems 27 (2002) 365–389
33. Dardenne, A., van Lamsweerde, A., Fickas, S.: Goal-directed requirements acquisition. Science of Computer Programming 20 (1993) 3–50

Dynamic Agent Composition from Semantic Web Services

Michael Czajkowski, Anna L. Buczak, and Martin O. Hofmann

Lockheed Martin Advanced Technology Laboratories
3 Executive Campus, 6th Floor
Cherry Hill, NJ, USA 08002
{mczajkow, abuczak, mhofmann}@atl.lmco.com
http://www.atl.lmco.com

Abstract. The shift from Web pages to Web services enables programmatic access to the near limitless information on the World Wide Web. Autonomous agents should generate concise answers to complex questions by invoking the right services with the right data. However, traditional methods of programming automated query processing capabilities are inadequate for two reasons: as Web services become more abundant, it becomes difficult to manually formulate the query process; and, services may be temporarily unavailable – typically just when they are needed. We have created a tool called Meta-Planning for Agent Composition (MPAC) that dynamically builds agents to solve a user-defined goal using a select, currently available set of services. MPAC relies on a planning algorithm and semantic descriptions of services in the Web Ontology Language/Resource Description Framework (OWL/RDF) and the Web Ontology Language-Services (OWL-S) frameworks. Our novel approach for building these agents is domain independent. It assumes that semantic descriptions of services and a registry of currently available services will be available, as envisioned by the Semantic Web community. Once an information goal is expressed through the ontology of the Web service descriptions, MPAC determines the right sequence of service invocations. To illustrate our approach, we describe a proof-of-concept application in a maritime navigation domain.

1 Introduction

The semantic web is an ever growing repository of information and web services, providing access to the Web's near limitless amounts of data. Today, resources accessible by Resource Description Framework (RDF) [1] and Universal Description Discovery & Integration (UDDI) [2] are quite abundant [3-5]. Complex queries that involve multiple data sources can be formed by combining services together. The required inputs of some services might be the outputs of others. As the evolution of the semantic web continues, specific services come and go. What is considered a good data source today may be an improper source tomorrow. Determining which services to use in a given situation based on quality, reliability, and availability is becoming an important technical challenge. Emergent technologies [6-8] are able to perform semantic composition of services, but few can adapt to the ever-changing sources of information found throughout the Web.

C. Bussler et al. (Eds.): SWDB 2004, LNCS 3372, pp. 27–40, 2005.
© Springer-Verlag Berlin Heidelberg 2005

To address these challenges, Lockheed Martin's Advanced Technology Laboratories (ATL) has developed an agent-based approach to semantic service composition. Meta-Planning for Agent Composition (MPAC) is our new approach to building composite web services through meta-planning. We compose agents that locate web services, access databases, gather information, etc. to satisfy the informational needs of our clients with the resources currently available on the semantic web. In order to do this, the agent composition tool must have certain elements of self-awareness (i.e. situation assessment), and planning. While building agents, our approach takes into account that the semantic web is ever changing, service availability is dynamic, and our clients may suddenly have new information gathering constraints.

The paper is organized in seven sections. Section 2 discusses related approaches to performing semantic web service composition. Section 3 defines the terms and technology on which our method is based. Section 4 describes in detail our meta-planning approach to dynamic composition of service-based agents. Section 5 describes an application of MPAC: gathering information pertinent to collision avoidance of maritime vessels and selecting actions based on information found. In Sections 6 and 7, we conclude and describe topics of future work.

2   Related Work

Semantic composition of web services has been addressed by several researchers. We will briefly describe the most promising approaches by Narayanan and McIlraith [6], Sycara et al. [7], and Wu et al. [8].

The work of Srini Narayanan and Shiela A. McIlraith [6] focuses on simulating, validating, and composing composite web services. Their approach is to take the DARPA Agent Markup Language-Services (DAML-S) [9] description of composite semantic web services and represent them as Petri nets. Using a simulation tool, a human user composes atomic services together to form larger composite services that achieve desired goals. Through encoding situational-logic, the Petri net-based approach ensues that any composed set of web services is a valid one.

Katia Sycara et al. at Carnegie Mellon University (CMU) approach the problem of automated composition of semantic web services in [7]. They create a DAML-S Virtual Machine (DS-VM) which relies upon the Java™ Expert System Shell (JESS) [10] inferencing engine. The DS-VM follows the workflow of a composite DAML-S service, invoking its atomic services through a series of control constructs: if-then-else, sequence, iteration, choice, and split+join. By relying upon JESS, the DS-VM keeps track of the necessary preconditions and side effects of invoking DAML-S services.

The work done by Wu et al. [8], in James Hendler's MindLab at the University of Maryland involves using semantic markup and the Simple Hierarchical Ordered Planner 2 (SHOP2) [11], a hierarchical task network (HTN) planner for agent composition. They maintain a repository of currently available services with their semantic descriptions. Wu et al. developed a general method that translates DAML-S descriptions of individual services into SHOP2. The method involves translating composite and simple DAML-S processes into SHOP2 methods, and atomic processes into SHOP2 operators. Then, SHOP2 is used to determine which services to invoke given the service that we want to achieve and the current data instances. The semantic service description acts like a template that can be executed based on current situation and availability; planning is performed with current data at run time. According to MindLab [8], "The goal of automatic web service composition is to develop software to manipulate DAML-S definitions, find a sequence of web service invocations thus to achieve the task automatically."

3   Background

Dynamic agent composition is the just-in-time building of agents from semantic web services to achieve the desired goals. Dynamically composed agents can be tailored to solve new problems (i.e. achieve new goals or assist other entities in the system). Our approach to dynamic composition of agents is based two technologies: the Web Ontology Language-Services (OWL-S) [12] and the Extensible Mobile Agent Architecture (EMAA) [13].

3.1   OWL and OWL-S

The Web Ontology Language (OWL) [14] has been created from the DARPA Agent Markup Language (DAML) and the Ontology Interface Layer (OIL) [15]. OWL provides an ontology framework for the web using RDF [1] technology. OWL ontologies use RDF to locate similar definitions of terminology with definite Uniform Resource Indicators (URIs). For example, the semantic term "database query" is important to agree upon. Using RDF, we agree that at http://www.database.com/query.owl#query the semantic description of a "database query" is forever bound. Thus, when two semantic applications discuss the act of querying a database, by pointing to this definite location, they know they are talking about the same concept.

OWL is a fundamental language for describing semantic web terminology. The OWL Services Coalition of semantic web researchers has used OWL as a basis for creating Web Ontology Language-Services (OWL-S), a popular semantic language describing web services. OWL-S is a collection of OWL ontologies that describe web services based upon DAML-S [9]. An OWL-S service provides three important characteristics that enable our agents to perform dynamic composition of informational services:

→ A breakdown of a web service's description into a *profile* document (describing what the service does), a *process model* document (describing how the service does it), and a *grounding* document (describing how to invoke the service).
→ A complete semantic description of a service including its inputs, outputs, preconditions, and effects (IOPEs).
→ The ability to bind the IOPEs of one service with another forming composite services executed by following control constructs.

3.2 EMAA

ATL developed the Extensible Mobile Agent Architecture (EMAA) and applied it in about two dozen projects covering a full range of intelligent systems, including information management for time-sensitive strike [16], situation awareness for small military units, and executing user requests entered via spoken language dialogue. Starting with the Domain Adaptive Information System (DAIS) [17] in 1996, experimentation with prototypes in military exercises has guided our research and development towards the adaptable EMAA agent architecture. EMAA was used in the US Navy Fleet Battle Experiment series as a human aiding tool.

EMAA agents are designed with a composable workflow model for agent construction. The EMAA workflow architecture enables a new approach to agent development called agent composition, characterized by choosing, configuring, and assembling elementary agent tasks into workflows. System programmers typically generate agent workflows that consist of agent components arranged in conditional (Boolean) and unconditional (open) execution paths as in Figure 1. If a path is open, tasks on that path are always executed; tasks on a Boolean path are only executed when the argument is true. In EMAA, tasks are the atomic components representing the lowest building block of an agent's process flow. Typical agent tasks include queries to relational databases, retrieval of content from Web pages, reading and sending e-mail, waiting and testing for conditions, and invoking processing services external to the agent. The ovals in Figure 1 depict agent tasks. Figure 1 is an example of a composed agent workflow that persistently queries a database until results have been found.

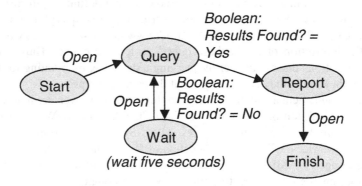

Fig. 1. An example workflow of a database query agent

4   Technical Approach

MPAC is a methodology we developed for dynamic, on-the-fly agent composition of composite semantic web-services. Our approach allows an almost arbitrary agent to be composed at run-time without user intervention. The main steps of our technical approach to agent composition are as follows:

1. Semantically describe individual components/services in OWL-S. We assume services on the Semantic Web will provide semantic descriptions, but it is possible to manually add mark-up for Web services where none exists.
2. Maintain a registry of currently available services or access an existing registry, such as the registry on the Network-Centric Enterprise Services (NCES) being developed by the Defense Information Systems Agency (DISA) [18].
3. Translate semantic descriptions of services into a domain description usable by a planner.
4. Give the planner the goal (desired output) to be achieved. We make the assumption that the ontologies of the service input, output, and query goal descriptions are compatible or that services exist that translate data between incompatible ontologies. The planner inserts these translator services as needed in the normal planning process.
5. Find the "best" sequence of components to invoke (the "best" plan) given the desired goal, using the planner. "Best" is application dependent and is defined by an evaluation function. OWL-S has no default measurement of service quality or cost. However, the translator (step 3) can provide this information to the planner if an application dependant value is present.
6. "Best" plan results take the form of an agent workflow where each task executes a service.
7. Compose the agent from components specified in the plan.
8. Execute the agent.

Steps 1-2 are performed by the service locator (see Figure 2), steps 3-5 are performed by the meta-planner, and steps 6-8 are executed by the agent composer.

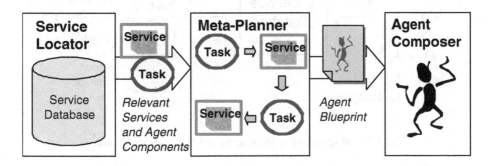

Fig. 2. The components of the MPAC system

4.1   Service Locator

The service locator uses the information contained in the service profile, i.e. it knows the inputs, outputs, pre-conditions, and effects of all services registered. It also contains information about their present availability. A query to the service locator is formulated to describe inputs and/or outputs of interest. The service locator determines which services match the request, and lists all services that have the desired terms in their inputs or outputs. In order to maintain an accurate list of available services, MPAC requires that as new services become available, they are added to the service locator as potential data sources. Services that become unavailable are removed. Our service locator is a conceptually simplified version of the MatchMaker in [7] and we discuss its limitations in Section 7.

To illustrate the operation of MPAC's components we query cargo information of merchant ships throughout Section 4. Imagine that we have a service locator containing information about services that provide cargo ship content data. These services are located at different places on the internet, but each has its own OWL-S service description. In Figure 3, a user/client asks MPAC to compose an agent that can get information about European ships from databases located within North America. The client sends a description of the goal (desired output of 'Ship Report Data') using terms from an OWL ontology to the service locator. All available web services registered with service locator, gather information on European cargo ships and return with 'Ship Report Data' output. Relevant services can include the Global Transport Analysis™ (GTA) [19], and PIERS™ [20] that both return the type 'Ship Report Data'. Furthermore, the service locator identifies agent tasks related to databases that could be of use, such as the, 'Generate Database Connection Task' and the 'Report Results Task'.

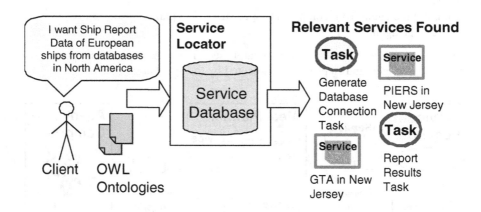

Fig. 3. Locating cargo ship information using the service locator

4.2   Meta-planning

A planner is invoked once the service locator has provided a list of all services that could be useful to achieve a given goal. The planner creates a plan, i.e. a sequential list of web-services and tasks that need to be invoked in order to achieve a given goal. As mentioned previously the goal to achieve is the desired type of output (e.g. 'Report Data'). The planner has also the list of existing inputs. The planner needs to make sure it is possible to achieve the desired output(s) with the input services in the order defined in the plan. We call this plan the blueprint of an agent.

The possible building blocks for the planner are provided by the service locator. The planner uses backward chaining to build the agent's blueprint. Using backward chaining means the end-goal is asserted as the desired goal first. In Figure 4, this is the 'Report Data' goal. The planner looks at all possible services returned by the service locator that produce 'Report Data' as their output. In our example, only the 'Report Data Task' produces 'Report Data' meaning that 'Report Data Task' is the last step of the plan. The input to component 'Report Data', i.e. 'Query Result Set', is asserted as the desired goal. The planner finds two components, 'GTA Database Service' and 'PIERS Database Service' that produce the 'Query Result Set'. It tries both of them. When the planner tries 'GTA Database Service', its input 'GTA Password' is asserted as the desired goal. Since there is no component (including the client's information) that produces 'GTA Password' as output, the planner backtracks, and chooses component 'PIERS Database Service', and asserts 'Database Connection' as desired goal. Continuing, the planner looks for services that produce a 'Database Connection'. It finds that there is only one component, 'Generate Database Connection Task' that produces a 'Database Connection' as output. The planner chooses 'Generate Database Connection Task' and asserts its inputs 'Username' and 'SQL' as desired goals. Since both a 'Username' and 'SQL' are given by the client, these goals are satisfied. The planner generates an agent blueprint that invokes in order: Generate Database Connection Task → PIERS Database Service → Report Results Task.

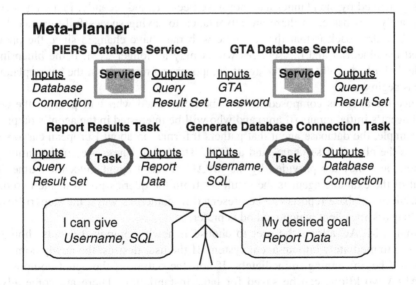

Fig. 4. Building an agent blueprint to find *Report Data*

When several plans (blueprints) are found, a heuristic is used to choose the best blueprint. The heuristics are problem dependent: some heuristics select plans based on the fewest service tasks that are to be invoked, while others might exclude services that exist on certain web servers due to network latency or security.

Our service-composition approach uses certain elements from the method developed at MindLab [8]. The chief difference between the two methods is that while UMD is performing planning, we are performing meta-planning. Planning (standard service composition) implies using an existing service to achieve a certain task automatically. In planning, the service is described semantically and acts like a template that an agent can execute based on the current situation, availability, and the current data instances. We are performing meta-planning; our system builds the template (the agent blueprint) that produces the desired output type (goals), and reasons over the input and output types of the services contained within. In contrast, the planner in MindLab's method reasons over the current data instances.

4.3   Agent Composition

MPAC takes the blueprint of the agent generated by the planner and composes it into an EMAA agent. During this step, the agent tasks are realized into activities and put into an EMAA agent workflow. Web services are contacted through the *grounding* instructions provided by their OWL-S descriptions. Usually this involves sending Simple Object Access Protocol (SOAP) [21] messages over Web Service Description Language (WSDL) [22].

As an option, the MPAC's agent composer checks the existence of all of the services before composing them into an agent. This may be necessary because the blueprints generated by the planner may not have been created recently. Planning is computationally expensive, so there are advantages to saving successfully created blueprints. The drawback is that the semantic web may have changed since the planner created the blueprint and the services within may no longer exist. If the blueprint is decidedly broken or obsolete, the agent composer can request that the entire planning process begin again.

Once the agent is composed, it must be determined who will provide the composed agent's initial inputs (if any) and who will be interested in the agent's output. In our example, the database agent that gathers information about European cargo ships requires the client's 'Username' and a 'SQL' statement. These are configuration parameters, and they are provided by the MPAC client at agent invocation time. The output of the example agent is the result set from the queries posed to the two databases. Since database reports can be presented in numerous ways, the Report Results Task may ask the client which method is preferred.

Finally, MPAC allows the user to choose if newly composed agents should be deployed immediately into an agent system. If the user desires, the newly composed agent will begin running immediately. If not, the output of the agent composition, an EMAA workflow, can be saved for later instantiation. There are some advantages to saving the workflow at this point rather than after the planning phase. The workflow out of the Agent composer is concrete, existing as a set of objects ready to be invoked. However, if the agent workflow is saved there is no guarantee that the informational web services will be available to execute later; the semantic web may have changed.

4.4 Novelty of MPAC

MPAC composes agents that invoke semantic web services to gather information and EMAA tasks to perform actions on that information. The EMAA tasks make a number of useful information processing tasks available across a number of applications, but are typically too narrowly defined to be provided on the Web. The addition of these tasks greatly enhances the variety of agents that MPAC can create. Each task used by our agents has its own semantic description as a web service in OWL-S. Thus MPAC can only distinguish between informational resources and acting agent tasks through their semantic descriptions. The term 'service' applies to any web service and any EMAA task described in OWL-S.

The main difference between the MPAC and the MindLab method is that UMD is performing planning and we are performing meta-planning. Planning requires that a composite service template already exist. Through some method an agent can locate and invoke services based on the current situation, availability, and the current data instances. In the UMD method, the template is described in DAML-S, and realized through hierarchical task decomposition. We are performing meta-planning; MPAC has no knowledge of the template upon construction time. We build the template that reasons over individual semantic input and output types. In contrast, the planner in MindLab's method reasons over the current data instances.

The advantages to our approach are twofold. First, we effectively merge the capabilities of our agent technology with the massively distributed databases across the internet. Since ATL has proven the viability of EMAA agent technology [16-17], we believe the semantic web and agent technology complement one another. The other advantage is a new sense of agent robustness. If a certain service becomes unavailable for any reason, other similar services (either agent component or informational) could serve as substitutes. Whenever new web services become available, they can be used to compose the next generation agent through dynamic agent composition. Services that use a semantic description in OWL-S could provide useful information about their service quality and costs, all of which can be decided when composing the agent dynamically.

5   Example Application

We have created a proof-of-concept implementation of MPAC geared towards a maritime navigation domain where dynamic agent composition has been determined as very valuable by the dynamic nature of the problems solved. We have been working with Lockheed Martin Marine Systems in Baltimore to create dynamically composed agents that help a ship navigate safely through a harbor. The goal of the composed agent is to correct a ship's voyage plan, a series of turn points and waypoints that a ship must follow as it navigates. Because of the dynamic nature of maritime navigation, an initial voyage plan often becomes invalid and may lead the ship aground or too close to other vessels (ultimately leading to collisions with other vessels). The scenario is complicated by the changing availability of ship sensors and navigation services. Additionally, the own ship must also adhere to maritime law governing safe distance passing, obvious turning, giving 'right of way', etc. [23].

MPAC agent composition for Collision Avoidance works over a domain of three types of services as shown on the left side of Figure 5. The service types are *land collision detection*, *route crossing detection*, and *voyage planning*. The land collision services represent the instruments that a ship has to help it determine where static obstacles are. Some examples of land collision services are infra-red cameras, fathometers, and vector based charts. The land collision services require as input the current Voyage Plan (VP), and they produce informational reports if the instrument determines there are static obstacles in the VP of own ship such as shorelines, shallows, minefields, etc. The route crossing services are instruments a ship uses to determine if it will collide with another ship. Some examples of route crossing services are radars, and the Automated Information System (AIS). The route crossing services require the knowledge of the own ship's speed and location. The route crossing service produces a ship crossing report detailing potential areas where the vessel may collide with another vessel. Finally, the voyage planning services take the potential land and ship collision reports, as well as the broken voyage plan, and generate new voyage plans for the own ship to follow. These services use the maritime Rules of the Road [23] which dictate how ships should avoid one another according to maritime law. When combined, an agent invoking a sequence of collision, route crossing, and voyage plan adjustment services provides us with new voyage plans to follow when the current voyage plan would have caused the ship to collide into land or another ship.

Our demonstration tool operates on a simulated environment of the "Demo-Ship" and its journey through a New York harbor. Our informational services (*land collision*, and *route crossing*) present data based on the simulated environment. We wrote EMAA tasks to handle simple implementations of the *voyage planning* services. Because we have separated the implementation of the service from its semantic description, it is easy to write new implementations of the ship services for the same semantic descriptions. This allows transition from our demonstration to real ships services in a live demonstration.

The first step in dynamic agent composition for maritime scenario was developing the semantic mark up of services that a ship can have. Since OWL-S was not created when we built the prototype, the MPAC demonstration tool used the OWL-S predecessor DAML-S. For our proof-of-concept demo for each ship service, a DAML-S service description was developed. MPAC takes the semantic descriptions of the ship's services and registers them with our service locator. We simulated the availability/unavailability of ship sensor services through the checkboxes as shown on the left side of Figure 5.

The planner that MPAC uses is called JSHOP, a Java™ variant of SHOP2 in [11]. We use UMD's translation algorithms [8] to translate the DAML-S descriptions of services into JSHOP processes. Along the bottom of Figure 5 is the current voyage plan agent composed of the currently available services. The current agent invokes the services: Fathometer → Channel Follower → Laser Range Finder → AIS → Complex Turning. Five out of seven existing services are used to compose the agent.

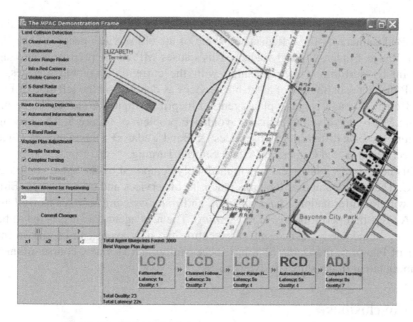

Fig. 5. The MPAC Collision Avoidance demonstration tool

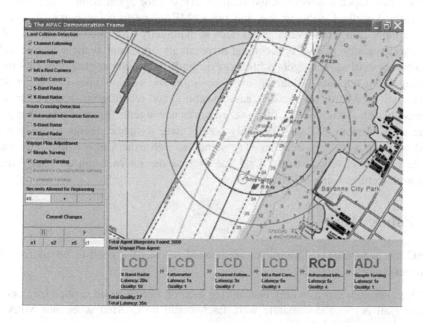

Fig. 6. The result of creating a new voyage plan agent and invoking it

As seen in the center of Figure 5, the Demo-Ship is about to have a direct collision with another ship, "Tokyo Express". The ship uses its current VP agent to build a new voyage plan that won't collide with any obstacles. The new VP is determined by the agent. As the situation changes in the environment, new services become available (Infra-Red Camera, X-Band Radar) and some of the old services become unavailable (Laser Range Finder, S-Band Radar). This causes MPAC to prepare a new agent blueprint by performing meta-planning with the currently available services. The JSHOP planner took the list of available services as denoted on the left side of Figure 6, and created a new voyage plan agent's blueprints. Figure 6 shows the result of running MPAC to solve the collision avoidance problem of Figure 5. The new agent in Figure 6 uses a different set of services: X-Band Radar → Fathometer → Channel Follower → Infra-Red Camera → AIS → Simple Turning.

This new voyage plan agent was immediately composed by the agent composer of MPAC. The agent composer took this blueprint of services and created a new EMAA agent with the informational *land collision,* and *route crossing* services as well as the EMAA tasks that performed *voyage planning.* The new agent was instructed to begin executing immediately. The result of executing the new agent can be shown in the center of Figure 6; the Demo-Ship has successfully plotted a new course around the oncoming threat of the ship, "Tokyo Express".

6 Conclusions

We have developed a novel method (named MPAC) for agent composition from semantically described web-services and tasks. MPAC performs dynamic, on-the-fly agent composition from available services semantically described and registered in our service registry. MPAC is becoming increasingly important as the semantic web's data sources evolve. The agent's blueprint is built by a planner that performs meta-planning using backward chaining over the input and output types of the services. Agents built by MPAC are flexible, easy to rebuild and reconfigure should their components change. Additionally, if the user requires new agents that perform other goals in the same domain, MPAC can easily create these dynamic agents to solve goals based on the client's requirements. The semantic web ushers in a whole new era of service use. Massively distributed services across the internet can connect through agent architectures using MPAC.

7 Future Work

MPAC has a number of limitations, mentioned below, that need to be addressed in future research:

→ Our approach assumes only one service locator, but multiple service locators can exist all across the semantic web. Each could be queried whenever MPAC is looking for candidate services.

→ When domains become too large, it is difficult for a service locator to discover services that are of use to the meta-planner. Simply looking for services that have something to do with "cargo ships" and "databases" might yield hundreds if not thousands of services. Even though OWL-based taxonomies that describe "cargo ships" and "databases" might exist, hundreds of services might be doing things that the meta-planner should not be interested in. To address this problem a MatchMaker is needed similar to the one developed by Sycara et al. at CMU [7].

→ Our service locator works primarily off of a service's inputs and outputs, and neglects the important preconditions and effects. The approaches discussed in Section 2 all work with preconditions and effects through reasoning systems.

→ A backward-chaining meta-planner only creates agent blueprints that are sequential. The OWL-S *process model* allows for more complicated agent blueprints that involve control constructs such as if-then-else, iterate, and split+join. As a result, MPAC could benefit from more powerful planning techniques to dynamically compose semantic agents with arbitrary control constructs.

→ The blueprints generated by the meta-planner could be made into their own OWL-S services. Blueprints have no specific ties to EMAA until they are given to the agent composer. MPAC could create an OWL-S service description of an agent and publish it to the internet as another available semantic web service.

Acknowledgements

We thank Vera Zaychik from ATL for the initial work on the meta-planner for our MPAC prototype. We would like to acknowledge the use of the DAML-S to J-SHOP translator provided to us by Professor James Hendler from the University of Maryland and the several fruitful discussions that we had with him and his MindLab team. Our sincere thanks go also to Mike Orlovsky from LM MS2 for his help in definition of the maritime domain scenario.

References

1. Beckett, D., McBride, B.: W3C: Resource Description Framework (RDF) syntax specification. http://www.w3.org/TR/2004/REC-rdf-syntax-grammar-20040210/ (2004)
2. Bellwood, T., Clément, L., Ehnebuske, D., Hately A., Hondo, M., Husband, Y. L., Januszewski, K, Lee, S., McKee, B., Munter, J., von Riegen, C.: OASIS: Universal Description Discovery & Integration version 3.0. http://uddi.org/pubs/uddi-v3.00-published-20020719.htm (2002)
3. Microsoft Universal Description Discovery & Integration (UDDI) Business Registry (UBR) node. http://uddi.microsoft.com/ (2004)
4. IBM Universal Description Discovery & Integration (UDDI) Registry v2: Overview. https://uddi.ibm.com/ubr/registry.html (2004)
5. SAP Universal Description Discovery & Integration (UDDI) Registry. http://uddi.sap.com/ (2004)
6. Narayanan, S., McIlraith S. A.: Simulation, Verification and Automated Composition of Web Services. In: Proceedings of the Eleventh International World Wide Web Conference (WWW-11) (2002)
7. Sycara, K., Paolucci, M., Ankolekar, A. Srinivasan, N.: Automated Discovery, Interaction and Composition of Semantic Web services. In: Journal of Web Semantics, Vol. 1, Iss. 1, September (2003) 27-46

8. Wu, D., Sirin, E., Hendler, J., Sirin, E., Parsia, D.: Automatic Web Services Composition Using SHOP2. In: Proceedings of 2nd International Semantic Web Conference (ISWC2003), (2003)
9. DARPA Agent Markup Language services (DAML-S): Semantic Markup for Web Services v0.9. http://www.daml.org/services/daml-s/0.9/daml-s.html (2003)
10. Java™ Expert System Shell (JESS) Rule Engine for the Java™ Platform. http://herzberg.ca.sandia.gov/jess/index.shtml (2004)
11. Nau, D. Munoz-Avila, H., Cao, Y., Lotem, A., and Mitchell, S.: Total-order planning with partially ordered subtasks. In: Proceedings of the Seventeenth International Joint Conference on Artificial Intelligence (2001)
12. The OWL Services Coalition: OWL-S: Semantic Markup for Web Services. http://www.daml.org/services/owl-s/1.0/owl-s.html (2004)
13. Lentini., R., Rao, G., Thies, J., and Kay, J.: EMAA: An Extensible Mobile Agent Architecture. In: Fifteenth National Conference on Artificial Intelligence (AAAI98), Technical Report WS-98-10:Software Tools For Developing Agents, ISBN 1-57735-063-4 (1997)
14. OWL Web Ontology Language Overview. http://www.w3.org/TR/2004/REC-owl-features-20040210/ (2004)
15. Horroks, I., van Harmelen, F., Patel-Schneider, P., Berners-Lee, T., Brickley, D., Connoly, D., Dean, M., Decker, S., Fensel, D., Hayes, P., Heflin, J., Hendler, J., Lassila, O., McGuinness, D., Stein, L.A.: DAML+OIL. http://www.daml.org/2001/03/daml+oil-index.html (2001)
16. Hofmann, M.O., Chacón, D., Mayer, G., Whitebread, K.R., Hendler, J.: CAST Agents: Network-Centric Fires Unleashed. In: Proceedings of the 2001 National Fire Control Symposium (2001) 12-30
17. Hofmann M.O., McGovern, A., Whitebread, K.R.: Mobile Agents on the Digital Battlefield. In: Proceedings of the Second International Conference on Autonomous Agents (Agents '98) (1998) 219-225
18. DSIA Fact Sheets Net-Centric Enterprise Services (NCES). http://www.disa.mil/pao/fs/nces3.html (2004)
19. Journal of Commerce, Commonwealth Business Media: Global Transport Analyzer (GTA). http://www.joc.com/gta/pointsearch.html (2004)
20. Commonwealth Business Media: Port Import Export Reporting Service (PIERS). http://www.piers.com (2004)
21. Mitra, N.: Simple Object Access Protocol (SOAP) version 1.2 Part 0: Primer. http://www.w3.org/TR/soap12-part0/ (2003)
22. Chinnichi, R., Gudgin, M., Moreau, J., Weerawarana, S.: Web Service Description Language (WSDL) version 1.2. http://www.w3.org/TR/2003/WD-wsdl12-20030303/ (2003)
23. Rules of the Road, Public Law 95-75, 91 Stat. 308 (33 U.S.C. 1601-1608). http://www.navcen.uscg.gov/mwv/navrules/international.html (2003)

Ontology-Extended Component-Based Workflows: A Framework for Constructing Complex Workflows from Semantically Heterogeneous Software Components

Jyotishman Pathak, Doina Caragea, and Vasant G. Honavar

Artificial Intelligence Research Laboratory,
Department of Computer Science,
Iowa State University,
Ames, IA 50011-1040, USA
{jpathak, dcaragea, honavar}@cs.iastate.edu

Abstract. Virtually all areas of human endeavor involve workflows - that is, coordinated execution of multiple tasks. In practice, this requires the assembly of complex workflows from semantically heterogeneous components. In this paper, we develop ontology-extended workflow components and semantically consistent methods for assembling such components into complex ontology-extended component-based workflows. The result is a sound theoretical framework for assembly of semantically well-formed workflows from semantically heterogeneous components.

Keywords: Workflows, Ontologies, Components.

1 Introduction

Almost all areas of human activity - education, business, health care, science, engineering, entertainment, defense - involve use of computers to store, access, process, and use information. The term *workflow* typically refers to coordinated execution of multiple tasks or activities [16,1,12]. Processing of an invoice, the protocol for data acquisition and analysis in experimental science, responding to a natural disaster, could all be viewed as workflows.

Examination of workflows in specific domains reveals that many activities (e.g., the task of credit evaluation in financial services workflows) are common to several workflows. Encapsulation of such activities in the form of reusable modules or workflow *components*, which can be assembled to create complex workflows, can greatly reduce the cost of developing, validating, and maintaining such workflows [21]. Hence, component-based approaches to designing workflows has begun to receive considerable attention in the literature [6,8,15,21].

A component [10,19] is a piece of software that can be independently developed and delivered as a unit. Well-defined interfaces allow a component to be connected with other components to form a larger system. Component-based

C. Bussler et al. (Eds.): SWDB 2004, LNCS 3372, pp. 41–56, 2005.

software development [9] provides a flexible and cost-effective framework for reuse of software components. Compositionality ensures that global properties of the resulting system can be verified by verifying the properties of the constituent components. By analogy with software components, a workflow component can be viewed as a workflow module (i.e., an executable piece of software) which can be connected to other workflow modules through well-defined interfaces.

A simple workflow consisting of two simple components: F-Sensor and Weather Description is shown in Figure 1. The function of this workflow is to

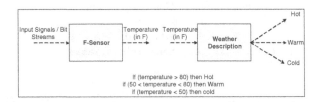

Fig. 1. Weather Description with F-Sensor

determine whether the day is hot, or warm or cold based upon the temperature. The input to the F-Sensor component consists of signals from one or more sensors and its output is the current temperature (in degree F) and the input to the Weather Description component is the current temperature (in degree F from the output of F-Sensor component) and its output is a description of the day (hot or warm or cold). Note that in this example, the output produced by the F-Sensor component has the same semantics as the input of the Weather Description component; furthermore, the name *Temperature* used in the vocabulary associated with the F-Sensor component has the same *meaning* as the term *Temperature* in the vocabulary associated with the Weather Description component. In the absence of syntactic or semantic mismatches between components, their composition is straightforward.

However, it is unrealistic to expect such syntactic and semantic consistency across independently developed workflow components libraries. Each such workflow component library is typically based on an implicit *ontology*. The workflow component ontology reflects assumptions concerning the objects that exist in the world, the properties or attributes of the objects, the possible values of attributes, and their intended meaning from the point of view of the creators of the components in question. Because workflow components that are created for use in one context often find use in other contexts or applications, syntactic and semantic differences between independently developed workflow components are unavoidable. For example, consider a scenario where we replace the F-Sensor component with a new component: C-Sensor. Suppose C-Sensor behaves very much like F-Sensor except that it outputs the temperature, denoted by *Temp*, and measured in degrees Centigrade instead of degrees Fahrenheit. Now we can no longer compose C-Sensor and Weather-Description components into a simple workflow, because of the syntactic and semantic differences between the two components. Effective use of independently developed components in a given context requires reconciliation of such syntactic and semantic differences between the components. Because of the need to define workflows in different application contexts in terms of vocabulary familiar to users of the workflow, there is no single privileged ontology that will serve all users, or for that matter, even a single user, in all context.

Recent advances in networks, information and computation grids, and WWW have made it possible, in principle, to assemble complex workflows using a diversity of autonomous, semantically heterogeneous, networked information sources and software components or services. Existing workflow management systems (WfMS) allow users to specify, create, and manage the execution of complex workflows. The use of standard languages for defining workflows [1] provides for some level of portability of workflows across different WfMS. A major hurdle in the reuse of independently developed workflow components in new applications arise from the *semantic* differences between the independently developed workflow components. Hence, realizing the vision of the Semantic Web [2], i.e., supporting seamless access and use of information sources and services on the web, in practice calls for principled approaches to the problem of assembly of complex workflows from semantically heterogeneous components - the *workflow integration* problem.

The workflow integration problem can be viewed as a generalization of the *Information Integration* problem [14]. Hence, we build on recent developments in component-based workflow design [6, 8, 15, 21] to extend ontology-based solutions of the information integration problem [7, 18] to develop principled solutions to the workflow integration problem. Specifically, in this paper, we develop *ontology-extended workflow components* and *mappings* between ontologies to facilitate assembly of *ontology-extended component-based workflows* using semantically heterogeneous workflow components. The proposed ontology-extended component-based workflows provide a sound theoretical framework for assembly of semantically well-formed workflows from semantically heterogeneous information sources and software components.

2 Ontology Extended Component Based Workflows

2.1 Ontologies and Mappings

An *ontology* is a specification of *objects*, *categories*, *properties* and *relationships* used to conceptualize some domain of interest. In what follows, we introduce a precise definition of ontologies.

Definition (Hierarchy) [4]: Let S be a partially ordered set under ordering $\leq$. We say that an ordering $\preceq$ defines a *hierarchy* for S if the following three conditions are satisfied:

(1) $x \preceq y \rightarrow x \leq y$; $\forall x, y \in S$. We say $(S, \preceq)$ is *better than* $(S, \leq)$),

(2) $(S, \leq)$ is the reflexive, transitive closure of $(S, \preceq)$,

(3) No other ordering $\sqsubseteq$ satisfies (1) and (2).

Example: Let $S = \{Weather,\ Wind,\ WindSpeed\}$. We can define the partial ordering $\leq$ on S according to the *part of* relationship. For example, *Wind* is part of the *Weather* characteristics, *WindSpeed* is part of the *Weather* characteristics, and *WindSpeed* is also part of *Wind* characteristics. Besides, everything is part of itself. Thus, $(S,\ \leq) = \{(Weather,\ Weather),\ (Wind,\ Wind),\ (WindSpeed,\ WindSpeed),\ (Wind,\ Weather),\ (WindSpeed,\ Weather),\ (WindSpeed,\ Wind)\}$. The reflexive, transitive closure of $\leq$ is the set: $(S,\ \preceq) = \{(Wind,\ Weather),\ (WindSpeed,\ Wind)\}$, which is the only hierarchy associated with $(S,\ \leq)$.

Definition (Ontologies) [4]: Let Δ be a finite set of strings that can be used to define hierarchies for a set of terms S. For example, Δ may contain strings like *isa, part-of* corresponding to *isa* or *part-of* relationships, respectively. An *Ontology O* over the terms in S with respect to the partial orderings contained in Δ is a mapping Θ from Δ to hierarchies in S defined according to the orderings in Δ. In other words, an ontology associates orderings to their corresponding hierarchies. Thus, if *part-of* $\in \Delta$, then $\Theta(part\text{-}of)$ will be the *part-of* hierarchy associated with the set of terms in S.

Example: Suppose a company K_1 records information about weather in some region of interest (see Figure 2). From K_1's viewpoint, weather is described by the attributes *Temperature, Wind, Humidity* and *Outlook* which are related to weather by *part-of* relationship. For example, *Wind* is described by *WindSpeed*. The values *Cloudy, Sunny, Rainy* are related to *Outlook* by the *is-a* relationship. In the case of a measurement (e.g., *Temperature, WindSpeed*) a unit of measurement is also specified by the ontology. In K_1's ontology, O_1, *Temperature* is measured in degrees Fahrenheit and the *WindSpeed* is measured in miles per hour. For contrast, an alternative ontology of weather O_2 from the viewpoint of a company K_2 is shown in Figure 3.

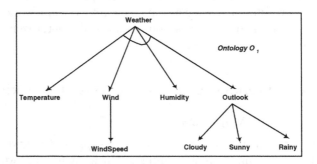

Fig. 2. Weather Ontology of Company K_1

Suppose $O_1,...,O_n$ are ontologies associated with components $C_1,...,C_n$, respectively. In order to compose workflow using those semantically heterogeneous components, the user needs to specify the mappings between these ontologies of the various components. For example, a company K_3, with ontology O_3 uses meteorology workflow components supplied by K_1 and K_2. Suppose in O_3, *Weather*

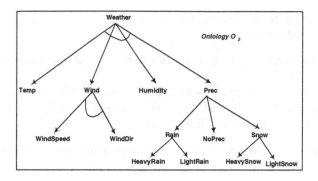

Fig. 3. Weather Ontology of Company K_2

is described by *Temperature* (measured in degrees Fahrenheit), *WindSpeed* (measured in mph), *Humidity* and *Outlook*. Then, K_3 will have to specify a suitable mapping $M_{O_1 \mapsto O_3}$ from K_1 to K_3 and a mapping $M_{O_2 \mapsto O_3}$ from K_2 to K_3. For example, *Temperature* in O_1 and *Temp* in O_2 may be mapped by $M_{O_1 \mapsto O_3}$ and $M_{O_2 \mapsto O_3}$ respectively to *Temperature* in O_3. In addition, conversion functions to perform unit conversions (e.g. *Temp* values in O_2 from degrees Centigrade to degrees Fahrenheit) can also be specified. Suppose K_3 considers *Precipitation* in O_2 is equivalent to *Outlook* in O_3 and maps *Rain* in O_2 to *Rainy* in O_3. This would implicitly map both *LightRain* and *HeavyRain* in O_2 to *Rainy* in O_3. These mappings between ontologies are specified through *interoperation constraints*.

Definition (Interoperation Constraints) [7,4]: Let $(H_1, \preceq_1)$ and $(H_2, \preceq_2)$, be any two hierarchies. We call the set of *Interoperation Constraints (IC)* the set of relationships that exists between elements from two different hierarchies. For two elements, $x \in H_1$ and $y \in H_2$, we can have *one* of the following Interoperation Constraints:

- $x : H_1 = y : H_2$
- $x : H_1 \neq y : H_2$
- $x : H_1 \leq y : H_2$
- $x : H_1 \not\leq y : H_2$

Example: For the weather domain, if we consider *part-of* hierarchies associated with the companies K_1 and K_2, we have the following interoperation constraints, among others- *Temperature* : 1 = *Temp* : 2, *Outlook* : 1 = *Prec* : 2, *Humidity* : 1 ≠ *Wind* : 2, *WindDir* : 2 $\not\leq$ *Wind* : 1, and so on.

Definition (Type, Domain, Values) [7,4]: We define $T = \{\tau \mid \tau \text{ is a string}\}$ to be a set of *types*. For each type τ, $D(\tau) = \{v | v \text{ is a value of type } \tau\}$ is called the *domain* of τ. The members of $D(\tau)$ are called *values* of type τ.

Example: A type τ could be a predefined type, e.g. *int* or *string* or it can be a type like *USD* (US Dollars) or *kmph* (kilometers per hour).

Definition (Type Conversion Function) [7,4]: We say that a total function $f(\tau_1, \tau_2): D(\tau_1) \mapsto D(\tau_2)$ that maps the values of τ_1 to values of τ_2 is a *type* *conversion function* from τ_1 to τ_2. The set of all type conversion functions satisfy the following constraints:

- For every two types τ_i, $\tau_j \in T$, there exists *at most* one conversion function $f(\tau_i, \tau_j)$.
- For every type $\tau \in T$, $f(\tau, \tau)$ exits. This is the identity function.
- If $f(\tau_i, \tau_j)$ and $f(\tau_j, \tau_k)$ exist, then $f(\tau_i, \tau_k)$ exists and $f(\tau_i, \tau_k) = f(\tau_i, \tau_j)$ $\circ$ $f(\tau_j, \tau_k)$ is called a composition function.

In the next few sections, we incorporate these definitions into our framework.

2.2   Component-Based Workflows

Definition (Primitive Component): A *primitive component* is a coherent package of software, that can be independently developed and delivered as a unit, and that offers interfaces by which it can be connected, unchanged, with other components.

Definition (Component): A *component* can be recursively defined as follows:

- A primitive component is a component.
- The composition of two or more components is a component.

Definition (Component-Based Workflow): A *component-based workflow* can be recursively defined as follows:

- A component is a workflow.
- The composition of two or more workflows is a workflow.

We can see that components are the building blocks upon which a workflow can be designed and composed.

Workflow Languages [1] facilitate precise formal specification of workflows. *Graph-Based Workflow Language* (GBWL) [20] allows us to model various aspects of traditional workflows which are relevant to our work. A GBWL specification of a workflow, known as *workflow schema* (WFS), describes the components of the workflow and the characteristics of the environment in which the workflow will be executed. The workflow schemas are connected to yield directed graphs of workflow schemas, called *workflow schema graphs* (WSG). The nodes of a WSG correspond to the workflow components and edges specify the constraints between the components. Figure 4 shows a WSG consisting of three components. Note that each workflow component trivially has a WSG description. When a workflow is to be executed, a WFS is instantiated resulting in the creation of a *workflow instance* (WFI). Each WFI created from a well-formed WFS is guaranteed to conform to the conditions specified by the WFS. The *functional aspect* of a workflow schema specifies the task to be performed by the corresponding workflow instances. The *information aspect* of a WSG specifies the data flow between the individual components. Associated with each component is a set of typed inputs and outputs. At the initiation of a workflow, the inputs are read, while on termination the results of the workflow are written to the outputs. The

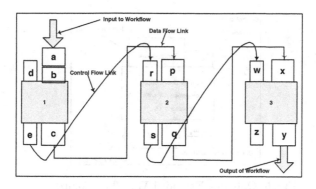

Fig. 4. Workflow Schema Graph

data flow which is defined in terms of the inputs and outputs, models the transfer of information through the workflow. For example, in Figure 4, component 1 has inputs a and b and an output c, and component 2 has an input p and an output q. Note that the data flow between components 1 & 2 is represented by the data flow link (c, p). The *behavioral aspect* of a WFS specifies the conditions under which an instance of the component will be executed. The behavior of a workflow is determined by two types of conditions: *Control* conditions and *Instantiation* conditions. The relation between the components is determined by the control conditions, which are expressed by the control flow links. These control flow links specify the execution constraints. For example, Figure 4 shows control flow links (e, r) specifying that the execution of component 1 has to precede the execution of component 2. In order for a workflow component to be executed, its instantiation conditions have to be set to $True$. Specifically, the existence of a control flow link from 1 to 2 does not imply that 2 will necessarily be executed as soon as 1 is executed (unless the instantiation conditions are satisfied). In general, it is possible to have cyclic data and control flow links. However, in the interest of simplicity, we limit the discussion in this paper to acyclic WSG.

2.3   Ontology-Extended Workflow Components

From the preceding discussion it follows that a workflow can be encapsulated as a component in a more complex workflow. Thus, to define *ontology-extended component-based workflows*, it suffices to show how components can be extended with ontologies and how the resulting ontology-extended components can be composed to yield more complex components (or equivalently, workflows).

Recall that a component has associated with it, input, output and control flow attributes. The control flow attributes take values from the domain $D(CtrlType)$ = {true, false, ϕ}, where the value of ϕ corresponds to the initial value of a control flow attribute indicating that the control flow link is yet to be signaled.

Definition (Ontology-Extended Workflow Component): An *ontology-extended workflow component*, s, consists of (see Figure 5):

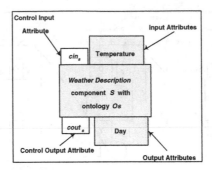

Fig. 5. Ontology-Extended Workflow Component

- An associated ontology O_s.
- A set of data types $\tau_1, \tau_2,..., \tau_n$, such that $\tau_i \in O_s$, for $1 \leq i \leq n$.
- A set of input attributes $input_s$ represented as an r-tuple $(A_{1_s}:\tau_{i_1},...,A_{r_s}:\tau_{i_r})$ (e.g., *Temp:C* is an input attribute of type Centigrade).
- A set of output attributes $output_s$ represented as a p-tuple $(B_{1_s}:\tau_{j_1},...,B_{p_s}:\tau_{j_p})$ (e.g., *Day:DayType* is an output attribute of type *DayType* whose enumerated domain is {*Hot, Warm, Cold*}).
- A control input attribute, cin_s, such that $\tau(cin_s) \in CtrlType$. A true value for cin_s indicates that the component s is ready to start its execution.
- A control output attribute, $cout_s$, such that $\tau(cout_s) \in CtrlType$. A true value for $cout_s$ indicates the termination of the execution of component s.

The composition of two components specifies the data flow and the control flow links between the two components. In order for the meaningful composition of ontology-extended workflow components to be possible, it is necessary to resolve the semantic and syntactic mismatches between such components.

Definition (Ontology-Extended Workflow Component Composition): Two components s (source) (with an associated ontology O_s) and t (target) (with an associated ontology O_t) are *composable* if some (or all) outputs of s are used as inputs for t. This requires that there exists:

- A directed edge, called control flow link, $C_{link}(s,t)$, that connects the source component s to the target component t. This link determines the flow of execution between the components. We have:

$$C_{link}(s,t) \in cout_s \times cin_t,$$

  which means that there exists $x \in cout_s$ and $y \in cin_t$ such that $\tau(x) \in CtrlType$ and $\tau(y) \in CtrlType$. For example, in Figure 4, (e, r) is a control flow link between the components 1 and 2.
- A set of data flow links, $D_{link}(s,t)$ from the source component s to the target component t. These links determine the flow of information between the components. We have:

$$D_{link}(s,t) \subseteq output_s \times input_t,$$

which means that there exist attributes $x \in output_s$ and $y \in input_t$, such that $\tau(x) = \tau_i \in O_s$ and $\tau(y) = \tau_j \in O_t$. For example, in Figure 4, (c, p) is a data flow link between the components 1 and 2.

- A set of (user defined) interoperation constraints, $IC(s, t)$, that define a mappings set $MS(s, t)$ between outputs of s in the context of the ontology O_s and inputs of t in the context of the ontology O_t. Thus, if $x : O_s = y : O_t$ is an interoperation constraint, then x will be mapped to y, and we write $x \mapsto y$.

- A set of (user defined) conversion functions $CF(s, t)$, where any element in $CF(s, t)$ corresponds to one and only one mapping $x \mapsto y \in IC(s, t)$. The identity conversion functions may not be explicitly specified. Thus, $|IC(s, t)| \leq |CF(s, t)|$.

Note that, in general, a component may be connected to more than one *source* and/or *target* component(s). The mappings set $MS(s, t)$ and the conversion functions $CF(s, t)$ together specify a *mapping component*, which performs the mappings from elements in O_s to elements in O_t.

Definition (Mapping Component): A *mapping component*, $MAP(s, t)$, which maps the output and the control output attributes of the source s to the input and the control input attributes of the target t respectively, consists of:

- Two ontologies, O_s and O_t, where O_s is associated with the inputs of $MAP(s, t)$, and O_t is associated with its outputs.
- A set of mappings $MS(s, t)$ and their corresponding conversion functions $CF(s, t)$ that perform the actual mappings and conversions between inputs and outputs.
- A set of data inputs $input_{map} = (A_{1_M} : \tau_{s_1}, \cdots, A_{p_M} : \tau_{s_p})$, which correspond to the output attributes of component s, that is, $input_{map} \equiv output_s$. Also, $\tau_{s_1}, ..., \tau_{s_p}$ is a set of data types such that $\tau_{s_i} \in O_s, \forall 1 \leq i \leq p$.
- A set of data outputs $output_{map} = (B_{1_M} : \tau_{t_1}, ..., B_{r_M} : \tau_{t_r})$, which correspond to the input attributes of component t, that is, $output_{map} \equiv input_t$. Also, $\tau_{t_1}, ..., \tau_{t_r}$ is a set of data types such that $\tau_{t_i} \in O_t, \forall 1 \leq i \leq r$.
- A control input cin_{map}, which corresponds to the control output attribute, $cout_s$ of component s. Also, $\tau(cin_{map}) = CtrlType$.
- A control output $cout_{map}$, which corresponds to the control input attribute, cin_t of component t. Also, $\tau(cout_{map}) = CtrlType$.

Ontology-extended workflow component instances (see Figure 6) are obtained by instantiating the ontology-extended workflow components at execution time. This entails assigning values to each of the component attributes. These values need to be of the type specified in the component schema. If a component instance *ins* is based on a component schema *sch* of the component s, we say that $hasSchema(ins) = sch$. We also say that for a given attribute, p, $v(p) \in D(t)$ refers to its value, if $\tau(p) = t \in O_s$.

Definition (Ontology-Extended Workflow Component Instance): The instance corresponding to an ontology-extended workflow component s has to satisfy the following constraints:

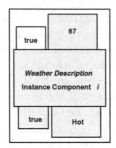

Fig. 6. Ontology-Extended Workflow Component Instance

- For every input attribute $x \in input_s$, $v(x) \in D(t)$, if $\tau(x) = t \in O_s$ (e.g., *Temperature = 87*).
- For every output attribute $y \in output_s$, $v(y) \in D(t)$, if $\tau(y) = t \in O_s$ (e.g., *DayType = Hot*).
- For the control input attribute, $cin_s \in \{\text{true, false, } \phi\}$, a true value indicates that the component s is ready for execution.
- For the control output attribute, $cout_s \in \{\text{true, false, } \phi\}$, a true value indicates that the component s has finished its execution.
- For an instantiation condition, $insc_s \in \{true, false\}$. If the evaluation of this condition returns *true*, then the execution of the component begins. This condition is defined as:

$$insc_s \equiv \{(cin_s) \; \Lambda \; (\forall \; x \in input_s, \; \exists \; v(x) \;)\},$$

such that $\tau(x) = t$ and $t \in O_s$.

Semantic Consistency of composition of ontology extended workflow components is necessary to ensure the soundness of component-based workflow assembly.

Definition (Consistent Workflow Component Composition): The composition of any two ontology-extended workflow components s (source) and t (target) is said to be *consistent*, if the following conditions are satisfied:

- The *data & control flow* between s and t must be consistent, i.e., control flow should follow data flow.
- The data and control flow links must be *syntactically consistent* i.e., there should be no syntactic mismatches for data flow links.
- The data and control flow links must be *semantically consistent*, i.e., there should be no unresolved semantic mismatches along the data & control flow links. (Semantic mismatches between workflow components are resolved by mapping components)
- Data & control flow links should be *acyclic* (free of cycles).

Definition (Ontology-extended Workflow Consistency): An ontology-extended workflow W is semantically consistent if the composition of each and every pair of *source* and *target* components is consistent.

Recall that the composition of two components s and t is consistent if it ensures data and control flow, syntactic, semantic and acyclic consistencies.

– *Data and Control Flow Consistency*: By the definition of the ontology-extended component composition, for any composition there exists a set of data flow links $\in D_{link}(s,t)$ and there exists a control link $\in C_{link}(s,t)$. According to the definition of the ontology-extended component instance, the instantiation conditions $insc_t$ for t have to be satisfied, which means that all the inputs $\in input_t$ are instantiated when cin_t becomes true (it also means that $cout_s = true$). Thus, the control flow follows the data flow.

– *Syntactic and Semantic Consistency*: For every data flow link $(x,\ y) \in D_{link}(s,t)$, there exists a conversion function corresponding to a mapping introduced by an interoperation constraint (if such a function is not defined, it is assumed to be the identity). Thus, all the syntactic and semantic mismatches are resolved by the mapping component corresponding to the components s and t, and the syntactical and semantical consistency is ensured. Note that, for $C_{link}(s,t)$ there exists no syntactic differences.

– *Acyclic Consistency*: Our framework does not allow any cycles for data or control flow links.

3   Weather Description Workflow Example

In this section we illustrate ontology-extended component-based workflows using a sample workflow whose goal is to determine whether the day is hot, or warm or cold based upon the temperature (see Figure 7). This workflow is composed of two main components: C-Sensor component which calculates the current temperature upon the reception of the signals/bit streams from some external sensors and Weather Description component which determines the type of day (hot, warm, cold) based on the temperature. The two components are semantically heterogeneous and we show how they can be composed into a workflow using our framework.

Ontology-Extended Workflow Components: The components used in the sample workflow are described as follows:

– For the *source* component, C,
  • O_C is the associated ontology, which describes a *Sensor* by *Signals* and *Temp*, where $\tau(Signals) = Bits$ and $\tau(Temp) = Centigrade$.
  • *Bits, Centigrade* $\in O_C$ are the data types.
  • $input_C = (Signals : Bits)$.
  • $output_C = (Temp : Centigrade)$.
  • c_1 and c_2 are the control input and control output attributes, respectively.
– For the *target* component, W,
  • O_W is the associated ontology, which describes the *Weather* by *Temperature* and *Day*, where $\tau(Temperature) = Fahrenheit$ and $\tau(Day) = DayType$ and $D(DayType) = \{\text{Hot, Warm, Cold}\}$.
  • *Fahrenheit, DayType* $\in O_W$ are the data types.
  • $input_W = (Temperature : Fahrenheit)$.

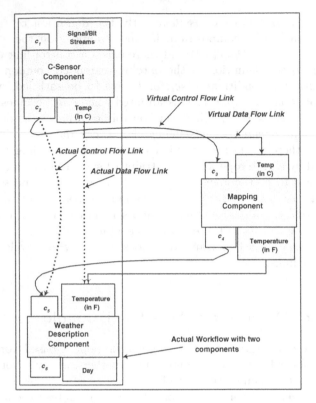

Fig. 7. Sample Workflow for Weather Description

- $output_W = (Day : DayType)$.
- c_5 and c_6 are the control input and control output attributes, respectively.

Composition of Ontology-Extended Workflow Components: The composition of the components C and W is defined as follows:

- Ontologies O_C and O_W (defined above).
- The control flow link, $(c_2, c_5) \in C_{link}(C, W)$, where $c_2 \in cout_C$ and $c_5 \in cin_W$.
- The data flow link, $(Temp, Temperature) \in D_{link}(C, W)$, where $Temp \in output_C$ and $Temperature \in input_W$.
- The interoperation constraint, $Temp{:}O_C = Temperature{:}O_W$. Thus, there also exist a mapping from $Temp$ to $Temperature$, denoted as, $(Temp \mapsto Temperature) \in MS (C, W)$.
- The conversion function, $f (Temp, Temperature) \in CF (C, W)$, which converts a value in Centigrade ($Temp$) to Fahrenheit ($Temperature$).

Mapping Component: Based on the interoperation constraints mentioned above, the mapping component, $MAP (C, W)$, can be defined as follows:

- Ontologies O_C and O_W are associated with its inputs and outputs, respectively.
- $(Temp \mapsto Temperature) \in MS(C, W)$ and $f\ (Temp,\ Temperature) \in CF(C, W)$ are the mapping and conversion function.
- $input_{map} = (Temp : Centigrade)$.
- $output_{map} = (Temperature : Fahrenheit)$.
- Attribute $c_3 \in cin_{map}$ is the control input attribute.
- Attribute $c_4 \in cout_{map}$ is the control output attribute.

Instances of Ontology-Extended Workflow Components: The instantiation condition for each of the component are shown below:

- *C-Sensor component*: The instantiation condition of the C-Sensor component is given by:

$$insc_C \equiv \{(c_1)\ \Lambda\ (\ \exists\ v(signals)\ )\} = \text{true}$$

The value of c_1 is considered to be true whenever the C-Sensor receives signal/bit streams from some external sensor(s). That is, the instantiation condition of the component instance is evaluated when the component receives signals, and if it evaluates to true, the execution of the instance begins. The component does some internal processing with its input *signal streams* and outputs the current temperature *Temp*. Also, a true value at c_2 indicates the termination of execution of the component instance.

- *Mapping component*: The instantiation condition of the Mapping component is given by:

$$insc_{map} \equiv \{(c_3)\ \Lambda\ (\ \exists\ v(Temp)\ )\} = \text{true}$$

The presence of a true value at c_2 (when C-Sensor component terminates its execution), results in a true value at c_3, of the mapping component. Upon successful evaluation of the instantiation condition of the component instance, the execution is initiated. On the termination of the component instance, it writes its output attribute *Temperature* (in degree F). Also, a true value at c_4, indicates the termination of execution of the component instance.

- *Weather Description component*: The instantiation condition for the Weather Description component is given by:

$$insc_W \equiv \{(c_5)\ \Lambda\ (\ \exists\ v(Temperature)\ )\} = \text{true}$$

The termination of the execution of the mapping component places a true value in c_5 at an instance of the workflow component. A true evaluation of the instantiation condition of the component instance, initiates its execution. The input attribute of this component, *Temperature*, corresponds to the output attribute of the mapping component. Note that both these attributes are syntactically and semantically identical. On termination of instance, it writes its output attribute *Day*. Finally, a true value at c_6 indicates the termination of execution of the component instance and also the termination of the workflow.

From the definitions above, the workflow is *consistent* because:

- The instantiation conditions ascertain that the control flow follows data flow.
- The mapping component guarantees that there are no syntactic and semantic mismatches.
- There are no cycles between data or control flow links.

4   Summary and Discussion

4.1   Summary

Recent advances in networks, information and computation grids, and WWW have made it possible, in principle, to access and use multiple, autonomous, semantically heterogeneous, networked information sources and software components or services. Development of tools that can contribute to substantial gains in productivity in specific application domains such as scientific discovery (e.g., bioinformatics), national defense (e.g., security informatics), business (e.g., e-commerce), manufacturing (e.g., virtual enterprises) and government calls for theoretically sound approaches for assembly of complex networks of coordinated activities or workflows from independently developed, semantically heterogeneous information sources and software components. Against this background, the framework of ontology-extended component-based workflows developed in this paper builds on recent advances in ontology-driven information integration [7,4,18,17] and component-based workflows [6,8,15,21] to address the need for a theoretically sound basis for composition of semantically heterogeneous workflow components into semantically consistent workflows.

4.2   Related Work

Benatallah *et al.* [3] introduce the Self-Serv framework for Web services composition. Their approach is based on two main concepts, namely, *composite service* and *service container*. The function of a composite service is to bring together various other services that collaborate to implement a set of operations, whereas, a service container facilitates the composition of a potentially large and changing set of services. However, the emphasis in this work has been more on the dynamic and scalable aspects of web service composition, and less on resolving semantic heterogeneity among the Web services, which remains as a major challenge in realizing the vision of the Semantic Web [2]. Cardoso *et al.* [8] provide metrics to select web services for composition into complex workflows. These metrics take into account various aspects like purpose of the services, quality of service (QOS) attributes, and the resolution of structural and semantic conflicts. Fileto [11] designed the POESIA framework for Web service composition using an ontological workflow approach. POESIA uses domain specific ontologies for ensuring semantic consistency in the composition process.

Our approach is similar to the approach in [11], where ontologies are used for component (or Web service) composition, and hence, for bridging the semantic gap between them. However, we allow users to specify the interoperation constraints and define the type conversion functions between attributes in different domains, thereby supporting flexible resolution of semantic mismatches between the distributed, heterogeneous and autonomous components.

4.3   Future Work

Some directions for future work include:

- Design and implementation of an environment for workflow assembly and execution from semantically heterogeneous software components, ontologies, and user-supplied mappings between ontologies.
- Development of an approach to verification of consistency of user-specified interoperation constraints using Distributed Description Logics [13, 5].
- Development of workflows for specific data-driven knowledge acquisition from autonomous, distributed information sources in computational molecular biology applications (e.g., discovery of protein sequence-structure-function relationships).
- Analyzing the dynamics and behavioral aspects of workflow execution.

Acknowledgment. This research was supported in part by grants from the National Science Foundation (0219699) and the National Institutes of Health (GM066387) to Vasant Honavar.

References

[1] The Workflow Reference Model: ⟨http://www.wfmc.org/⟩
[2] Berners-Lee, T., Hendler, J., Lassila, O.: The semantic web. Scientific American (2001)
[3] Benatallah, B., Sheng, Q., Dumas, M.: The self-serv environment for web services composition. IEEE Internet Computing **7** (2003) 40–48
[4] Bonatti, P., Deng, Y., Subrahmanian, V.: An ontology-extended relational algebra. In: Proc. IEEE International Conference of Information Reuse and Integration. (2003)
[5] Borgida, A., Serafini, L.: Distributed description logics: Assimilating information from peer sources. Journal of Data Semantics (2003) 153–184
[6] Bowers, S., Ludascher, B.: An ontology-driven framework for data transformation in scientific workflows. In: Intl. Workshop on Data Integration in the Life Sciences. (2004)
[7] Caragea, D., Pathak, J., Honavar, V.: Learning from Semantically Heterogeneous Data. In: 3rd International Conference on Ontologies, Databases, and Applications of Semantics for Large Scale Information Systems (2004)
[8] Cardoso, J., Sheth, A.: Semantic e-workflow composition. Journal of Intelligent Information Systems **21** (2003) 191–225
[9] Cox, P., Song, B.: A formal model for component-based software. In: Proc. IEEE Symposia on Human Centric Computing Languages and Environments. (2001)
[10] D'Souza, D., Wills, A.: Object, Components and Frameworks with UML - The Catalysis Approach. Addison-Wesley, Reading, MA (1997)

[11] Fileto, R.: POESIA: An Ontological approach for Data And Services Integration on the Web. PhD thesis, Institute of Computing, University of Campinas, Brazil (2003)

[12] Fischer, L.: Workflow Handbook. Future Strategeis Inc., Lighthouse Point, FL (2004)

[13] Ghidini, C., Serafini, L.: Distributed first order logics. In: Frontiers of Combining Systems 2. Volume 7. (2000) 121–139

[14] Levy, A.: Logic-Based Techniques in Data Integration. Kluwer Academic Publishers, Norwell, MA (2000)

[15] Ludascher, B., Altintas, I., Gupta, A.: A modeling and execution environment for distributed scientific workflows. In: 15th Intl. Conference on Scientific and Statistical Database Management. (2003)

[16] Marinescu, D.: Internet-Based Workflow Management: Toward a Semantic Web. Wiley, New York (2002)

[17] Reinoso-Castillo, J.: Ontology driven information extraction and integration from autonomous, hetergoneous, distributed data sources - a federated query centric approach. MS. thesis, Department of Computer Science, Iowa State University, USA (2002)

[18] Reinoso-Castillo, J., Silvescu, A., Caragea, D., Pathak, J., Honavar, V.: Information extraction and integration from heterogeneous, distributed and autonomous sources: A federated ontology-driven query-centric approach. In: Proc. IEEE International Conference of Information Reuse and Integration. (2003)

[19] Szyperski, C.: Component Software: Beyond Object-Oriented Programming. Addison-Wesley Longman, Reading, MA (1998)

[20] Weske, M.: Workflow Management Systems: Formal Foundation, Conceptual Design, Implementation Aspects (Habilitationsschrift). PhD thesis, Fachbereich Mathematik und Informatik, Universitt Mnster, Germany (2000)

[21] Zhuge, H.: Component-based workflow systems development. Decision Support Systems **35** (2003) 517–536

Data Procurement for Enabling Scientific Workflows: On Exploring Inter-ant Parasitism*

Shawn Bowers[1], David Thau[2], Rich Williams[3], and Bertram Ludäscher[1]

[1] San Diego Supercomputer Center, UCSD, La Jolla, CA, USA
[2] University of Kansas, Lawrence, KS, USA
[3] National Center for Ecological Analysis and Synthesis,
UCSB, Santa Barbara, CA, USA

1 Introduction

Similar to content on the web, scientific data is highly heterogeneous and can benefit from rich semantic descriptions. We are particularly interested in developing an infrastructure for expressing explicit semantic descriptions of ecological data (and life-sciences data in general), and exploiting these descriptions to provide support for automated data integration and transformation within scientific workflows [2]. Using semantic descriptions, our goal is to provide scientists with: (1) tools to easily search for and retrieve datasets relevant to their study (i.e., data *procurement*), (2) the ability to select a subset of returned datasets as input to a scientific workflow, and (3) automated integration and restructuring of the selected datasets for seamless workflow execution.

As part of this effort, we are developing the *Semantic Mediation System* (SMS) within the SEEK project[1], which aims at combining knowledge representation and semantic-web technologies (e.g., OWL and RDF) with traditional data-integration techniques [3, 8, 9]. We observe that along with these traditional approaches, mediation of ecological data also requires external, special-purpose services for accessing information not easily or conveniently expressed using conceptual modeling languages, such as description logics. The following are two specific examples of ecologically relevant, external services that can be exploited for scientific-data integration and transformation.

Taxonomic Classification and Mapping. There is an extensive body of knowledge on species (both extinct and existing) represented in a variety of different taxonomic classifications, and new species are still being discovered [7]. The same species can be denoted in many ways across different classifications, and resolving names of species requires mappings across multiple classification hierarchies [6]. Within SMS we want to leverage operations that exploit these existing mappings, e.g., to obtain synonyms of species names, without explicitly representing the mappings or simulating the associated operations within the mediator.

Semantics-Based Data Conversion. We are interested in applying operations during mediation that can transform and integrate data based on their implied meaning. How-

---

* This work supported in part by NSF grant ITR 0225674 (SEEK).
[1] *Science Environment for Ecological Knowledge*, http://seek.ecoinformatics.org

C. Bussler et al. (Eds.): SWDB 2004, LNCS 3372, pp. 57–63, 2005.

ever, for scientific data, the nature of these conversions are often difficult to express explicitly within a conceptual model. A large number of ecological datasets represent real-world observations (like measuring the abundance of a particular species), and therefore often have slightly different spatial and temporal contexts, use different measurement protocols, and measure similar information in disparate ways (e.g., area and count in one dataset, and density, which is a function of area and count, in a second dataset). As with taxonomic classification, we want the mediator to exploit existing conversion operations when possible.

This short paper describes an initial logic-based SMS prototype that leverages ontologies, semantic descriptions, and simple external services (primarily taxonomic) to help researchers find relevant datasets for ecological modeling. In Section 2 we describe our motivating scenario. In Section 3 we discuss details of the prototype through examples. And in Section 4 we conclude with future work.

2   Motivation: Ant Parasitism and Niche Modeling

A diverse and much studied group of organisms in ecology is the family *Formicidae*, commonly known as ants. Ants account for a significant portion of the animal biomass on earth and churn much of the earth's soil. Ants are also social animals that provide insights into the evolution of social behaviors. One such complex social behavior is parasitism between ant species [4].

The environment in which parasitism is likely to occur provides important data on how parasitism arises. For example, one theory states that inter-ant parasitism is more likely to arise in colder climates than in warmer ones. Thus, an ecological researcher may be interested in the question: *In California, what environmental properties play a role in determining the ranges of ants involved in inter-ant parasitism?*

Answering this question requires access to a wide array of data: (1) the types of parasitic relationships that exist between ants, (2) the names of species of ants taking part in these parasitic relationships, (3) georeferenced observations of these species of ants, and (4) the climate and other environmental data within the desired locations.

Today, these datasets are typically sought out by the researcher, retrieved, and integrated manually. The researcher analyzes the data by running it through an appropriate ecological model, the result of which is used to help test a hypothesis. In our example, an ecological niche model [10] can be used, which takes data about the presence of a species and the environmental conditions of the area in question, and produces a set of rules that define a "niche" (i.e., the conditions necessary for the species to exist) relative to the given environmental conditions and presence data. The rest of this paper describes a first step towards helping a researcher to collect the datasets needed to test inter-ant parasitism, and similar high-level questions.

3   The Prototype

Our dataset-discovery architecture is shown in Figure 1. A set of repositories store ontological information, datasets, and semantic descriptions (of the datasets). A semantic

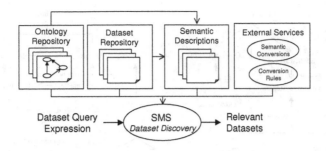

Fig. 1. The initial SMS architecture for ecological data mediation

d_1

genus	species	count	lat	lon
Manica	parasitica	2	37.85	-119.57
Manica	bradelyi	1	38.32	-119.67

d_2

genus	species	cnt	lt	ln
Camponotus	fornasinii	1	-29.65	26.18

d_3

man-para-cnt	aph-cald-cnt	lt	ln
3	6	37.56	-120.03

d_4

genus1	species1	genus2	species2
Manica	parasitica	Aphaenogaster	calderoni

Fig. 2. Four heterogeneous datasets d_1 through d_4

description logically annotates a dataset using concepts and roles in the ontology repository. Semantic descriptions are expressed as sound *local-as-view* mappings [3, 8], which can succinctly represent mappings from information within a dataset to corresponding ontological information. We also consider external services in the architecture, which currently consist of synonym and unit-conversion operations. The SMS engine accepts a user query and returns the set of relevant datasets that satisfy the given query.

Figure 2 shows example portions of four datasets that can be used to help answer ant and inter-ant parasitism queries. Dataset d_1 in Figure 2 contains georeferenced ant data from AntWeb[2] and consists of approximately 1,700 observations, each of which consist of a genus and species scientific name, an abundance count, and the location of the observation. Dataset d_2 in Figure 2 contains similar georeferenced ant data from the Iziko South African Museum (ISAM),[3] consisting of about 12,000 observations. Dataset d_3 in Figure 2 is a typical representation used for georeferenced co-occurrence data, where species are encoded within the schema of the table. This dataset contains only five tuples. Dataset d_4 in Figure 2 describes specific ants that participate in inquilinism inter-ant parasitism. The first two columns denote the parasite and the last two columns denote the host. Over two-hundred pairs of ants are described using four distinct datasets, each representing a particular parasitic relationship (all data were derived from Table 12-1 of [4]). Finally, Figure 3 shows a simplified fragment of the measurement and parasitism ontologies currently being developed within SEEK.

The following conjunctive queries define semantic descriptions of datasets d_1, d_3, and d_4 (the semantic description of d_2 is identical to d_1).

---

[2] See www.antweb.org
[3] Provided by Hamish Robertson, Iziko Museums of Cape Town

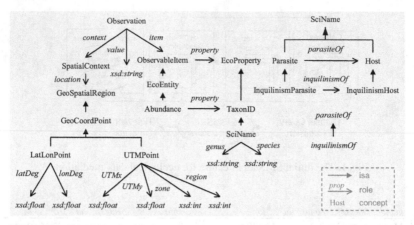

Fig. 3. Simplified ontologies for measurement observations and inter-ant parasitism

d_1(Ge,Sp,Co,Lt,Ln) :-
    Observation(O), value(O,Co), context(O,S), location(S,P), LatLonPoint(P),
    latDeg(P,Lt), lonDeg(P,Ln), item(O,A), Abundance(A), property(A,N), SciName(N),
    genus(N,Ge), species(N,Se).
d_3(Mp, Cf, Lt, Ln) :-
    Observation(O_1), value(O_1,Mp), context(O_1,S), location(S,P), LatLonPoint(P),
    latDeg(P,Lt), lonDeg(P,Ln), item(O_1,A_1), Abundance(A_1), property(A_1,N_1),
    SciName(N_1), genus(N_1,'Manica'), species(N_1,'parasitica'), Observation(O_2),
    value(O_2,Cf), context(O_2,S), item(O_2,A_2), Abundance(A_2), property(A_2,N_2),
    SciName(N_2), genus(N_2,'Aphaenogaster'), species(N_2,'calderoni').
d_4(G_1,S_1,G_2,S_2) :-
    InquilinismParasite(P), SciName(P), genus(P,G_1), species(P,S_1), InquilinismHost(H),
    genus(H,G_2), species(H,S_2), inquilinismOf(P,H).

The following example is a dataset-discovery query defined in terms of the ontology
that asks for all datasets containing georeferenced abundance measurements of Manica
bradleyi ants observed within California (as defined by the given bounding box). Dataset-
discovery queries allow predicates to be annotated with dataset variables, given as D
below. Each semantic description is also implicitly annotated with its dataset identifier,
e.g., every predicate in the body of the first description above would be annotated with
d_1. A dataset handle is returned by the query below if each formula annotated with D
is satisfied by the dataset, assuming the given inequality (i.e., the latitude-longitude)
conditions also hold.

q_1(D) :- Observation(O)^D, context(O,S)^D, location(S,P)^D, LatLonPoint(P)^D,
    latDeg(P,Lt)^D, lonDeg(P,Ln)^D, item(O,A)^D, Abundance(A)^D, property(A,N)^D,
    SciName(N)^D, genus(N,'Manica')^D, species(N,'bradleyi')^D, $Lt \geq 33$, $Lt \leq 42$,
    $Ln \geq -124.3$, $Ln \leq -115$.

Using a standard data-integration query-answering algorithm [8], the query above is
answered by (1) finding *relevant* information sources, i.e., sources whose view mappings
overlap with the given query, and (2) using the relevant sources, rewriting the user query,
producing a sound query expressed only against the underlying data sources, possibly
containing additional conditions. We extend this approach by also considering dataset

annotations on query formulas. In our example, d_1 and d_2 are the only relevant datasets for the above query, giving the following query rewritings. Note that after executing the queries below, only d_1 is returned; the ISAM dataset does not contain the given species.

$q_1(d_1)$:- d_1('Manica','bradleyi',Ct,Lt,Ln), Lt $\geq$ 33, Lt $\leq$ 42, Ln $\geq$ -124.3, Ln $\leq$ -115.
$q_1(d_2)$:- d_2('Manica','bradleyi',Ct,Lt,Ln), Lt $\geq$ 33, Lt $\leq$ 42, Ln $\geq$ -124.3, Ln $\leq$ -115.

The following query is similar to q_1, but uses an external service (prefixed with 'ext:') for computing synonymy of species names.

$q_2(D)$:- Observation(O)^D, context(O,S)^D, location(S,P)^D, LatLonPoint(P)^D, latDeg(P,Lt)^D, lonDeg(P,Ln)^D, item(O,A)^D, Abundance(A)^D, property(A,N)^D, SciName(N)^D, genus(N,Ge)^D, species(N,Sp)^D, Lt $\geq$ 33, Lt $\leq$ 42, Ln $\geq$ -124.3, Ln $\leq$ -115, ext:synonym('Manica','bradleyi',Ge,Sp).

The synonymy operation, encapsulated as a logical formula above, draws from descriptions in the Hymenoptera Name Server [5], and supports over 2,500 taxa of ants and their synonymy mappings. In the operation, a given genus-species pair is always a synonym of itself. In the prototype, we equate synonyms between taxa as equivalence relations. This assumption is often an oversimplification [1] and in future work we intend to explore different synonymy relations between taxa.

The following rewritings are obtained from the above query. After execution, the rewritten q_2 query will return dataset d_1 as well as dataset d_3; the latter because Aphaenogaster calderoni is a synonym of Manica bradleyi. Note that we could have discarded the third rewriting below since all arguments of the synonym operation are ground, and for the particular binding, the species' are not valid synonyms.

$q_2(d_1)$:- d_1(Ge,Sp,Ct,Lt,Ln), Lt $\geq$ 33, Lt $\leq$ 42, Ln $\geq$ -124.3, Ln $\leq$ -115, ext:synonym('Manica','bradleyi',Ge,Sp).
$q_2(d_2)$:- d_2(Ge,Sp,Ct,Lt,Ln), Lt $\geq$ 33, Lt $\leq$ 42, Ln $\geq$ -124.3, Ln $\leq$ -115, ext:synonym('Manica','bradleyi',Ge,Sp).
$q_2(d_3)$:- d_3(Mp,Cf,Lt,Ln), Lt $\geq$ 33, Lt $\leq$ 42, Ln $\geq$ -124.3, Ln $\leq$ -115, ext:synonym('Manica','bradleyi','Manica','parasitica').
$q_2(d_3)$:- d_3(Mp,Cf,Lt,Ln), Lt $\geq$ 33, Lt $\leq$ 42, Ln $\geq$ -124.3, Ln $\leq$ -115, ext:synonym('Manica','bradleyi','Aphaenogaster','calderoni').

Finally, the following query finds datasets containing georeferenced measurements of parasites of Manica bradleyi within California. Thus, the query finds the relevant ant presence data needed for our original parasitism question, for a single host species. The query uses the external synonym operation and projects the latitude, longitude, and genus and species names of the relevant observations so that the result (with additional pre-processing) can be fed into a scientific workflow, such as a niche model.

$q_3(D,Lt,Ln,Ge,Sp)$:- Observation(O)^D, context(O,S)^D, location(S,P)^D, LatLonPoint(P)^D, latDeg(P,Lt)^D, lonDeg(P,Ln)^D, item(O,A)^D, Abundance(A)^D, property(A,N)^D, SciName(N)^D, genus(N,Ge)^D, species(N,Sp)^D, Lt $\geq$ 32, Lt $\leq$ 42, Ln $\geq$ -124.3, Ln $\leq$ -115, Host(Ho), genus(Ho,Ge$_1$), species(Ho,Sp$_1$), ext:synonym('Manica','bradleyi',Ge$_1$,Sp$_1$), Parasite(Pa), genus(Pa,Ge$_2$), species(Pa,Sp$_2$), parasiteOf(Pa,Ho), ext:synonym(Ge$_2$,Sp$_2$,Ge,Sp).

The rewritings of q_3 are shown below. The result includes the tuples (d_1,37.85,-119.57,'Manica','parasitica') and (d_3,37.56,-120.03,'Manica','parasitica'), where only datasets d_1 and d_3 contain possible answers. In particular, Manica parasitica are inquilinism parasites of Manica bradleyi, which is derived from dataset d_4 by computing Manica bradleyi synonyms.

$q_3(d_1,Lt,Ln,Ge,Sp)$:- $d_1(Ge,Sp,Ct,Lt,Ln)$, $Lt \geq 33$, $Lt \leq 42$, $Ln \geq -124.3$, $Ln \leq -115$,
    ext:synonym('Manica','bradleyi',Ge_1,Sp_1), $d_4(Ge_1,Sp_1,Ge_2,Sp_2)$,
    ext:synonym(Ge_2,Sp_2,Ge,Sp).

$q_3(d_1,Lt,Ln,Ge,Sp)$:- $d_2(Ge,Sp,Ct,Lt,Ln)$, $Lt \geq 33$, $Lt \leq 42$, $Ln \geq -124.3$, $Ln \leq -115$,
    ext:synonym('Manica','bradleyi',Ge_1,Sp_1), $d_4(Ge_1,Sp_1,Ge_2,Sp_2)$,
    ext:synonym(Ge_2,Sp_2,Ge,Sp).

$q_3(d_1,Lt,Ln,Ge,Sp)$:- $d_3(Mp,Cf,Lt,Ln)$, $Lt \geq 33$, $Lt \leq 42$, $Ln \geq -124.3$, $Ln \leq -115$,
    ext:synonym('Manica','bradleyi',Ge_1,Sp_1), $d_4(Ge_1,Sp_1,Ge_2,Sp_2)$,
    ext:synonym(Ge_2,Sp_2,'Manica','parasitica').

$q_3(d_1,Lt,Ln,Ge,Sp)$:- $d_3(Mp,Cf,Lt,Ln)$, $Lt \geq 33$, $Lt \leq 42$, $Ln \geq -124.3$, $Ln \leq -115$,
    ext:synonym('Manica','bradleyi',Ge_1,Sp_1), $d_4(Ge_1,Sp_1,Ge_2,Sp_2)$,
    ext:synonym(Ge_2,Sp_2,'Aphaenogaster','calderoni).

4   Summary and Future Work

We have described an initial prototype that enables semantic-based dataset-discovery queries and supports mixing external services with traditional query-answering techniques. The prototype is written in Prolog and has an accompanying web interface for queries over geographic region, species, and parasitic relationship. We are extending the prototype by adding additional ontology-based query answering techniques including support for external services that perform transformation operations. To illustrate, the semantic description below is for a dataset similar to d_1, but uses an external service UTM2LatLon(Ux,Uy,Re,Zo,Lt,Ln) that converts UTM to latitude-longitude degree coordinates.

$d_5(Ge,Sp,Co,Ux,Uy,Re,Zo)$:-
    Observation(O), value(O,Co), context(O,S), location(S,P), UTMPoint(P),
    UTMx(P,Ux), UTMy(P,Uy), region(P,Re), zone(P,Zo), item(O,A), Abundance(A),
    property(A,N), SciName(N), genus(N,Ge), species(N,Se).

To answer query q_1, we want to (1) return d_5 as a relevant source, since UTM points can be converted to latitude-longitude points using UTM2LatLon, and (2) correctly insert a call to UTM2LatLon into the resulting query as part of the query rewriting. We are currently exploring *parameter dependency* specifications for this purpose, in which the domain and range of an external service are semantically described. In general, we believe incorporating external services into mediator architectures provides a powerful framework to support complex integration and transformation of scientific data.

References

1. W. Berensohn. The concept of "Potential Taxa" in databases. *Taxon*, vol. 44, 1995.
2. S. Bowers and B. Ludäscher. An ontology-driven framework for data transformation in scientific workflows. In *Proc. of Data Integration in the Life Sciences*, LNCS, vol. 2994, 2004.

3. A. Y. Halevy. Answering queries using views: A survey. In *VLDB Journal*, 10(4), 2001.

4. B. Hölldobler and E. O. Wilson. *The Ants*. Harvard University Press, 1990.

5. N. F. Johnson. The Hymenoptera Name Server. http://atbi.biosci.ohio-state.edu:210/hymenoptera/nomenclator.home_page

6. T. Paterson and J. Kennedy. Approaches to storing and querying structural information in botanical specimen descriptions. To appear in *Proc. of BNCOD*, LNCS, July, 2004.

7. A. Purvis and A. Hector. Getting the measure of biodiversity. *Nature*, vol. 405, 2000.

8. A. Y. Levy, A. Rajaraman, and J. J. Ordille. Query-answering algorithms for information agents. In *Proc. of AAAI*, 1996.

9. B. Ludäscher, A. Gupta, and M. E. Martone. Model-based mediation with domain maps. In *Proc. of ICDE*, IEEE Computer Society, 2001.

10. D. R. B. Stockwell and D. P. Peters. The GARP modelling system: Problems and solutions to automated spatial prediction. *Intl. J. of Geographic Information Systems*, vol. 13, 1999.

XSDL: Making XML Semantics Explicit*

Shengping Liu, Jing Mei, Anbu Yue, and Zuoquan Lin

Department of Information Science, Peking University,
Beijing 100871, China
{lsp, mayyam, yueanbu, lz}@is.pku.edu.cn

Abstract. The problem that "XML formally governs syntax only - not semantics" has been a serious barrier for XML-based data integration and the extension of current Web to Semantic Web. To address this problem, we propose the XML Semantics Definition Language(XSDL) to express XML author's intended meaning and propose a model-theoretic semantics for XML. Consequently, XML becomes a sub-language of RDF in expressiveness and XML data can be semantics-preserving transformed into RDF data. We further discuss the semantic entailment and validity of the XML documents.

1 Introduction

XML[1] has achieved great success as standard document format for writing and exchanging information on the Web. However, one of the limitations of XML has been well recognized: "XML formally governs syntax only - not semantics"[2]. The tags in an XML document are only meaningful to human, but meaningless to machine. For example, humans can predict the information underlying between the tags in the case of <price></price>, but for any generic XML processor, the tag <price> is equal to the HTML tag <H1>, because nowhere in an XML document, or DTD and XML Schema, does it say what these tags mean. Therefore, XML cannot express formal semantics by itself. Nonetheless, there are implicitly semantic information lied in the tags and structure of an XML document. For example[1],

Example 1. An XML fragment with implicit semantics

```
<wineMerchant name="Bristol Bottlers" >
    <wine id="w100">
        <name>Vielles Bottes</name>
        <color>black</color>
    </wine>
</wineMerchant>
```

---

* This work was supported by the National Natural Science Foundation of China under grant numbers 60373002 and 60496323.
[1] This XML fragment is modified from examples in SWAD-Europe Deliverable 5.1: http://www.w3.org/2001/sw/Europe/reports/xml_schema_tools_techniques_report.

C. Bussler et al. (Eds.): SWDB 2004, LNCS 3372, pp. 64–83, 2005.

The above XML fragment expresses rich semantic information: there is a wine merchant called "Bristol Bottlers" who sells a kind of wine whose name is "Vielles Bottes" and the color is black. The facts and relationship represented by the XML document is called XML Semantics[3].

In fact, the XML semantics is implicitly expressed in the XML documents. The semantics is conveyed on the basis of a shared understanding derived from human consensus. If there is an implicitly shared consensus about what the tags mean, then people can hardcode this implicit semantics into applications. The disadvantage of implicit semantics is that they are rife with ambiguity[4]. People often disagree with the meaning of a term. For example, prices come in different currencies and they may or may not include various taxes. The hardcoding of the XML semantics into applications make the interoperation and integration difficult.

Moreover, due to the implicit XML semantics, XML is not suitable to represent the content in the next generation of Web, Semantic Web[5]. The metadata language RDF[6] with a formal semantics was proposed as the standard to fulfil the task[7], and the techniques from knowledge representation field, such as the Web ontology language OWL[8], was introduced to represent the domain knowledge. Consequently, the semantic discontinuity between XML and RDF is formed; most XML data on the current Web cannot be smoothly transformed to the Semantic Web. This is a serious barrier for one of the statements by Semantic Web: being an extension of the current Web, and is also a barrier for the wide acceptance of Semantic Web in industry.

Therefore, for broad applications of XML and developments of Semantic Web, the XML semantics is required to be formally and explicitly specified. To this end, P. Patel-Schneider and J. Siméon proposed the XML model-theoretic semantics[9] and later the Yin/Yang Web[10], in which the data model of XML and RDF are unified and the XML document is given a direct RDF-compatible meaning. However, because there is no specification for expressing the XML semantics, hence the author of XML document can express the same meaning in almost arbitrary ways and the intended meaning of author is hidden in the tags and structure of the XML document without any formal description. Therefore, without the author's intervention, the direct interpretation for XML is difficult to capture the author's intended meaning and thus decrease the Yin/Yang Web's value in practical applications. For example, in the interpretation of XML in the Yin/Yang Web, an element node is mapped to an individual of the class with the same name. But, in fact, an element node in XML may represent an individual, a property and even a literal. Sometimes even worse, a node can have different meaning under different conditions. Thus, it is nearly impossible to capture the author's intended meaning by only syntactic analysis and a language to specify XML semantics by author is required. MDL(Meaning Definition Language,[11]) is such a language that defines the XML semantics in terms of UML class model and defines how to extract the meaning in terms of XPath[12]. The main disadvantage of MDL is that it has no formal semantics and thus provides no much help to bridge the gap between XML and Semantic Web.

Motivated by the Yin/Yang Web and MDL, we propose a novel approach. First, we propose the XML Semantics Definition Language (XSDL)[2], in which the XML semantics is defined in terms of OWL DL ontology and is extracted in terms of XPath (namely XPath 2.0) path expression. The XML authors can use XSDL to define the intended meaning of an XML document. Second, we propose the XML model-theoretic semantics that gives XML meaning by two steps: we firstly define the XML's simple interpretation that gives a rough meaning of an XML document, for example, an element node is interpreted as an individual in the universe; then we define the XML's XSDL-interpretation that gives the exact meaning of the XML document by taking the XML's XSDL definition into account, for example, the individual is further interpreted as an instance of some class according to the XSDL definition.

After XML document having XSDL to define the semantics, XML can express OWL DL's fact assertions, i.e., the statement about a particular individual in the form of classes that the individual belongs to plus properties and values of that individual[17]. Therefore, XML can be viewed as a knowledge representation language which is less expressive than RDF. Furthermore, we introduce the semantic validity of XML document to check whether the document satisfies the semantic integrity constraints and show that this problem is equivalent to the satisfiability of the knowledge base in the description logic language $\mathcal{SHOIN}(\mathcal{D})$. In addition, we discuss one important reasoning task about XML: the semantic entailment between XML documents, and show that the entailment problem can be reduced to the same satisfiability problem of $\mathcal{SHOIN}(\mathcal{D})$ [13].

The paper is organized as follows. We describe the syntax of XSDL with some examples in Section 2. The XML model-theoretic semantics that give XML meaning by simple interpretation and XSDL-interpretation is presented in Section 3. In Section 4, we discuss some related works. Finally, we conclude this paper in the concluding section.

2   XML Semantics Definition Language(XSDL)

The XML semantics is implicitly expressed in almost arbitrary ways, so it is difficult to extract the semantic information in a purely syntactic way. A language is required to define the semantics by human. The language should at least include two parts: a formal language to represent the semantic information in XML and a mapping language to specify the mapping from XML constructs to the formal language. In XSDL, OWL DL is selected as the formal language because it is the standard Web ontology language and have a formal logic foundation; the mapping language is based on Schema Adjuncts Framework(SAF, [14]), which extends the XML's structural model given by XML schema with additional information about the meaning of XML instances. In SAF, information items are selected by means of XPath path expressions; the additional information is given

---

[2] In the XML Schema specification, a term "XML Schema definition language" is used, but "XSDL" is not proposed as the term's acronym by W3C.

by reference to an external schema. XSDL is the SAF implementation with the external schema as OWL DL ontology's XML presentation syntax[15].

Now we briefly introduce the XML syntax and abstract syntax of XSDL. For more detailed information about XSDL, refer to XSDL specification[25].

The XSDL document structure is as follows:

```
<schema-adjunct target="http://foo.org/myschema.xsd"
    xmlns:owlx="http://www.w3.org/2003/05/owl-xml">
  <document>
    <!-- global ontology definition: any legal syntax of OWL DL-->
    <owlx:Ontology owlx:name="http://foo.org/wine">
    ...
    </owlx:Ontology>
  </document>
  <!-- mapping rules definitions: mapping XML constructs to
        the global ontology -->
  <element context ="/wineMerchant">
    <owlx:Class owlx:name="WineMerchant" />
  <!--or:DataValue,Individual,ObjectProperty,DatatypeProperty-->
  </element>
  ...
  <attribute context ="/wineMerchant/wine/name">
    <owlx:DatatypeProperty owlx:name="name" />
    <!--or:ObjectProperty-->
  </attribute>
  ...
</schema-adjunct>
```

where the "target" attribute value is the XML Schema for which XSDL defines the semantics. Semantic information are given at all levels: document, element and attribute: the "document" node includes a global ontology definition; in "element" and "attribute" nodes, the "context" attribute selects the instance data by XPath 2.0 path expression, the child elements can be references to the individuals, classes, datatype properties and object properties defined in the global ontology. The global ontology is sometimes called the *ontology in XSDL*.

XSDL is defined at schema level and the XSDL definition can be applied to all XML documents conforming to the schema. But to be intuitive, the following examples are XML fragments when introducing the XSDL definitions.

2.1   Class Definition

In XML, individual is always denoted by XML element node, and then class is denoted by a set of element nodes. To define class in XSDL, we need an XPath path expression to select the set of nodes, and a reference to the class name in the global ontology. In addition, because URI reference is used to identify resources in Semantic Web, so we need a URI constructor to assign URI references to the resources mapped from XML nodes.

In Example 1, the set of wine nodes represent a *Wine* Class, every instance in the class have an URIref like "http://foo.org/wine#w100", this can be defined in XSDL as:

```
<element context="/wineMerchant/wine">
    <URIFunction>concat("http://foo.org/wine#",
        string("/wineMerchant/wine[$i]/@id"))</URIFunction>
    <owlx:Class owlx:name="Wine"/>
</element>
```

where the "context" attribute select the "wine" nodes; the "URIFunction" element is an XPath 2.0 function for URI construction, the parameter $i denote the ith node in the set selected by XPath expression, *string, concat* are both XPath built-in functions, other functions, such as *document-uri, namespace-uri*, can also be used to construct the URI; the "owlx:Class" node refers to a class that has been already defined in the global ontology.

Note that the use of URI function partially solves one of the limitations of OWL DL: datatype property cannot be inverseFunctional, so if ID-typed attribute is mapped to datatype property, it cannot identify the individual. Now we can construct URIref through the ID-typed attribute, and use URIref to identify individual. If the URI function is not given, the nodes will be interpreted as anonymous individuals.

The abstract syntax for class definition is:

<CtxPath^^element, urifn, cn^^Class>,

where "CtxPath" is the context path, "^^element" means the type of nodes return by context path are element nodes, "urifn" is the URI constructor function and "cn" is the class name. "^^Class" means that "cn" is a name of class.

2.2   Individual Definition

Sometimes we need to make assertions about individual or define enumerated class in the global ontology. Then we need to define individual in XSDL. In Example 1, one specific wine node represents an individual of class *Wine*, the syntax is:

```
<element context ="/wineMerchant/wine[@id='w100']">
    <owlx:Individual owlx:name="w100" />
</element>
```

Note that all nodes selected by context path are interpreted as the same individual, whereas every node is interpreted as different individual of the same class in above class definition.

The abstract syntax for individual definition is:

<CtxPath^^element, uri^^Individual>,

where "uri" is the individual's name or URIref.

2.3   Literal Definition

In XSDL, the values of attribute and text nodes are predefined as literal values. However, sometimes element node that has no attribute may also represent a literal. For example:

Example 2. An XML fragment about literal definition

```
<Mathematics>
    <student name="John" grade="87" id="100" />
</Mathematics>
```

where the "Mathematics" node can be viewed as a literal "maths" and be the value of "courseName" attribute of student, the equivalent XML fragment is:

```
<student name="John" grade="87" id="100" courseName="maths"/>
```

This can be defined in XSDL as:

```
<element context="/Mathematics">
   <owlx:DataValue  owlx:datatype="&xsd;string">
   maths</owlx:DataValue>
</element>
```

The asbtract syntax for literal definition is:
    <CtxPath^^element, literal^^ddd>,
where "ddd" is literal's data type.

2.4   Datatype Property Definition

In XML, attribute nodes and some element nodes with PCDATA type always represent datatype properties. To define this in XSDL, we need to further define the path attribute of "domainContext" and "rangeContext", which are the relative paths related to context path and define the way to extract the node pairs of the property.

In Example 1, node "id" and "name" represent datatype properties of class *Wine*, the syntax in XSDL is

```
<attribute context ="/wineMerchant/wine/@id">
    <domainContext path=".." />
    <rangeContext path="." />
    <owlx:DatatypeProperty owlx:name="wineID" />
</attribute>
<element context ="/wineMerchant/wine/name">
    <domainContext path=".." />
    <rangeContext path="text()" />
    <owlx:DatatypeProperty owlx:name="wineName" />
</element>
```

Note that the property *wineID* and *wineName* should have been defined in the global ontology. Because the range of datatype property must be literal values, so the node in the path of range context should be attribute node, text node or element node defined as literal. In addition, the context path is just a convenient way to locate the nodes that interpreted as individuals or literal values in the domain and range of the property. For the *wineName* definition, the context path can also be "/wineMerchant/wine", then the path of domain context should be "." and the path of range context should be "name/text()".

In the Yin/Yang Web, there must be a property between element node and its child attribute nodes, by contrast, XSDL provides a way to define the datatype property on any node pairs not limited by the document order. For example, in Example 2, we can relate the "student" node to its parent "Mathematics" node by a *courseName* property, the syntax is:

```
<element context ="/Mathematics/student">
    <domainContext path="." />
    <rangeContext path=".." />
    <owlx:DatatypeProperty owlx:name="courseName" />
</element>
```

Sometimes the document order in XML has significant meaning, for example, in the individual normal form for XML representations of structured data[3],

Example 3. An XML fragment extracted from the individual normal form

```
<Address>
        <string>US</string>
        <string>Alice Smith</string>
        <string>123 Maple Street</string>
</Address>
```

The "string" nodes have different meaning at different positions. Fortunately, XPath expressions can select nodes by position, for example, the first "string" node represents a *country* property, this can be defined in XSDL as:

```
<element context ="/Address/string[position()=1]">
    <domainContext path=".." />
    <rangeContext path="text()" />
    <owlx:DatatypeProperty owlx:name="country" />
</element>
```

As can be seen from the above example, XPath expression bridges the gap between ordered XML document and unordered semantic representation.

The abstract syntax for datatype property definition is:

$$<CtxPath\char`^\char`^ nodeType, DPath, RPath, dpn\char`^\char`^ DatatypeProperty >,$$

where "nodeType" can be "element" and "attribute" ,"DPath","RPath" are the "path" attribute of "domainContext" and "rangeContext" respectively, "dpn" is the name of datatype property.

---

[3] Henry S. Thompson, http://www.ltg.ed.ac.uk/~ht/normalForms.html

2.5   Object Property Definition

In XML, the nesting of elements always represent object property. In Example 1, the nesting of "wineMerchant" and "wine" nodes represent a "sell" object property. The definition is similar to datatype property definition, the syntax is:

```
<element context ="/wineMerchant">
    <domainContext path="." />
    <rangeContext path="wine" />
    <owlx:ObjectProperty owlx:name="sell" />
</element>
```

In addition, object property may be represented by reference in XML. The explicit referencing mechanism uses the ID/IDREF attribute combination, for example,

Example 4. An XML fragment with explicit reference by ID/IDREF

```
<wine id="w1001" name="Vielles Bottes" color="black" />
<wineMerchant name="Bristol Bottlers"  wineID="w1001" />
```

where "wineID" node is an IDREF-typed attribute node and refers to an ID-typed "id" attribute in a wine node. This ID/IDREF combination establishes a relationship between the "wine" individual and the "wineMerchant" individual, although XML does not say what is the relationship.

However, there are also implicit references by shared value in XML, for example[4],

Example 5. An XML fragment with implicit reference by shared value

```
<student name = "James Smith">
  <course>101</course>
</student>
<department name = "Mathematical Sciences">
  <courses>
    <course code = "101" name = "basic algebra"/>
  </courses>
</department>
```

The "attend" relationship between student and course is represented by the sharing of a value (the course code 101) between node < course>101</course> and node <course code="101" />.

To define object property by reference, we need further define the "IDPath" that is always the path of ID-typed nodes or the nodes implicitly referred outside and the "IDREFPath" that is always the path of IDREF-typed nodes or the nodes implicitly referring to other nodes by shared value. For implementation convenience, the "IDREFPath" should be relative XPath expression with respect

---

[4] This example is modified from an example in SWAD-Europe Deliverable WP5.2 : http://www.w3.org/2001/sw/Europe/reports/xslt_schematron_tool/".

to the context path, the "IDPath" should be absolute XPath expression and the
"path" attribute of "rangeContext" should be relative XPath expression with
respect to the "IDPath". The syntax for Example 4 is:

```
<attribute context="/wineMerchant/@wineID">
    <domainContext path=".." />
    <rangeContext path=".." IDPath="/wine/@id"  IDREFPath="."/>
    <owlx:ObjectProperty owlx:name="sell" />
</attribute>
```

where the path attribute in domain context selects the "wineMerchant" nodes
and the path attribute in range context selects the corresponding "wine" nodes.

The syntax for Example 5 is similar:

```
<element context="/student/course/text()">
    <domainContext path="../.." />
    <rangeContext path=".."
     IDPath="/department/courses/course/@code" IDREFPath="."/>
    <owlx:ObjectProperty owlx:name="attend" />
</element>
```

The abstract syntax for object property definition is:
<CtxPath^^nodeType, DPath, RPath, IDPath, IDREFPath,
opn^^ObjectProperty>,
where "opn" is the name of object property.

3   XML Model-Theoretic Semantics

After XML document having XSDL to specify the semantics, XML documents
not only carry the data, but also the data semantics. To make the semantics machine understandable, we now define XML's model-theoretic semantics.
First, we define XML's simple interpretation; second, we define XML's XSDL-
interpretation that is an extension on simple interpretation; third, we introduce
the semantic validity of XML document; finally, we discuss entailment problem
for XML.

3.1   Simple Interpretation of XML

After parsing, XML document is validated against DTD or XML Schema and
an XML XQuery 1.0 and XPath 2.0 Data Model[16] can be constructed. The
data model serves as the vocabulary for XML's simple interpretation. Because
the data model contains information about data type, we first introduce the
interpretation of datatype.

Definition 1 (Datatype). *A datatype d is characterized by a lexical space,
$L(d)$, which is a set of Unicode strings; a value space, $V(d)$; and a total mapping
$L2V(d)$ from the lexical space to the value space. A datatype map D is a partial
mapping from URI references to datatypes.*

Definition 2 (XML Vocabulary). *An XML vocabulary V is the data model of XML that consists of:*

1. *N: the node set of XML document, $N = N_e \cup N_a \cup N_t$, where N_e, N_a and N_t denote the set of element nodes, attribute nodes and text nodes, respectively, other kinds of nodes are ignored by the interpretation;*
2. *NP: the set of node pairs, $NP = N \times N$.*

Definition 3 (Simple Interpretation). *A simple interpretation I of an XML vocabulary V is defined by:*

1. *R: a non-empty set of resources, called the universe of I;*
2. *LV: the literal values of I, is a subset of R that contains the set of Unicode strings, the set of pairs of Unicode strings and language tags, and the value spaces for each datatype in D;*
3. *O: a subset of R, is disjoint with LV and contains the individuals of I;*
4. *$S : V_{I_0} \rightarrow O$: a total mapping from URIrefs in XML, denoted as V_{I_0}, into O;*
5. *$M_c : N_e \rightarrow O \cup LV$: a partial mapping from element nodes into individuals and literal values;*
6. *$M_c : N_a \cup N_t \rightarrow O \cup LV$: a total mapping from attribute nodes and text nodes into individuals or literal values. For each node $m \in N_a \cup N_t$:*
   - *(a) if the type of m is xsd:anyURI, then $M_c(m) \in O$ and $M_c(m) = S(dm : typed\text{-}value(m))$, where the "dm"-prefixed functions are the XML Data Model's accessor functions and the set of all URIrefs here is V_{I_0};*
   - *(b) if the type of m is supported by OWL(except xsd:anyURI), then $M_c(m) \in LV$ and $M_c(m) = dm : typed\text{-}value(m)$;*
   - *(c) if the type of m is not supported by OWL, then $M_c(m) \in V(D(xsd : string))$ and $M_c(m) = dm : string\text{-}value(m)$;*
7. *$M_o : NP \rightarrow R \times R$: a partial mapping from node pairs into pairs of resources, i.e., every node pair $< m, n > \in NP$ is interpreted as a resource pair $< M_c(m), M_c(n) >$ within an unknown relationship.*

The simple interpretation of XML has given a primary meaning to nodes and document order in XML Document, for example, an element node may represent an individual, but it cannot tell which class the individual belongs to. This information is further provided by XSDL interpretation.

3.2   XSDL-Interpretation of XML

XSDL provides further information about the author's intended meaning of XML document. The interpretation of XSDL is considered as extensions on XML's simple interpretation.

Definition 4 (XSDL Vocabulary). *An XSDL vocabulary V_X consists of:*

1. *V_0: the vocabulary of global OWL DL ontology, $V_0 = (V_L, V_C, V_D, V_I, V_{DP}, V_{IP}, V_{AP}, V_O)$, for the detailed meaning of OWL vocabulary items, refer to OWL Direct Model-Theoretic Semantics[17];*

2. XP: an XPath path expressions set, $XP = AXP \cup RXP$, where AXP and RXP denote the set of absolute path expressions and relative path expressions, respectively;
3. FN: the set of URI construction functions in XSDL class definitions.

Definition 5 (XSDL-Interpretation). *An XSDL-Interpretation I of XML vocabulary V extends XML's simple interpretation with:*

1. $M_{ap} : AXP \to 2^N$: *a mapping from absolute XPath path expression into a node set[5] that must be obtained according to W3C specification[26];*
2. $M_{rp} : N \times RXP \to 2^N$: *a mapping from relative XPath path expression with respect to node n into a node set that must be obtained according to W3C specification[26];*
3. $M_{fn} : N \times FN \to V_{IX}$: *a mapping from URI function, with respect to node n, into an URIref. This set of URIrefs is denoted as V_{IX};*
4. $S : V_{I_0} \cup V_0 \cup V_{IX} \to R$: *$S$ is extended to map all URIrefs in the global ontology and URIrefs constructed by URI functions into R, and $S(V_{IX} \cup V_{I_0}) \subseteq O$;*
5. I_0: *the global ontology's interpretation, $I_0 = (R_0, LV, O_0, S, L, EC, ER)$, where $O_0 = S(V_I)$, $R_0 = S(V_0)$, L, EC and ER are OWL's interpretations of typed literals, classes and properties, respectively;*

The meaning of XPath path expression is provided by mapping into a node set, and then the nodes are mapped into the universe of interpretation by M_c in the simple interpretation. For simplification, we avoid analyzing the detailed syntax of XPath expressions and providing a model-theoretic semantics for them.

The XSDL definitions, such as class definitions, are interpreted as semantic conditions on XML's XSDL-Interpretation:

Definition 6 (Semantic Conditions). *The semantic conditions on XML's XSDL-Interpretation are:*

1. *if there is literal definition: $<CtxPath\char`^\char`^element, literal\char`^\char`^ddd>$, then:*

$$literal \in V_L, M_{ap}(CtxPath) \subseteq N_e,$$

for each $n \in M_{ap}(CtxPath)$, such that

$$M_c(n) = L2V(D(ddd))(literal);$$

2. *if there is individual definition:$<CtxPath\char`^\char`^element, uri\char`^\char`^Individual>$, then:*

$$uri \in V_I, M_{ap}(CtxPath) \subseteq N_e,$$

for each $n \in M_{ap}(CtxPath)$, such that

$$M_c(n) = S(uri);$$

---

[5] In XPath 2.0, the value of an expression is always a sequence. For path expression, the value is a sequences of nodes by eliminating duplicate nodes and sorting in document order. so the node sequence can be viewed as a node set.

3. *if there is class definition:$<CtxPath\hat{\ }\hat{\ }element,\ urifn,\ cn\hat{\ }\hat{\ }Class>$, then:*

$$cn \in V_C, M_{ap}(CtxPath) \subseteq N_e,$$

for each $n \in M_{ap}(CtxPath)$, such that

$$M_c(n) = S(M_{fn}(n, urifn)) \ if \ urifn \ is \ given,$$
$$M_c(n) \in EC(cn);$$

4. *if there is datatype property definition:$<CtxPath\hat{\ }\hat{\ }nodeType,\ DPath,\ RPath,$
dpn$\hat{\ }\hat{\ }DatatypeProperty>$, then:*

$$dpn \in V_{DP}, M_{ap}(CtxPath) \subseteq N(nodeType),$$

$$where\ N(nodeType) = \begin{cases} N_e, & if\ nodeType="element"; \\ N_a, & if\ nodeType="attribute"; \end{cases}$$

for each $n \in M_{ap}(CtxPath)$,

$$|M_{rp}(n, DPath)| = 1 \ or \ |M_{rp}(n, RPath)| = 1,$$

i.e., for any context node n, there cannot be both more than one node in domain and range path; let the property's range is datatype d, for each $m \in M_{rp}(n, DPath)$, and for each $t \in M_{rp}(n, RPath)$, such that

$$M_c(t) \in V(d), M_c(t) = L2V(d)(dm : string\text{-}value(t))$$
$$M_o(<m,t>) = <M_c(m), M_c(t)> \in ER(dpn);$$

5. *if there is object property definition without reference: $<CtxPath\hat{\ }\hat{\ }nodeType,$
DPath, RPath, opn$\hat{\ }\hat{\ }ObjectProperty>$, then:*

$$opn \in V_{IP}, M_{ap}(CtxPath) \subseteq N(nodeType),$$

for each $n \in M_{ap}(CtxPath)$,

$$|M_{rp}(n, DPath)| = 1 \ or \ |M_{rp}(n, RPath)| = 1,$$

for each $m \in M_{rp}(n, DPath)$, and for each $p \in M_{rp}(n, RPath)$, such that

$$M_o(<m,p>) = <M_c(m), M_c(p)> \in ER(opn);$$

6. *if there is object property definition with reference:$<CtxPath\hat{\ }\hat{\ }nodeType,$
DPath, RPath, IDPath, IDREFPath), opn$\hat{\ }\hat{\ }ObjectProperty>$, then:*

$$opn \in V_{IP}, M_{ap}(CtxPath) \subseteq N(nodeType),$$

for each $n \in M_{ap}(CtxPath)$,

$$|M_{rp}(n, DPath)| = 1 \ or \ |M_{rp}(n, IDREFPath)| = 1,$$

for each $m \in M_{rp}(n, DPath)$, and for each $p \in M_{rp}(n, IDREFPath)$, there is one $q \in M_{ap}(IDPath)$ with $M_c(p) = M_c(q)$, then there is one $k \in M_{rp}(q, RPath)$, such that

$$M_o(<m,k>) = <M_c(m), M_c(k)> \in ER(opn).$$

According to the semantic conditions, XSDL further make assertions in the form of: $M_c(n) \in EC(cn)$, $M_c(t) \in V(d)$ and $M_o(< m, n >) = < M_c(m), M_c(n) > \in ER(pn)$, then, XML document is interpreted as a set of fact assertions with respect to the ontology in XSDL. we call this assertion set *XML Facts*. From a view of description logic, the ontology in XSDL is a TBox[6], an XML document conforming to the XSDL definition is an ABox with respect to the TBox.

The XML Facts should be consistent with the ontology in XSDL, otherwise, from the viewpoint of logic, one could draw arbitrary conclusions from it. In terms of our model-theoretic semantics we can easily give a formal definition of consistency.

Definition 7 (Model). *An XML document's XSDL-Interpretation I is the XML's model, if I satisfies both the semantic conditions and the ontology in XSDL.*

Therefore, if an XML's XSDL-Interpretation I is the XML document's model, the XML Facts represented by the document is consistent with the ontology in XSDL. Note that XML model is only meaningful with respect to the XML's XSDL definition.

3.3   Semantic Validity of XML Documents

The XML's model satisfies both the XML Facts and ontology in XSDL. If the XML document has no model, there must be inconsistent between the XML document and the ontology, so having a model is an important property of XML document, this property is called semantic validity[7].

Definition 8 (Semantic Validity). *An XML document is semantically validated with respect to its XSDL definition, if there is a model of the XML document.*

As well-formness and syntactic validity enable XML's syntax checking, semantic validity further enable checking XML's semantic integrity constraints.

To check the semantic validity of XML documents, we first introduce the notion of "corresponding ontology". Because the XML Facts are fact assertions with respect to the global ontology, so we can merge the XML Facts and the global ontology in XSDL to form a new ontology.

Definition 9 (Corresponding Ontology). *For an XML document D, let O_0 denote the global ontology in D's XSDL definition, the corresponding ontology of D is the ontology merged by O_0 with the XML Facts represented by D.*

Second, we introduce the notion of extension and expansion[18]. The first-order language L' is an *extension* of language L if every nonlogical symbol of L

---

[6] Strictly speaking, the counterpoint of OWL DL ontology in description logic is knowledge base, because the ontology includes fact assertions.

[7] The "semantic validity" is comparable to the (syntactic) validity of XML document and the meaning of "validity" is not in logical sense.

is an nonlogical symbol of L'. A theory T' is an *extension* of theory T if $L(T')$ is an extension of $L(T)$ and every theorem of T is a theorem of T'. Let I' be the interpretation of L', by omitting some interpretation of nonlogical symbol we obtain a interpretation for I. We call I the *restriction* of I' on L and I' an *expansion* of I to L'. We have the following lemma:

Lemma 1 (J. Shoenfield[18]). *If theory T' is an extension of T, M' is a model of T', then the restriction of M' on language $L(T)$ is a model of T.*

Applied this notion to our problem, XML plus XSDL is our language and an XML document plus the XSDL definition is a theory of our language. Obviously, our language is an extension of OWL DL language and the theory of our language is also an extension of the theory of OWL DL language.

Third, we introduce a lemma about the relation between XML's model and the corresponding ontology's model.

Lemma 2. *The restriction of an XML's model on OWL DL language is a model of the XML's corresponding ontology; a model of XML's corresponding ontology can be expanded to the XML's model.*

Proof. 1)By Lemma 1,the restriction of an XML's model on OWL DL language is a model of the XML's corresponding ontology. 2) Denote the corresponding ontology's model as M, then M includes an OWL DL interpretation I_0 whilst the interpretation functions are M_c and M_o. Because M satisfies XML facts, there must be some M_{ap}, M_{rp}, M_{fn} and S satisfy the semantics condition (about M_c and M_o). Trivially $(M_c, M_o, M_{ap}, M_{rp}, M_{fn}, S, I_0)$ is a model of the XML Document. □

Finally, we have the following theorem to decide the semantic validity of XML document.

Theorem 1. *An XML document is semantically validated with respect to its XSDL definition iff the corresponding ontology of XML document is satisfiable.*

The theorem is an obvious consequence of Lemma 2.

According to Theorem 1, if the corresponding ontology of XML document is not satisfiable, then the XML document is semantically invalid. There are two problems resulting in semantic invalidity: first, the ontology in XSDL is not satisfiable; second, there are inconsistences between XML Facts and the ontology in XSDL. Below are some examples to illustrate the inconsistence.

Example 6. A semantically invalid XML fragment

```
<book>
    <author>Jerry</author>
    <author>Tom</author>
    <price>illegal price</price>
</book>
```

If the property *author* is defined as functional property in the global ontology and the XSDL definition for *author* is:

```
<element context = "/book/author" >
   <domainContext path=".." />
   <rangeContext path="text()" />
   <owlx:DatatypeProperty owlx:name="author"/>
</element>
```

then for each XSDL-interpretation I of the XML document, denote the book node as n, if I satisfy the semantic conditions:

$$< M_c(n), \text{"Jerry"} >\in ER(author)$$
$$< M_c(n), \text{"Tom"} >\in ER(author)$$

then I cannot satisfy the global ontology because this is contrary to the ontology definition of "author" property as functional property. Therefore, this XML document is semantically invalid.

In addition, the ill-typed literal will lead to semantic inconsistence too. In example 6, if the *price* node is defined as a datatype property with range as *float* in XSDL, then for each XSDL-interpreation I, if I satisfy:

$$M_c(\text{"illegal price"}) \in V(D(xsd:float))$$

I cannot satisfy the global ontology because "illegal price" cannot in the value space of data type *float*, so I is not the model of XML document.

Sometimes, semantic invalidity can be avoided by enforcing syntactic checking, such as define the *price* node type as *float* in XML Schema, then (syntactically) validated XML document will also be semantically validated. But semantic validity checking can further decide whether XML instance satisfy the integrity constraints that cannot expressed by DTD and XML Schema. For example,

Example 7. Another semantically invalid XML fragment about pedigree:

```
<person id="s1" gender="male" name="John"/>
<person id="s2" gender="female" name="Jane"/>
<person id="s3" gender="male" name="Tom" father="s2" mother="s1"/>
```

where "id" is an ID-typed attribute, "father" and "mother" are IDREF-typed attributes, this XML document is semantically invalid, because the value of "father" attribute in the third "person" node is referred to a female person. But both DTD and XML Schema cannot invalidate this kind of error reference, because they cannot assert that the "father" attribute must refer to an "id" attribute accompanied with a "gender" attribute whose value is "male".

However, this constraint can be expressed in XSDL as follows:

```
(1) <"/person[@gender='male']"^^element, urifn1, "Man"^^Class>
(2) <"/person[@gender='female']"^^element, urifn2, "Woman"^^Class>
(3) <"/person/@father"^^attribute, "..","..", "/person/@id", ".",
    "hasFather"^^ObjectProperty>,
```

The "person" nodes with gender's value as male are defined as instances of class Man and the "person" nodes with gender's value as female are defined as instances of class $Woman$, attribute node "father" represent an object property $hasFather$ with reference. In addition, in the global ontology, we define:

(4) <hasFather, rdfs:range, Man>,
(5) <Man, owl:disjointWith, Woman>,

Denote the person with "id" equals to "s2" as p_2, and the person with "id" equals to "s3" as p_3, then according to the semantic conditions of XSDL-Interpretation, one part of the XML Facts is:

by (2): $p_2 \in EC(Woman)$,
by (3): $< p_3, p_2 > \in ER(hasFather)$,

Combined with the global ontology, we can easily infer that:

$p_2 \in EC(Man)$,
$p_2 \in EC(Man) \cap EC(Woman)$.

This is contrary to the disjointness between class Man and $Woman$. By Theorem 1, the pedigree.xml is semantically invalid with respect to the above XSDL definition.

3.4 Reasoning About XML

After XML has a formal semantics, we can define entailment of XML documents. However, the definition is somehow different from classical logic. If XML document D_2 have different nodes from document D_1, then any D_1's model cannot be a model of D_2, because D_1's interpretation do not give meaning to the different nodes in D_2. So we need extend D_1's vocabulary to some one(eg. D') that contains D_2's vocabulary. D_1's model M is simultaneously expanded to an interpretation M' defined on D' by keeping the universe and the interpretation of individuals unchanged.

Definition 10 (Entailment). *Assumed that XML document D_1 and D_2 have the same XSDL definition, D_1 entails D_2, if for every D_1's model, there exists an expansion that is a model of D_2. Denoted as $D_1 \models D_2$.*

Definition 11 (Equivalence). *Assumed that XML document D_1 and D_2 have same XSDL definition, D_1 is equivalent with D_2, if $D_1 \models D_2$ and $D_2 \models D_1$. Denoted as $D_1 \equiv D_2$.*

To reduce the XML entailment problem to ontology entailment problem, we have the following theorem:

Theorem 2. *Let the corresponding ontology of XML document D_1 and D_2 are O_1 and O_2, respectively, then $D_1 \models D_2$ iff $O_1 \models O_2$.*

Proof. $\Rightarrow$Let M_1' be an arbitrary model of O_1, by Lemma 2, M_1' can be expanded to D_1's model, denoted as M_1. Since $D_1 \models D_2$, we have M_1's expansion M_2, which is a model of D_2. By Lemma 1, the restriction of M_2 to OWL language is a model of O_2. On the other hand, M_2 is an expansion of M_1 and then is an expansion of M_1', hence the restriction of M_2 to OWL language is M_1', so M_1' is also a model of O_2. That is, $O_1 \models O_2$.

$\Leftarrow$: Let M_1 be an arbitrary model of D_1, by Lemma 1, the restriction of M_1 to OWL language is a model of O_1, denoted as M_0', since $O_1 \models O_2$, so M_0' is also a model of O_2. By Lemma 2, M_0' can be expanded to a model of D_2, denoted as M_2, in addition, M_2 can be further expanded to model M_2' by adding the interpretation of nodes in D_1, obviously, M_2' is an expansion of M_1 and is the model of D_2, that is, $D_1 \models D_2$. $\square$

Theorem 3 (I. Horrocks and P. Patel-Schneider[13]). *OWL DL ontology entailment problem can be reduced to knowledge base satisfiability in description logic language $\mathcal{SHOIN}(\mathcal{D})$ in polynomial time.*

Corollary 1. *The XML entailment problem can be reduced to knowledge base satisfiability in $\mathcal{SHOIN}(\mathcal{D})$ in polynomial time.*

Example 8. Assume XML document D_1 simply is:

```
<man id="p1234" />
```

and XML document D_2 is :

```
<person id="p1234" />
```

If the XSDL definition is:

```
<"/man"^^element,"concat('http://foo.org/person#',
        string('/man[$i]/@id'))", "Man"^^Class>
<"/person"^^element,"concat('http://foo.org/person#',
        string('/person[$i]/@id'))", "Person"^^Class>
<Man, rdfs:subClassOf, Person>
```

Proposition 1. $D_1 \models D_2$ *with respect to the above XSDL definition.*

Proof. The corresponding ontology O_1 of D_1 is:

```
<Man, rdfs:subClassOf, Person>
<"http://foo.org/person#p1234",rdf:type, Man>
```

The corresponding ontology O_2 of D_2 is:

```
<Man, rdfs:subClassOf, Person>
<"http://foo.org/person#p1234", rdf:type, Person>
```

Obviously, $O_1 \models O_2$, by Theorem 2, XML document D_1 entails D_2. $\square$

Unfortunately, the complexity for the satisfiability problem is in NExpTime and there are yet no known optimized inference algorithms or implemented systems for $\mathcal{SHOIN}(\mathcal{D})$. However, if the ontology language is restricted to OWL Lite, then the problem can be reduced to knowledge base satisfiability in $\mathcal{SHIF}(\mathcal{D})$, whose complexity is in ExpTime[13]. The highly optimized reasoner RACER[19] can provide efficient reasoning services for $\mathcal{SHIF}(\mathcal{D})$.

4   Related Works

The "semantics" of XML have different understanding. The analogy between a document tagged by XML and a source string generated by a BNF grammar is noticed and thus enable adding semantic attributes and functions to XML[20]. From the SGML field, the BECHAMEL project[3] are trying to apply knowledge representation technologies to the modelling of meaning and relationship expressed by XML markup. The prototype formalization language and implementation environment is based on Prolog[21]. The formalization is complex and difficult to fulfill the requirement of Semantic Web.

Recently, P. Patel-Schneider and J. Siméon propose the idea of Yin/Yang Web [10], in which XML XQuery 1.0 and XPath 2.0 Data Model is regarded as a unified model for both XML and RDF, and a RDF-compatible semantics is developed based on this data model. However, because XML author can express semantics by almost arbitrary ways, the direct interpretation for XML in Yin/Yang Web is difficult to capture the author's intended meaning. We introduce XSDL to specify XML's semantics and gives XML meaning by two steps: the simple interpretation and the XSDL-interpretation. The two-step semantics is of more clarity and closer to XML author's intended meaning.

XSDL is similar to MDL[11] in adoption of Schema Adjuncts Framework and definition of XML semantics by conceptual model. However, MDL has proprietary syntax and takes UML as modelling language, in contrast, XSDL's syntax are mostly the standard XPath and OWL's XML syntax, hence XSDL is simple, easy to learn and implement; XSDL takes OWL DL as modelling language, thus XSDL has formal semantics, enables reasoning about XML and helps to bridge the gap between XML and Semantic Web.

XSDL defines XML semantics by mapping XML to ontology. There are other efforts: M. Erdmann and R. Studer[22] present a tool to generate DTD from ontology, then the tags of XML instances conforming to this DTD can be mapped to concepts and properties in the ontology; B. Amann, et al. [23]propose a rule-based language to map XML fragments into general ontology and later I. Fundulakil and M. Marx[24] provide a formal semantics by interpreting XML sources into ER models. The rule language does not support literal, individual definition and object property definition by reference in XSDL, and the ontology path in mapping rule is not supported by OWL. Besides, their work is intended for the querying of heterogeneous XML resources using an ontology-based mediator. In contrast, our work is intended to bridge the gap between XML and Semantic Web and is believed to be more tightly integrated with the Semantic Web architecture.

5   Conclusion and Future Works

In this paper, to address the problem that XML have no formal semantics, we propose XML Semantics Definition Language(XSDL) and a model-theoretic semantics for XML. XSDL is a simple language with which syntax mainly come from XPath, OWL XML syntax and SAF. There are only three additional constructs in XSDL: URI constructor, domain context and range context. The more significant work is the formal semantics for XML, which gives XML meaning by simple interpretation and XSDL-interpretation and is close to XML author's intended meaning. The semantics is compatible with a subset of RDF supported by OWL DL, hence, XML becomes a sub-language of RDF in expressive power and XML data can be semantics-preserving transformed to RDF data.

The expressive power of XML is the same as ABox in description logic language, thus is limited compared to general formal language. Therefore, XSDL is suitable to represent the semantics of data-centric XML document.

One limitation of our work is that XSDL document for XML need to be defined manually and the authoring is a laborious, time-consuming task. Note that XML Schema also has rich implicit semantic information, such as datatypes, cardinality constraints. The solution is to generate XSDL definition from XML Schema for author's further reviews and to develop user-friendly XSDL editor.

As Yin/Yang Web, our work can also be applied to semantic query of XML data, XML data integration and Semantic Web Services. In addition, XSDL is more natural and powerful to represent XML data integrity constraints than in a syntactic way, such as XML Schema. We will explore these application areas in future works.

Acknowledgement. We are grateful to Wei Song and the anonymous reviewers for their helpful suggestions for the improvements of this paper.

References

1. Bray, T., Paoli, J., Sperberg-McQueen, C.M., Maler, E.: Extensible Markup Language (XML) 1.0 (second edition) W3C recommendation (2000)
2. Cover, R.: XML and semantic transparency (1998)
3. Allen, R., Dubin, D., Sperberg-McQueen, C.M., Huitfeldt, C.: Towards a semantics for XML markup. In: the 2002 ACM Symposium on Document Engineering, 119–126
4. Uschold, M.: Where are the semantics in the Semantic Web? AI Magazine **24** (2003) 25–36
5. Berners-Lee, T., Handler, J., Lassila, O.: The Semantic Web. Scientific American **184** (2001) 34–43
6. Klyne, G., Carroll, J.J.: Resource Description Framework (RDF):concepts and abstract syntax,W3C recommendation 10 february 2004 (2004)
7. Berners-Lee, T.: Why RDF is more than XML (1998)
8. Patel-Schneider, P.F., Hayes, P., Horrocks, I.: OWL Web ontology language reference, W3C recommendation 10 february 2004 (2004)
9. Patel-Schneider, P.F., Simeon, J.: Building the Semantic Web on XML. In: the Twelfth International World Wide Web Conference, ACM Press (2003)
10. Patel-Schneider, P.F., Simeon, J.: The Yin/Yang Web: A unified model for XML syntax and RDF semantics. IEEE Transactions on Knowledge and Data Engineering **15** (2003) 797–812
11. Worden, R.: MDL: A Meaning Definition Language, version 2.06 (2002)

12. Berglund, A., Boag, S., Chamberlin, D., et al.: XML Path Language (XPath) 2.0 W3C working draft 12 november 2003 (2003)
13. Horrocks, I., Patel-Schneider, P.F.: Reducing OWL entailment to description logic satisfiability. In: the 2003 International Semantic Web Conference. 17–29
14. Vorthmann, S., Buck, L.: Schema Adjunct Framework draft specification 24 february 2000 (2000)
15. Hori, M., Euzenat, J., Patel-Schneider, P.F.: OWL Web ontology language XML presentation syntax . W3C note 11 june 2003 (2003)
16. Fernandez, M., Malhotra, A., Marsh, J., Nagy, M., Walsh, N.: XQuery 1.0 and XPath 2.0 data model, W3C working draft. (2003)
17. Patel-Schneider, P., Hayes, P., Horrocks, I.: OWL Web ontology language semantics and abstract syntax, W3C recommendation 10 february 2004 (2004)
18. Shoenfield, J.R.: Mathematical Logic. Addison-Wesley Publisher (1967)
19. Haarslev, V., Moller, R.: Racer system description. In: International Joint Conference on Automated Reasoning (IJCAR'2001), Siena, Italy (2001) 18–23
20. Psaila, G., Crespi-Reghizzi, S.: Adding semantics to XML. In: Second Workshop on Attribute Grammars and their Applications, (1999) 113–132
21. Dubin, D., Sperberg-McQueen, C.M., Renear, A., Huitfeldt, C.: A logic programming environment for document semantics and inference. Literary and Linguistic Computing **18** (2003) 225–233
22. Erdmann, M., Studer, R.: How to structure and access XML documents with ontologies. Data and Knowledge Engineering **36** (2001) 317–335
23. Amann, B., Fundulaki, I., Scholl, M., Beeri, C., Vercoustre, A.: Ontology-Based Integration of XML Web Resources. In: International Semantic Web Conference 2002. (2002) 117–131
24. Fundulaki, I., Marx, M.: Mediation of XML Data through Entity Relationship Models. In: First International Workshop on Semantic Web and Databases. (2003) 357–380
25. Liu S.P., Mei J., Lin Z.Q.: XML Semantics Definition Language(XSDL) draft specification(In Chinese). PKU-TCL lab techonology report. (2004)
26. Draper D., Fankhauser P., Fernedez M., et al.: XQuery 1.0 and XPath 2.0 Formal Semantics, W3C Working Draft 20 February 2004 (2004)

Refining Semantic Mappings from Relational Tables to Ontologies

Yuan An[1], Alexander Borgida[2], and John Mylopoulos[1]

[1] Department of Computer Science, University of Toronto, Canada
{yuana, jm}@cs.toronto.edu
[2] Department of Computer Science, Rutgers University, USA
borgida@cs.rutgers.edu

Abstract. To support the Semantic Web, it will be necessary to construct mappings between legacy database schemas and ontologies. We have developed a prototype tool which starts from a simple set of correspondences from table columns to ontology components, and then helps derive algorithmically candidate logical mappings between complete tables and the ontology. We report here some refinements of this algorithm inspired by an analysis of the ways in which relational schemas are standardly derived from Extended Entity Relationship diagrams, and relate this to the main heuristic used by the Clio system [6], which maps between relational database schemas.

1 Introduction

In order to make the vision of the Semantic Web a reality, it will be necessary to find semantic mappings between existing databases (the "deep web") and existing ontologies. Building such connections is nontrivial task because: (i) the ontologies and schemas will have been derived *independently*; (ii) the ontologies (and schemas) could be very large; (iii) there will be relatively few people who will be thoroughly familiar with any one of them; (iv) the construction would have to be repeated when encountering new ontologies. For this reason, it would be desirable to have computer tools to help find the logical mappings between database schemas and ontologies.

Specifically, we assume a framework where we are given

1. An ontology, expressed in some language, such as OWL or UML, which has a semantics that can be captured by First Order Predicate Logic through the use of unary and binary predicates, representing concepts and properties. The ontology language should support domain, range and cardinality restrictions on properties and their inverses, and differentiate datatype valued properties ("attributes" in UML).
2. A relational schema, where for each table we have standard information available in SQL DDL declarations, including constraints concerning the primary key, foreign keys, and absence of null values.

C. Bussler et al. (Eds.): SWDB 2004, LNCS 3372, pp. 84–90, 2005.

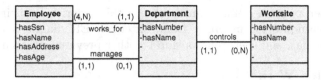

Fig. 1. Company Ontology

Our general objective is to find a mapping relating predicates in the ontology and relational tables [5]. Currently, we are obtaining for each table $T(A_1, \ldots, A_n)$ a formula ϕ that is a (disjunction of) conjunction of ontology atoms. For example, given the ontology in Figure 1, and relational table schema $Emp(ssn, name, dept, proj)$, we may expect an answer of the form

$T{:}Emp(ssn, name, dept, proj){:}-$
   $\mathcal{O} : Employee(x), \mathcal{O} : hasSsn(x, ssn), \mathcal{O} : hasName(x, name),$
   $\mathcal{O} : Department(y), \mathcal{O} : works\_for(x, y), \mathcal{O} : hasNumber(y, dept).$
   $\mathcal{O} : Worksite(z), \mathcal{O} : controls(y, z), \mathcal{O} : hasName(z, proj).$

where, for clarity, we use prefixes T and $\mathcal{O}$ to distinguish predicates in the relational schema and the ontology.

2   The MAPONTO Approach

To achieve the above objective, we envision a 2-step process, where (a) the columns A_i of each table are linked to elements in the ontology (mostly datatype-valued properties); then (b) a formula of the kind described above is proposed by the tool on the basis of heuristics. Since considerable effort has been devoted to step (a) in the database and ontology integration literature, we have concentrated on step (b). Because the answers produced are inherently heuristic, our tool offers a *partially ordered list* of formulae, where more highly ranked proposals are assumed to be more likely.

The basic idea underlying our current tool (detailed in [1]) is to represent the ontology as a graph consisting of nodes (corresponding to concepts) connected by edges (corresponding to properties). Semantic connections in the ontology, expressed in the formula ϕ, are then based on paths in this graph, and we hypothesize a version of Occam's razor: fewer connections are better. This has lead us to look for minimal-cost spanning trees connecting the concepts which have one or more properties corresponding to table columns — called *Steiner trees*. Such a tree is then translated to a logical formula by "joining" the concepts and properties encountered in it. For example, if concepts C and D are connected by the tree consisting of edges p and q, traversing intermediate node G, the formula produced is $C(x), p(x, y), G(y), q(y, z), D(z)$.[1]

---

[1] The algorithm in [1] is considerably more elaborate; among others, sometimes copies are made of certain nodes in the graph, so that more than one variable can range over a concept.

This paper presents some refinements to this algorithm, their motivation based on techniques for mapping from Extended ER diagrams to relational database schemas, and their relationship to other previous research.

2.1   Related Work

The framework of our approach is clearly inspired by the Clio system [6, 8], which attempts to find mappings between two relational schemas. In fact, in Section 4.2, we will relate the key heuristic underlying Clio to our work.

The general framework for connecting ontologies and relational schemas using logical formulas has a long history [2, 5], although in all previous cases the specification is done entirely by the designer.

Data reverse engineering is the process of taking an existing database schema (and instances), and recovering some corresponding conceptual schema. Various approaches have been proposed (e.g., [7]), with a comprehensive introduction provided by Hainaut [4]. Our problem differs in two ways: we are given an *existing* ontology, which needs to be connected to the database; and the ontology will likely contain much superfluous information that will not appear in the schema. (For example, a *City* might be *locatedIn* a *Province*, and a *Province locatedIn* a *Country*, yet the relational table may only have columns for *cityName* and *countryName*.) Conversely, we have to face the fact that some aspects of the database (e.g., aritificial identifiers), may not appear in the ontology.

3   From Extended ER to Relational Schema

Our new proposal is based on the methodology of relational schema design from Extended Entity-Relationship (EER) diagrams.[2] The principles behind this widely-understood and practiced technique are to create a small number of tables that are in Boyce-Codd Normal Form (assuming that the only dependencies are those due to keys in the EER diagram), preferring schemas where columns do not have null values, which might waste space. The basic methodology can be summarized as follows:

- For each regular entity type E create an "entity table" whose columns are the attributes of E, and whose primary key is the key of E.
- For each weak entity type E, create an "entity table" whose columns are the attributes of E, together with the key of the owner entity type O, and any attributes of the "identifying relationship". The primary key of the table consists of the concatenation of the key for O and the identifying attribute(s) of E.
- For each relationship type R create a "relationship table" whose columns are the primary keys of the participating entity types, together with attributes of R. The key of the table is determined by the cardinality of relationship: if R connects entities A and B, with keys K_A and K_B respectively then

---

[2] We assume the reader is familiar with standard EER terminology, e.g., [3].

- if R is an N:M relationship, then the key is the union of K_A and K_B;
- if R is a N:1 relationship, then the key is just K_A, while for 1:N relationships the key is K_B;
- if R is 1:1, the key should be that of the entity whose participation in the relationship is *total* (i.e., has cardinality lower bound 1); otherwise the choice of key is arbitrary.

– Repeatedly merge any pair of tables that have the same key by unioning the set of attributes and eliminating the duplicate key attributes. In some cases (e.g., merging a N:1 relationship which is not "total"), the result may have columns that could now be null. Such merges are less desirable.

Finally, an important aspect of the relational schema design is imposing appropriate foreign key and non-null constraints during the above construction.

The above mapping results in a schema that is very natural for humans to understand, and may well be the one encountered in practice, unless denormalized in order to improve query processing.

4   New Heuristics for Finding Mappings

The search for a low-cost Steiner tree[3] may return a number of results, some of which may be intuitively better than others, especially if the table is not "denormalized". For example, in the semantic mapping for the $T : Emp$ example earlier, the tool should prefer *works_for*, rather than *manages*, as the connection between *Employee* and *Department*. On the other hand, for a table $T : Project(name, supervisor, ...)$, the connection of $O : Worksite$ with $O : Employee$ would more likely involve the composition of $controls^{-1}$ with $manages^{-1}$ rather than with $works\_for^{-1}$.

To achieve this, we propose that the spanning sub-trees be ranked according to the following rules:

1. In growing a tree, edges with cardinality upper-bound 1 should be preferred. Edges which also have cardinality lower-bound 1 are given even higher preference.
2. If the relational table has a key that is the composite of foreign keys k_A, k_B,..., and there are single anchor nodes[4] for each of the keys k_A,..., then those trees are preferred in which every pair of anchor nodes is connected by a *path* on which some edge has cardinality upper bound higher than 1. (The simplest case of this is an edge for a property p such that the cardinality upper bound of p and its inverse are larger than 1.)
3. If the relational table has a key $K = K_C + A_1 + ...$, where K_C is a foreign key, and the A_i are not part of a foreign key appearing in K, then the real

---

[3] From our motivation, minimality is not strictly necessary, and it may be hard to ensure, since the problem is NP-hard.

[4] An anchor node is a concept which has datatype properties corresponding to columns in the table key

anchor node is not the node (call it C') which has properties matching K_C; instead, it is some other node D, which has a 1-upper bound path to C', such that D has some attributes for A_j.

4.1   Motivating the New Heuristics

Suppose the ontology corresponds *exactly* to the conceptual model used for database design, and the relational schema is obtained according to Section 3. Furthermore, let us restrict ourselves to the case when the EER diagrams that can be represented directly in ontologies, by mapping entity types into concepts, and binary relationship types and attributes into properties.

An analysis of the algorithm in Section 3 shows that every table produced by it will have key K of the form (i) K_E for an entity table, possibly merged with some N:1 or 1:1 relationship tables involving that entity; (ii) same as (i), but corresponding to N:1/1:1 relationships that were not merged in with the entity because the participation was not total; (iii) $K_A + K_B$, where entities A and B are in an N:M relationship; (iv) $K_E + A_1 + ...$, for a weak entity table, where $A_1...$ do not form a key; (v) the analogue of (ii) for weak entities.

Columns in tables of category (i) and (ii) correspond to datatype properties of a concept C_E (possibly a subclass), as well as properties of entities related to it by N:1/1:1 relationships. All of these appear as properties of C_E with upper bound 1 in the ontology. Moreover, the preference for total participation corresponds to lower-bound 1. Hence case 1 of our heuristic.

Tables in category (iii), which can be recognized from their key structure, and which have columns corresponding to N:M relationships between properties of anchor entities, would be miss-treated by the algorithm, which would prefer N:1/1:1 linking properties. Hence case 2 of our heuristic.

Tables corresponding to weak entities are another source of problems, since weak entities are an artifact of the EER data model, and are not specially marked in standard ontologies. Once again, we recognize weak entities from the table key structure, and then try to find the concept corresponding to the weak entity, and the (chain of) relationships/properties to the strong entity identifying it.

Our algorithm generalizes all these cases to the situation when a relationship in the EER model might be the composition of several properties in the ontology, by permitting the Steiner tree to traverse additional edges, if necessary, as long as their upper bound is 1.

4.2   Relationship to Clio Heuristics

Recall that Clio tries to find a logical mapping from a source to a target relational (or XML) schema, starting from correspondences between columns of tables in them. The core of Clio is the generation, in both the source and target schema, of "logical relations" [8] — maximal sets of logically related schema elements, particularly table columns. This is accomplished as follows: if table R has a foreign key to table T, then (a) R and T are joined over this foreign key to yield a larger table, R', and (b) the process is repeated on R'[5].

First, as we noted, in MAPONTO ontology subtrees give rise to formulas representing joins similar to Clio's logical relations.

Now suppose ontology properties $p(x, y)$ and $q(y, z)$ meet at concept $G(y)$. If these were relational tables, columns y of p and q would be foreign keys for G. Clio would only suggest $p(x, y) \bowtie G(y)$ or $G(y) \bowtie q(y, z)$ as joins building alternative logical relations. The reason for avoiding $p(x, y) \bowtie G(y) \bowtie q(y, z)$, is that from practical experience, this could lead to too many alternatives[6]. Step 1 of the new heuristics will make MAPONTO also downgrade such joins **if** the relationship corresponding to q is M:N. Moreover, if q represented a N:1/1:1 relationship then according to Section 3, table q could have been merged with E to yield $E'(y, z) \iff G(y) \bowtie q(y, z)$. In this schema, Clio would in fact join p and E', as would our algorithm, since q has cardinality upper bound 1.

The iterative nature of Clio's algorithm is also captured by our tree growing algorithm.

5   Conclusions and Future Work

Establishing manually semantic mappings between database schemas and ontologies is time-consuming and error-prone, especially, when the mappers are not fully cognizant of the ontology, which could be very large. We are developing a tool, MAPONTO, to support creating such mappings, and have carried out several experiments using it [1]. In this paper, we have presented certain refinements of the algorithm intended to deal with several problems we have encountered, together with explanations tying the heuristics to the well-known mapping of EER diagrams to relational schemas, and the heuristics used in Clio.

We defer to a later paper the treatment of n-ary relationships, the less standard tabular representations of semantic relationships (such as the representation of subclass hierarchies using concept names as values in columns), denormalized relations, and more complex mappings.

References

1. Y. An, A. Borgida, and J. Mylopoulos. Building Semantic Mappings between Database Schemas and Ontologies. Submitted for publication.
2. D. Calvanese, G. D. Giacomo, M. Lenzerini, D. Nardi, and R. Rosati. "Data integration in data warehousing", *J. Cooperative Information Systems. 10(3)*, 2001.
3. R. Elmasri and S. B. Navathe. *Fundamentals of Database Systems*. Addison-Wesley. 2000.
4. J.-L. Hainaut. Database reverse engineering. http://citeseer.ist.psu.edu/article/hainaut98database.html. 1998.

---

[5] This is related to the notion of "chase" in relational databases.

[6] Y. Velegrakis, personal communication, 2004.

5. J. Madhavan, P.A. Bernstein, P. Domingos, A.Y. Halevy. "Representing and Reasoning about Mappings between Domain Models", *AAAI 2002*: 80-86
6. R. J. Miller, L. M. Haas, and M. A. Hernandez. Schema mapping as query discovery. In 26th VLDB. 2000.
7. V. M. Markowitz and J. A. Makowsky. Identifying Extended Entity-Relationship Object Structures in Relational Schemas. IEEE Transactions on Software Engineering 16(8). 1990.
8. L. Popa, Y. Velegrakis, R. J. Miller, M. Hernandes, R. Fagin. "Translating web data", *VLDB 2002*.

Triadic Relations:
An Algebra for the Semantic Web

Edward L. Robertson

Computer Science Dept. and School of Informatics,
Indiana University, Bloomington IN 47405
Supported by NSF grant ISS-82407

Abstract. This paper introduces and develops an algebra over triadic
relations (relations whose contents are only triples). In essence, the algebra is a severely restricted variation of relational algebra (RA) that
is defined over relations with exactly three attributes and is closed for
the same set of relations. In particular, arbitrary joins and Cartesian
products are replaced by a single three-way join. Ternary relations are
important because they provide the minimal, and thus most uniform,
way to encode semantics wherein metadata may be treated uniformly
with regular data; this fact has been recognized in the choice of triples
to formalize the Semantic Web via RDF. Indeed, algebraic definitions
corresponding to certain of these formalisms will be shown as examples.

An important aspect of this algebra is an encoding of triples, implementing a kind of reification. The algebra is shown to be equivalent, over
non-reified values, to a restriction of Datalog and hence to a fragment
of first order logic. Furthermore, the algebra requires only two operators if certain fixed infinitary constants (similar to Tarski's identity) are
present. In this case, all structure is represented only in the data, that
is, in the encodings that these infinitary constants represent.

1   Introduction and Motivation

Relations are the minimal, and thus the most uniform, way to encode semantics
wherein metadata may be treated uniformly with regular data, a fact recognized
by C. S. Peirce in 1885.[6] Binary relations are sufficient to represent information
in a fixed schema, but the names of these relations are inaccessible from the
relation contents. Both a benefit and a disadvantage of binary relations is that
they are inherently closed in the algebra of unary and binary operators defined
by Tarski.[8] Join operations on triadic relations, on the other hand, must be
carefully defined, lest the results increase in arity (joining two triadic relations
on a single attribute results in a quintary relation).

As the World Wide Web has grown from presentation of information into
management and manipulation of that information, there has been a recognition
of the need for description of not only structure but also content of web artifacts.
This description is to be achieved via the Semantic Web. Central to the Semantic
Web is a simple, uniform representation mechanism RDF and central to RDF
is a formalization in terms of triples.[12]

C. Bussler et al. (Eds.): SWDB 2004, LNCS 3372, pp. 91–108, 2005.
© Springer-Verlag Berlin Heidelberg 2005

The following paragraphs move to a somewhat older perspective in order to introduce the notion of reification. Reification plays a central role in the following algebra, where it is "nonymous", as opposed to the *anonymous* reification of RDF; such reification is alluded to in [11], where it is called "Skolemization."

A natural use of triples, or "triangles", is in semantic nets, which are used to express the semantics of natural language. Semantic nets are represented by labeled graphs (often called Conceptual Graphs[7]) or, equivalently, families of binary relationships. Adapting an example from W3C efforts to address these same issues[11], "Chris is diagnosed with cancer" is represented relationally as diagnosis(Chris, cancer) and graphically as in Fig. 1.

$$\text{Chris} \xrightarrow{\text{diagnosis}} \text{cancer}$$

Fig. 1

The relational representation follows Tarski; other linear (textual) representations include the F-logic convention[4] "Chris(diagnosis→cancer)", observing one component as a dominant object and placing that first, and an RDF triple "Chris diagnosis cancer". RDF tends to write triples with no punctuation other than spaces and a period to indicate the end of a triples. We will henceforward use a form with parentheses and commas, writing the preceeding RDF triple as "(Chris, diagnosis, cancer)".

This notation is brittle, however, in that it cannot distinguish between different occurrences of "diagnosis" and does not allow statements about statements, such as observations about the reliability of Chris's diagnosis. This problem is addressed in two subtly different ways. The first is anonymous reification – equivalently object-id creation. The second is *"nonymous"* reification, which lifts the triple (Chris, diagnosis, cancer) to the single value Chris◻diagnosis◻cancer, allowing the representation of "Chris has cancer with high probability" as (Chris◻diagnosis◻cancer, likelihood, high).

Figure 2 shows three different variations of the "statements about statements" phenomenon. On the left is a semantic net, promoting an edge label to an item of discussion. In the center is reification as practiced in other Semantic Web discussions (a similar diagram appears in [11]). In this case the relationship between Chris and cancer is abstracted to a blank, or anonymous, node. On the right is reification as used in this paper, wherein the entire triad relating Chris, diagnosis, and cancer is represented by a single value. Intuitively, the construction in the center reifies the arrow and the right reifies the triangle.

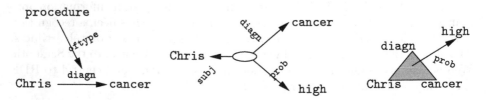

Fig. 2

While the representation of information by triples, as discussed above, is well-established, there has been no formal mechanism for manipulating information in exactly this format. Of course any query mechanism will extract information, but the result of this extraction may not be triples. That is, there is no natural way to restrict output of these mechanisms to triples, except by fiat. F-logic[4] has a triadic format at its outset, but it is used to define higher arity predicates; nonymous reification is integrated with F-logic in [13] as in the $ operator of $\mathcal{F}$lora [14]. Further from a triadic-to-triadic language is relational algebra (RA), although the algebra defined below is essentially a variation of RA which is naturally closed on triadic relations. Closest to a natural triadic-to-triadic query language is a variation of (nonrecursive) Datalog[9], which we call "Trilog"; Trilog is defined in the following section and is used later in this paper as a standard of comparison.

The rest of this paper therefore develops an algebra specifically defined over triadic relations. The next section presents some basic notation. Section 3 defines the algebra in its purest form, including operators for reification. The next section removes reification from the base algebra, replacing the reification operation with an encoding in a constant relation, and explores the impact of such constants by reducing the algebra to two operations. Section 5 proves the equivalence of the algebra to a fragment of first order logic (written as Datalog). Section 6 then returns to RDF, showing how a typical RDF rule is expressed in the algebra.

2   Notation

We assume that all values come from a countable fixed domain $\mathcal{D}$. It is, of course, possible to partition $\mathcal{D}$ into types and index the algebraic operators with respect to types, but this leads to unnecessarily cumbersome notation. Hence we globally assume a single domain $\mathcal{D}$. Toward the end of the paper, input values in $\mathcal{D}$ are distinguished from internal values, but all the operators are always over the single domain $\mathcal{D}$.

Lower case letters $(a, b, c, \ldots, x, y, z)$ are used as variables over $\mathcal{D}$. Where possible, letters from the beginning of the alphabet are used for manifest values, appearing in the final result, while letters from the end of the alphabet are used for intermediate values. Finally, i, j, and sometimes k are indices for relation coordinates, always with values restricted to $\{0, 1, 2\}$. For example, $*_i$, defined below, actually refers to three operators $*_0$, $*_1$, and $*_2$, which are the same except that they operate on columns 0, 1, and 2 respectively.

The basic structures are sets of triples over $\mathcal{D}$. We refer to these as *triadic relations*. It often aids perspicuity to view these triples in a triangular form. On these occasions (Chris,diagnosis,cancer) is written as $\begin{smallmatrix} & \text{diagnosis} & \\ \text{Chris} & & \text{cancer} \end{smallmatrix}$, or more generally (x_0, x_1, x_2) as $\begin{smallmatrix} & x_1 & \\ x_0 & & x_2 \end{smallmatrix}$. Occasionally, d^3 will be used to indicate the triple (d, d, d), for $d \in \mathcal{D}$.

Note the indexing of components in the triple above and its triangular presentation. By convention, indices are interpreted modulo 3, so that position $i+1$ is always one step clockwise from position i. The benefit of this notation is discussed in the context of ι and ρ below. The numbering (forgiving the "off by one" quirk) is suggestive of Peirce's *firstness, secondness,* and *thirdness*[6].

Set notations serve two purposes in this paper. Occasionally they are used to give definitions of formal constructs; such occasions are always marked with $\overset{def}{=}$.

More often, sets are used for exposition, particularly to provide intuition on the results of evaluating algebraic expressions. When used expositionally, set notation is somewhat informal, without explicit binding of variables (they are all over $\mathcal{D}$) and even using "$*$" as a placeholder for unique variables, emphasizing purpose (the traditional "don't care") rather than syntax.

We now return to Trilog, a restriction of (nonrecursive) Datalog[9] to triadic relations. The notions of *extensional database* (EDB) and *intensional database* (IDB) are borrowed from the discussion of Datalog in [9]. EDB relations are those given as input to the program (or later, algebra). The sets of EDB and IDB relations are disjoint.

Definition 1. The language *positive Trilog* is the fragment of Datalog subject to the following restrictions:

   i: rule bodies are either (a) conjuncts of triadic relations, where each variable in the head must also occur in the body, or (b) disjuncts of triadic relations, where each variable in the head must also occur in every disjunct,

   ii: rule heads are single triadic relations and may not be EDB relations,

   iii: definitions may not be recursive,

   iv: the reserved word "`result`" designates the result of the computation.

Parameters to relation occurrences, either in the head or body of a rule, may be constants or variables with the usual semantics.

The constraints on occurrences of variables force Trilog to be *safe*; that is, Trilog programs run on finite EDB always produce finite results.

Example 2. If the single table `Fact` contains the net information in the left of Fig. 2, then the query "What procedures have been performed?" is expressed by:
`result(pr,sb,rst) :- Fact("procedure","oftype",pr)&Fact(sb,pr,rst)`

Definition 3. Full Trilog is Trilog where negation is allowed in rule bodies. That is, restriction $i(a)$ is changed to "conjuncts of triadic relations and negations of triadic relations, where each variable in the head occurs in at least one (positive) relation in the body."

Trilog is of course equivalent to the use of fragment of first order logic to define ternary predicates, a fragment which has less convenient syntax and safety rules.

3   Definition of Trirel

The algebra begins with named variables (the EDB of an expression) and explicitly enumerated sets of triples. Its expressions are built inductively with certain unary and ternary operations.

The fundamental operation on triadic relations is a particular three-way join which takes explicit advantage of the triadic structure of its operands. This join of three triadic relations results in another triadic relation, thus providing the closure required of an algebra.

Definition 4. Let $\mathbf{R}$, $\mathbf{S}$, and $\mathbf{T}$ be triadic relations. The *tri-join* of $\mathbf{R}$, $\mathbf{S}$, and $\mathbf{T}$, is defined

$$\mathrm{trijoin}(\mathbf{R}, \mathbf{S}, \mathbf{T}) \overset{def}{=} \{ {}_a^b c : \exists x, y, z [{}_a^x z \in \mathbf{R} \ \& \ {}_x^b y \in \mathbf{S} \ \& \ {}_z^y c \in \mathbf{T}] \}$$

An equivalent notation for $\mathrm{trijoin}(\mathbf{R}, \mathbf{S}, \mathbf{T})$ is $\begin{smallmatrix} & \mathbf{S} & \\ & \diagup \diagdown & \\ \mathbf{R} & \!\!-\!\! & \mathbf{T} \end{smallmatrix}$.

Sometimes the three equality conditions implied in trijoin are too strong, so there are also three joins with only two equalities. That is, $\mathrm{trijoin}_i^*$ "breaks the bond" across from corner i.

Definition 5. (Definitions for subscripts 1 and 2 are symmetric.)

$$\mathrm{trijoin}_0^*(\mathbf{R}, \mathbf{S}, \mathbf{T}) \overset{def}{=} \{ {}_a^b c : \exists w, x, y, z [{}_a^x z \in \mathbf{R} \ \& \ {}_x^b y \in \mathbf{S} \ \& \ {}_z^w c \in \mathbf{T}] \}$$

An equivalent notation for $\mathrm{trijoin}_0^*(\mathbf{R}, \mathbf{S}, \mathbf{T})$ is $\begin{smallmatrix} & \mathbf{S} & \\ & \diagup * \diagdown & \\ \mathbf{R} & \!\!-\!\! & \mathbf{T} \end{smallmatrix}$.

Definition 6.

$$\mathcal{I}(\mathbf{R}) \overset{def}{=} \{ {}_x^x x : x \text{ occurs in the active domain of } \mathbf{R} \}$$

Notation. If we wish to emphasize the coincidence of values that occurs in a tri-join, we will often use a notation which collapses pairs of values forced to be equal by the join conditions and makes explicit the structure of the relational operands. Example 7 illustrates this convention and motivates the definition of $\mathcal{I}(\mathbf{R})$.

Example 7. Consider $\mathbf{B}$ to encoded labeled binary relationships, so that a triple of the form (x, ℓ, z) in $\mathbf{B}$ to indicates binary relationship (x, z) labeled ℓ holds. To compute one transitive step of all these relationships, it is necessary to to join $\mathbf{B}$ with itself, preserving the relationship label (ℓ component):

$$\textbf{Trans}(\textbf{B}) \overset{def}{=} \begin{array}{c} \mathcal{I}(\textbf{B}) \\ / \quad \backslash \\ \textbf{B} \text{------} \textbf{B} \end{array} = \begin{array}{c} \ell \\ \wedge \\ \ell - \ell \\ \wedge \vee \wedge \\ x - y - z \end{array}$$

Note that transitive <u>closure</u>, with its arbitrary iteration of **Trans**, is as impossible in Trirel as it is in RA, and for the very same reasons.

Example 8.

$$\begin{array}{c} \mathcal{I}(\textbf{R}) \\ / \quad \backslash \\ \textbf{R} \text{------} \mathcal{I}(\textbf{R}) \end{array} = \begin{array}{c} y \\ y\ y \\ / \quad \backslash \\ b \qquad z \\ a\ c - z\ z \end{array} = \begin{array}{c} b \\ \wedge \\ b - b \\ \wedge \vee \wedge \\ a - b - b \end{array} = \{\,{}_{a}^{\ b}{}_{b} : {}_{a}^{\ b}{}_{b} \in \textbf{R}\,\}$$

Definition 9. The (clockwise) *rotation* operator ρ is defined over triadic relations in the expected way: $\rho(\textbf{R}) \overset{def}{=} \{\,{}_{a\ b}^{\ a} : {}_{a\ c}^{\ b} \in \textbf{R}\}$

The conventional numbering of components of a triple, interpreting index expressions modulo 3, is matched by the fact that $\rho^i = \rho^{i+3}$ for any i. For example, if ${}_{y_0\ y_2}^{\ y_1} = \rho^j({}_{x_0\ x_2}^{\ x_1})$, then we can state $y_{i+j} = x_i$ for $i \in \{0,1,2\}$. The following definition also illustrates this convention.

Definition 10. The *flip* operators $\lambdabar_i$ fix the ith component of the elements of a triadic relation and interchange the other two. $\lambdabar_i(\textbf{R}) \overset{def}{=}$

$$\{\,{}_{y_0\ y_2}^{\ y_1} : \exists x_0, x_1, x_2 [{}_{x_0\ x_2}^{\ x_1} \in \textbf{R} \ \& \ y_i = x_i \ \& \ y_{i+1} = x_{i+2} \ \& \ y_{i+2} = x_{i+1}]\}$$

The final base operations of the algebra are the usual set operations $\cap, \cup$, and $-$ (relative complement). Relative complement is the only non-monotone operator in Trirel. Thus the fragment of Trirel that excludes only "$-$" is termed *positive Trirel*.

All the above are easily definable in RA (or relational calculus). For example, using $\textbf{R}[\textbf{i}]$ to denote the ith component of $\textbf{R}$, trijoin$(\textbf{R}, \textbf{S}, \textbf{T})$ is simply the RA expression $\prod_{\textbf{R}_0, \textbf{S}_1, \textbf{T}_2}(\sigma_{\textbf{R}_1 = \textbf{S}_0 \& \textbf{R}_2 = \textbf{T}_0 \& \textbf{S}_2 = \textbf{T}_1}(\textbf{R} \bowtie \textbf{S} \bowtie \textbf{T}))$.

On the other hand, the triadic algebra thus-far defined obviously omits operators of standard relational algebra: projection, selection, join, and Cartesian product. Join and Cartesian product have obviously been specialized to trijoin. Projection is of course not allowed, since it would break the fact that the algebra is closed on triadic relations. Selection – at least equality selection – is

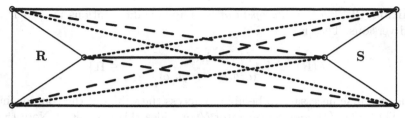

Fig. 3

unnecessary because of the equality test implicit in trijoin. Using the traditional notation of σ for selection and assuming that $d \in \mathcal{D}$ and that the attributes of $\mathbf{R}$ are named x_0, x_1, and x_2, Example 8 implements $\sigma_{x_1=x_2}(\mathbf{R})$ and $\text{trijoin}_1^*(\{\,(d,d,d)\,\},\mathbf{R},\mathcal{I})$ implements $\sigma_{x_0=d}(\mathbf{R})$.

Inequality selection can of course be derived from relative complement, but it is unseemly to require a non-monotone operator for such an obviously monotone construction. An alternative is to extend Trirel with the operators $\mathcal{N}_j$ (for Not equal), similar to $\mathcal{I}$, such that $\mathcal{N}_j(\mathbf{R})$ has the jth component different from the other two. Inequality selection is then easily expressed, as in $\sigma_{x_0 \neq x_2}(\mathbf{R}) = \text{trijoin}(\mathcal{N}_1(\mathbf{R}),\mathbf{R},\mathcal{I})$.

The language thus far is too restrictive. Expressions with varieties of trijoin, $\wr$, and ρ, are relentlessly planar. Thus it is not possible for these operators to simulate

```
result(x, y, z) :– R(x, y, z) & S(xx, yy, zz) &
        Link(x, "L1", xx) & Link(x, "L2", yy) & Link(x, "L3", zz) &
        Link(y, "L1", yy) & Link(y, "L2", zz) & Link(y, "L3", xx) &
        Link(z, "L1", zz) & Link(z, "L2", xx) & Link(z, "L3", yy)
```

This program essentially encodes the Kuratowski graph $K_{3,3}$ [3, Thm. 11.13], which is known to be non-planar. Figure 3 shows the connections required in the body of this program, with heavy lines representing L1 Links, dashed lines L2 Links, and dotted lines L3 Links.

Intersections, the other means to require equality, are of no help because intersections are limited to triads and expressing the above with intersection would require equality across coordinates of both $\mathbf{R}$ and $\mathbf{S}$.

The solution to this problem requires encoding triads in $\mathbf{R}$ and $\mathbf{S}$ as single values – the same encoding that supports reification. The term "tag" is used to name this encoding because it has an implementation flavor suitable for the algebra, avoiding semantic and philosophical concerns that accompany "reify". Tagging has been extensively studied in the context of binary relations in [10], which provided the seed of this paper.

Definition 11. The function τ is a *tagging function*, satisfying $\tau : \mathcal{D} \times \mathcal{D} \times \mathcal{D} \overset{1\text{–}1}{\to} \mathcal{D}$ and π_0, π_1, and π_2 are three *projection functions*, such that $\pi_i : \mathcal{D} \to \mathcal{D}$. These functions correspond so that, for arbitrary $x \in \mathcal{D}$, $x = \tau(\pi_0(x), \pi_1(x), \pi_2(x))$. Consistent with the usage described above, we will interpret subscripts to π_i mod 3.

Definition 12. The *tagging operator* $\mathcal{T}$ maps triadic relations into their fully tagged versions. That is,

$$\mathcal{T}(\mathbf{R}) \overset{def}{=} \{ \begin{array}{cc} & \tau(a,b,c) \\ \tau(a,b,c) & \tau(a,b,c) \end{array} : \begin{array}{c} b \\ a\ c \end{array} \in \mathbf{R} \}$$

It is of course necessary to be able to access the values of the components of a tag. The *untag* (or *unpack*) operator $\mathcal{U}$ provides this capability. Note that $\mathcal{U}$ cannot unpack a tuple either if that tuple does not have the same values in each component or if that value is not in the range of τ.

Definition 13. For $i, j \in \{0, 1, 2\}$, $\mathcal{U}_{i,j}(\mathbf{S}) \overset{def}{=}$

$$\{ \begin{array}{c} x_1 \\ x_0\ \ x_2 \end{array} : \exists y_0, y_1, y_2 [\tau(y_0, y_1, y_2)^3 \in S\ \& \tau(y_0, y_1, y_2) = x_{i+1} = x_{i+2}\ \& x_i = y_j] \}$$

Definition 14. Overloading $\mathcal{T}$ and $\mathcal{U}$, $\mathcal{T}_{i,j}(\mathbf{R}) \overset{def}{=} \mathcal{U}_{i,j}(\mathcal{T}(\mathbf{R}))$ and

$$\mathcal{U}(\mathbf{S}) \overset{def}{=} \begin{array}{c} \mathcal{I}(\mathbf{S}) \\ \diagup \quad \diagdown \\ \mathcal{I}(\mathbf{S}) \qquad * \\ * \quad \diagdown \qquad \diagdown \\ \mathcal{U}_{0,0}(\mathbf{S}) - \mathcal{U}_{1,1}(\mathbf{S}) - \mathcal{U}_{2,2}(\mathbf{S}) \end{array} = \{ \begin{array}{c} b \\ a\ c \end{array} : \tau(a,b,c) \in \mathbf{S} \}$$

Obviously, $\mathcal{U}(\mathcal{T}(\mathbf{R})) = \mathbf{R}$ (but $\mathcal{T}(\mathcal{U}(\mathbf{R})) \subsetneq \mathbf{R}$ unless $\mathbf{R}$ is already symmetric).

This completes the definition of Trirel. Because none of the above operators introduces new values, the following is immediate (the definition of "safe" is that all output values come from the input).

Proposition 15. *Trirel is safe.*

The set of operators introduced above is obviously not minimal. We agree with Peirce that "superfluity here, as in many other cases in algebra, brings with it great facility in working." [6, p. 191]. The one occasion where this superfluity is more an aesthetic issue than a notational convenience is in having distinct tag and untag operations (instead of having the $\mathcal{T}_{i,j}$, from 14, as primitive). Thus reification is a single primitive step rather than a construction, as is done in the binary case in [10].

4   Constants and Operators

The goal of this section is to support the claim that the trijoin operator is indeed "more fundamental" than the other operators. Although trijoin cannot alone express all other operators, it can express all those operators, except $-$, when used in conjunction with a few *constant* relations. These constants are infinite, but only finite subsets are required in the evaluation of any expression based on Trirel operators. The idea of such constants dates back to Tarski[8], who introduced four binary relations: empty, universality (all pairs), identity (all equal pairs), and diversity (all unequal pairs). He considered these four akin, even though three were infinite and the fourth is as small as a set can be.

This section first defines primitive constants $\triangle_{i,j}$ and $\mathcal{A}$. Then it defines a few additional constants in terms of the $\triangle_{i,j}$ and $\mathcal{A}$, only using trijoin. Then it proves the major result of this section alluded to above. Finally, it briefly returns to the issue of inequality selection.

Definition 16. For $i, j \in \{0, 1, 2\}$,

$$\triangle_{i,j} \stackrel{def}{=} \{ {}_{x_0}{}^{x_1}{}_{x_2} : x_0, x_1, x_2 \in \mathcal{D} \,\&\, x_j = \pi_i(x_{j+1}) \,\&\, x_{j+1} = x_{j+2} \}$$

The effect of $\triangle_{i,j}$ is to match up domain values in the jth position of a triangle and in the ith position of the tags. For example, $\triangle_{1,0}$ is ${}_a{}^{\tau x, a, z}_{\tau x, a, z} = \{(a, t, t) | \exists x, z[t = \tau(x, a, z)]\}$. In a sense, the three tagging sets $\triangle_{i,i}$ are more natural, in that they have the untagged value in the "right place." The sets $\triangle_{i,i+1}$ and $\triangle_{i,i+2}$ are merely rotations of $\triangle_{i,i}$. However, since rotation will subsequently be expressed in terms of the $\triangle_{i,j}$, all these constraints must be considered primitive.

Definition 17. The *alternative set* $\mathcal{A}$ explicitly expresses two-fold choices:

$$\mathcal{A} \stackrel{def}{=} \{ {}_a{}^y{}_c : y = a \vee y = c \}$$

The notation Trirel$^\infty$ is used for the algebra with only trijoin, relative complement, and the constants $\triangle_{i,j}$ and $\mathcal{A}$. Of course, positive Trirel$^\infty$ excludes "$-$". Observe that Trirel$^\infty$ is inherently unsafe.

There are a few other infinitary relations that are important. While these could be postulated as primitive, they can equally well be defined in terms of the various $\triangle$ constants. So that this definition is not circular, ρ is expressed below only in terms of $\triangle_{i,j}$ and trijoin. The notation $\triangle$ is overloaded to $\triangle_{i,i',j}$. Note that only j and not a corresponding j' is required in this extension because the i and i' components go into the j and $j+1$ positions of the result. $\mathcal{I}$ is the triadic identity relation (and is more properly written $\mathcal{I}_{\mathcal{D}}$, the first and only time we shall explicitly indicate domain). $\mathcal{D}^3$ is the "universal" relation: all triples of values in $\mathcal{D}$. The following gives the Trirel definition of these constants, followed by an explication in set notation.

Definition 18.

$$\mathcal{I} \stackrel{def}{=} \{ {\textstyle {a \atop a\;a}} : a \in \mathcal{D}\}, \quad \mathcal{D}^3 \stackrel{def}{=} \{ {\textstyle {b \atop a\;c}} : a, b, c \in \mathcal{D}\}$$

$$\triangle_{i,i',j} \stackrel{def}{=} \text{trijoin}(X_0, X_1, X_2), \text{ where } X_j = \triangle_{i,j} \& \; X_{j+1} = \triangle_{i',j+1} \& \; X_{j+2} = \mathcal{I}$$

In addition, borrowing the "star" notation, the $*_i$ operator puts don't-cares at i coordinates; $*_i(\mathbf{R})$ is defined as

$$\text{trijoin}(X_0, X_1, X_2), \quad \text{where } X_i = \mathcal{D}^3, \; X_{i+1} = \mathbf{R} \text{ and } X_{i+2} = \mathcal{I}$$

The $*_i$ operators obviously help in defining the "don't care" variants of trijoin.

Theorem 19. *Let $\mathcal{E}$ be an expression in positive Trirel. Then there is an equivalent $\mathcal{E}^*$ in positive Trirel$^\infty$.*

Proof. The following lemmas cover all the cases for the operators in Trirel. The theorem follows by simple induction using these lemmas.

Lemma 20.

Proof.

Lemma 21.

$$\ell_0(\mathbf{S}) = \begin{array}{c} \triangle_{1,2} \\ \diagup \quad \diagdown \\ \mathcal{T}(\mathbf{S}) \quad \diagdown \\ \diagup \quad \diagdown \quad \diagdown \\ \triangle_{0,0} \underline{\quad} \mathcal{T}(\mathbf{S}) \underline{\quad} \triangle_{2,1} \end{array} \quad , \quad \mathcal{U}_{0,0}(\mathbf{S}) = \begin{array}{c} \ell_0(\mathbf{S}) \\ \diagup \quad \diagdown \\ \triangle_{0,0} \underline{\quad\quad} \mathbf{S} \end{array}$$

$$and \quad \rho(\mathbf{S}) = \begin{array}{c} \triangle_{1,0} \\ \diagup \quad \diagdown \\ \mathcal{T}(\mathbf{S}) \quad \diagdown \\ \diagup \quad \diagdown \quad \diagdown \\ \triangle_{0,2} \underline{\quad}_*\underline{\quad} \mathcal{I} \underline{\quad} \triangle_{2,1} \end{array}$$

The use of ℓ_0 in the definition of $\mathcal{U}$ above guarantees, with the properties of $\triangle_{0,0}$, that only triples in **S** that have the same value in each coordinates are unpacked.

Lemma 22.

$$\mathbf{R} \cap \mathbf{S} = \mathcal{U}\left(\begin{array}{c} \mathcal{I} \\ \diagup \diagdown \\ \mathcal{T}(\mathbf{R}) \underline{\quad} \mathcal{T}(\mathbf{S}) \end{array} \right) \quad and \quad \mathbf{R} \cup \mathbf{S} = \mathcal{U}\left(\begin{array}{c} \mathcal{I} \\ \diagup \quad \diagdown \\ \mathcal{A} \quad \diagdown \\ \diagup \diagdown \quad \diagdown \\ \mathcal{T}(\mathbf{R}) \underline{\quad}_*\mathcal{T}(\mathbf{S}) \underline{\quad} \mathcal{I} \end{array} \right)$$

This completes the proof of Theorem 19. Extension to relative complement/ negation is immediate. Note that these constants are tightly linked to operators that generate finite sub-instances of the respective constants, as illustrated by $\mathcal{I}$ and $\mathcal{I}(\mathbf{R})$. Uses of $\triangle_{i,j}, \mathcal{I},$ etc. can be replaced by the corresponding operators; using the constants makes the expressions somewhat more readable.

Finally, Trirel$^\infty$ may be extended with an infinite diversity relation $\mathcal{N}$, that is $\mathcal{N} = \mathcal{D}^3 - \mathcal{I}$, in order to support inequality selection in extended positive Trirel$^\infty$. Note that $\mathcal{N}$ cannot be defined in positive Trirel$^\infty$. The addition of $\mathcal{N}$ accounts for all four constants considered essential by Tarski (empty is a constant defined trivially by explicit enumeration).

5   Equivalence of Trilog and Trirel

Two formalisms dealing with triadic relations have been discussed thus far: the operational Trirel in detail and the declarative Trirel more cursorily. It would be nice to have a result paralleling Codd's equivalence of relational algebra and relational calculus, but the presence of tagging makes an exact parallel impossible. However, a restricted equivalence does hold. The first step of this equivalence is to show that Trirel can simulate Trilog.

Theorem 23. *For every positive Trilog program* prog, *there exists a positive Trirel expression $\mathcal{E}$ that computes* result *of* prog *when given the same EDB.*

Proof. Because Trilog programs are not recursive, the rules may be ordered such that the relation in the head of each rule does not occur in the body of any preceeding rule. This is equivalent to the dependency graph technique of [9]. If a relation r occurs in the head of more than one rule, give these occurrences new, unique names and add a new rule defining r as the union of all these just introduced relations. Then this ordered, renamed program is translated a rule at a time according to lemmas 25 and 26, which deal with the two cases of rule formation.

Lemma 24. *The expression $\mathcal{L}$, defined below, is such that*

$$\mathcal{L}(\mathbf{Q}) = \{\tau(\tau(x,y,v),u,z) : (\tau(x,y,z),u,v) \in \mathbf{Q}\}$$

Proof. The construction of $\mathcal{L}$ is given in a sequence of steps, each step showing first the desired set and then an expression yielding that set, with variable bindings implicitly global until $\mathbf{Q}$ is introduced in step $\mathcal{L}_4$. The value $\tau(\tau(x,y,z),u,v)$ occurs frequently and is abbreviated by $\mathcal{T}$. The expression for $\mathcal{L}_1$ is showing is graphic form as well as typical algebraic notation as partial explication of the transformations implemented here.

step	desired result	expression
$\mathcal{L}_1$	$\{(\tau(x,y,v),\tau(x,y,z),x)\}$	$\text{trijoin}(\triangle_{1,0,1},\triangle_{0,1,2},\mathcal{I}) \equiv$
$\mathcal{L}_2$	$\{(\tau(x,y,v),\tau(x,y,z),v)\}$	$\text{trijoin}_1^*(\triangle_{1,1,1},\mathcal{L}_1,\mathcal{I})$
$\mathcal{L}_3$	$\{(\tau(x,y,v),\mathcal{T},*)\}$	$\text{trijoin}_1^*(\mathcal{L}_2,\triangle_{0,0},\mathcal{I})$
$\mathcal{L}_4$	$\{(\mathcal{T},u,\mathcal{T}) : (\tau(x,y,z),u,v) \in \mathbf{Q}\}$	$\mathcal{T}_{1,1}(\mathbf{Q})$
$\mathcal{L}_5$	$\{(\mathcal{T},\mathcal{T},z)\}$	$\text{trijoin}(\mathcal{D}^3, \triangle_{1,2}, \triangle_{2,2})$
$\mathcal{L}$	$\{(\tau(x,y,v),u,z) : (\tau(x,y,z),u,v) \in \mathbf{Q}\}$	$\text{trijoin}_1^*(\mathcal{I}, \text{trijoin}_1^*(\mathcal{L}_3,\mathcal{L}_4,\mathcal{I})\ \mathcal{L}_5)$

Lemma 25. *Let* $\text{R}(p_0,p_1,p_2)$:- $\text{S\_1}(q_{1,0},q_{1,1},q_{1,2})$ & $\cdots$ & $\text{S\_k}(q_{k,0},q_{k,1},q_{k,2})$ *be a Trilog statement defined over a set of variables* $\mathcal{V} = \{q_{j,i} : 1 \le j \le k \& 1 \le i \le 3\} \cup \{p_i : 1 \le i \le 3\}$. *Then there is an equivalent Trirel expression $\mathcal{E}$ that computes the value of* $\mathbf{R}$ *given instances of the* $\mathbf{S_j}$.

Proof. It is sufficient to give $\mathcal{E}_i$, $i \in \{0,1,2\}$, respectively containing triples of the form $(\text{s},\text{s},\text{eurm p})$, where s encodes an assignment satisfying the rule body and p is an assignment to p_i is consistent with s. With these $\mathcal{E}_i$,

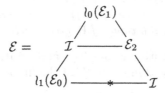

$$\mathcal{E} =$$

Without loss of generality, we assume that each variable occurs at most once as a parameter to any one $\mathbf{S}_j$. If that is not the case, then some v occurs more than once as a parameter to some $\mathbf{S}_j$, replace all but one of these v's by new, unique variables (in essence, don't cares) and, in the algebraic expression, intersect $\mathbf{S}_j$ with an expression forcing equality at the respected components.

The first step is to build a structure that encodes the contents of the $\mathbf{S}$'s. In the following the notation (x_j, y_j, z_j) is always restricted to tuples in $\mathbf{S}_j$. Define

$$Svect_1 \overset{def}{=} *_0(*_2(TAG(\mathbf{S}_1))) \qquad\qquad = \{(*, \tau(x_1, y_1, z_1), *)\}$$
$$Svect_j \overset{def}{=} \mathrm{trijoin}(*_1(*_2(Svect_{j-1})), TAG(\mathbf{S}_j), \mathcal{D}^3)$$
$$= \{(s, \tau(x_j, y_j, z_j), *) : s \in Svect_{j-1}\}, \text{ for } j > 1.$$

Thus $Svect_k$ encodes all structures of the form ("_" indicates a distinct placeholder variable)

$$((\cdots((_-, (x_1, y_1, z_1), _-), (x_2, y_2, z_2), _-), \cdots), (x_k, y_k, z_k), _-).$$

Similarly, we want to construct comparable structures that enforce agreement among the appropriate positions for each distinct variable $v \in \mathcal{V}$. Note that, in the following, v as a superscript to M is the variable name while v in the expository set expressions ranges over the possible values of the variable so named. This possibility is resolved to certainty in M_k^v. Also, $\hat{x}_j$ is v if $p_{j,0}$ is v and is $*$ otherwise. Similar usage holds for $\hat{y}$ and $\hat{z}$. Parallel to the above definition of $Svect$, define

$$M_1^v \overset{def}{=} *_0(\triangle_{i,2}) \text{ if } v = p_{j,i}, \mathcal{D}_3 \text{ otherwise}$$
$$M_j^v \overset{def}{=} \mathcal{L}(*_2(M_{j-1}^v)) \cap M_1^v$$

Thus $M_1^v = \{(*, (\hat{x}_1, \hat{y}_1, \hat{z}_1), v)\}$ and, for $j > 1$, $M_j^v = \{(s, (\hat{x}_j, \hat{y}_j, \hat{z}_j), v) : s \in *_2(M_{j-1}^v)\}$. M_1^v appears to do double duty in the above construction. In reality, it is the inductive step which is simply applied to a vacuous starting condition for the base step.

Thus M_k^v encodes the set of all structures which agree on the positions where v occurs and

$$\mathcal{E}_i = \mathcal{T}_{2,2}(Svect_k \cap \bigcap_{\substack{v \in \mathcal{V} \\ v \neq p_i}} *_2(M_k^v) \cap M_k^{p_i})$$

Lemma 26. *Let* $R(p_0, p_1, p_2)$:- $S_1(q_{1,0}, q_{1,1}, q_{1,2}) \vee \cdots \vee S_k(q_{k,0}, q_{k,1}, q_{k,2})$ *be a Trilog statement where* $q_{j,i} \in \{p_0, p_1, p_2\}$. *Then there is an equivalent Trirel expression* $\mathcal{E}$ *that computes the value of* $\mathbf{R}$ *given instances of the* $\mathbf{S}_j$.

Proof. A union of the $\mathbf{S}_j$, with relevant flips and rotations, suffices. Recall that p_0, p_1, and p_2 must occur within every S_j of the union.

This lemma completes the proof of Theorem 23. Now let us consider the other side of the equivalence issue: the degree to which Trilog can implement Trirel.

Because Trilog is inherently conservative, in that it does not introduce new values, it cannot implement tagging. One might consider restricting the output of Trirel expressions to triples over the active domain of the EDB. However, because all values in Trilog are atomic, it cannot implement any "higher order" algebraic operation, even something as simple as $\mathcal{T}(\mathbf{R}) \cap \mathbf{S}$. Thus the domain restriction must apply to inputs as well as outputs.

To this end, $\mathcal{D}$ is partitioned into $\mathcal{D}_b$ and $\mathcal{D}_t$, for "base domain" and "tagging domain". In particular, $\mathcal{D}_t \overset{def}{=} range(\tau)$ and $\mathcal{D}_b \overset{def}{=} \mathcal{D} - \mathcal{D}_t$. This partition induces a unique tree structure on any element of $\mathcal{D}$. That is, an element x of $\mathcal{D}_t$ is expanded into a node with three subtrees $\pi_0(x)$, $\pi_1(x)$, and $\pi_2(x)$, which are recursively expanded until element of $\mathcal{D}_b$ are reached for the leaves. For the next theorem, the EDB is assumed to contain only values from $\mathcal{D}_b$ and any values containing elements of $\mathcal{D}_t$ are deleted from the output.

Proposition 27. *Given a Triler expression* $\mathcal{E}$, *it is possible to tell whether* $\mathcal{E}$ *produces no, some, or only values in* $\mathcal{D}_b$.

Proof. The proof follows from constructions in the next theorem.

Theorem 28. *For each positive Triler expression* $\mathcal{E}$, *there exists a positive Trilog program* $\text{prog}_{\mathcal{E}}$ *such that* `result` *of* `prog` *is the value of* $\mathcal{E}$ *when given the same input instances.*

Proof. Let $\mathbf{S}_1, \cdots, \mathbf{S}_k$ be the occurrences of relations in $\mathcal{E}$; note that one relation may occur as multiple $\mathbf{S}_j$'s. Because unions are handled separately in Trilog, it is necessary to separate the cases whether or not unions occur in $\mathcal{E}$.

Case: $\mathcal{E}$ is a "simple expression" without $\cup$

The tree structure on elements of $\mathcal{D}$ carries over to $\mathcal{E}$. This and the exclusion of $\cup$ imply that, for each coordinate of the result of an expression, values are constructed in one and only one way. Each subexpression $\mathcal{F}$ of $\mathcal{E}$ is associated with three sets of labels. At the leaves, these sets are singletons, but they merge moving up the tree. This merging occurs, in programming jargon, by reference and not by value. That is, when sets associated with two positions are merged, the result is not two sets (one for each position) but one set associated with both positions. Consequently, any subsequent merges propagate directly to all positions associated with a set. To be precise, this set association is defined on the recursive structure of subexpressions $\mathcal{F}$ of $\mathcal{E}$, with the following cases:

$\mathcal{F}$ is a leaf, that is $\mathbf{S}_j$ for some j: associate with each parameter position i of $\mathcal{F}$ the set $\{\langle j, i \rangle\}$.

$\mathcal{F} = \hat{\mathcal{F}} \cap \check{\mathcal{F}}$: If the tree structures for $\hat{\mathcal{F}}$ and $\tilde{\mathcal{F}}$ do not match exactly, then $\hat{\mathcal{F}} \cap \tilde{\mathcal{F}}$ is empty. Otherwise, for each matching leaf in the trees of $\hat{\mathcal{F}}$ and $\tilde{\mathcal{F}}$, merge the two sets associated with those leaves.

$\mathcal{F}$ is defined using trijoin or $\mathcal{I}$: handled similarly in three cases corresponding to the three sides.

$\mathcal{F}$ is defined using $\wr$ or ρ: just reshape the tree structure.

$\mathcal{F}$ is defined using $\mathcal{T}$ or $\mathcal{U}$: these obviously affect the tree structure but do not change the associated sets.

Finally, the results of expression $\mathcal{E}$ are associated with sets. In particular, for each coordinate i of $\mathcal{E}$, examine its tree structure. If that tree is just a base value, it has an associated set and $\langle 0, i \rangle$ is added to that set. If the tree structure is not a base value, then $\mathcal{E}$ will always produce values in $\mathcal{D}_t$, which will be deleted. This observation is also the heart of the proof of Proposition 27.

The associated sets index relation coordinates that are joined, since these sets are merged whenever they overlap. Now construct the body of a Trilog rule as a conjunction of the $\mathbf{S}_j$'s. Assign a unique variable to each set and place that variable in each location in that set. That is, if v is assigned to a set containing $\langle j, i \rangle$, the ith parameter of S_j in the conjunction is v. The head of the rule is either result, if the expression stands by itself, or is a new, unique name if the expression is a subexpression of a union, as discussed below. In either case, the ith parameter of the head is the variable assigned to the set containing $\langle 0, i \rangle$.

Case: $\mathcal{E}$ contains $\cup$

Each expression will now correspond to a finite union of trees relating to simple expressions. Most algebra operations are accomplished by simply distributing across $\cup$. For example, if $\mathcal{E}$ is $\hat{\mathcal{E}} \cap \tilde{\mathcal{E}}$, and $\hat{\mathcal{E}}$ and $\tilde{\mathcal{E}}$ correspond to $\widetilde{\text{tree}}_1 \cdots \widetilde{\text{tree}}_k$ and $\widetilde{\text{tree}}_1 \cdots \widetilde{\text{tree}}_\ell$ respectively, then $\mathcal{E}$ corresponds to

$$\bigcup_{\substack{1 \le i \le k \\ 1 \le j \le \ell}} \widetilde{\text{tree}}_i \cap \widetilde{\text{tree}}_j$$

When a simple subexpression evaluates empty, it is dropped from the union.

6 Application to RDF

This section briefly considers the application of Triler to RDF, first to the model theory[12] and then to approaches for querying RDF.

RDF model theory contains variety of closure rules, rules that are applied to close any piece of RDF syntax E. For example, rule rdfs2 states that if E contains (xxx,aaa,yyy) and it contains (aaa,[rdfs:domain],zzz), then (uuu,[rdf:type], zzz) should be added to E. While the algebra itself does not provide a mechanism for doing updates, it is easy to use the algebra to define the increment to E.

In particular, let $\mathbf{C}$ be $\{(*, [\texttt{rdfs : range}], [\texttt{rdf : type}])\}$ (*i.e.* $\mathbf{C}$ is defined by applying $*_0$ to an explicitly enumerated constant). Then rule rdfs2 adds to E

$$l_0\left(\begin{array}{c} l_0(\mathrm{E}) \\ \diagup \qquad \diagdown \\ \mathrm{E} \text{———} \mathrm{C} \end{array}\right) = l_0\left(\begin{array}{c} zzz \\ \diagup \quad \diagdown \\ aaa \text{—} [\texttt{rdfs : range}] \\ \diagup \diagdown \diagup \qquad \diagdown \\ uuu \text{—} * \text{———} [\texttt{rdf : type}] \end{array}\right) = \begin{array}{c} [\texttt{rdf : type}] \\ uuu \qquad\quad zzz \end{array}.$$

Triler is not sufficient for RDF model theory since the latter includes a transitive closure (rule rdfs5). Any solution that augments Triler with transitive closure will handle this problem. The fixed arity of Triler is beneficial here; with relations of arbitrary arity, the question is which pair attributes encodes the binary relationship to be closed. With ternary relations, there is only one "extra" attribute and that in fact is actually useful to label the relationships to be closed, as was seen in **Trans** of example 7. Thus we define an operator $\mathcal{TC}$ (or the three rotations thereof) that computes the full closure of the operation of that example.

Definition 29. Let $\mathbf{R}$ be a triadic relation. Then

$$\mathcal{TC}_1 \overset{def}{=} \left\{ \begin{array}{c} \ell \\ x_0 \ x_k \end{array} | \exists x_1, \cdots, x_{k-1} [\&_{i=1}^{k} \begin{array}{c} \ell \\ x_{i-1} \ x_i \end{array} \in \mathbf{R}] \right\}$$

$\mathcal{TC}_0$ and $\mathcal{TC}_2$ are defined analogously or as rotations of $\mathcal{TC}_1$.

Note that the above definition has an implicit existential for k or equivalently an unbounded union over sets parameterized by that k. The other common definition of transitive closure, as the fixed point of **Trans**, has a similar unbounded union nature.

Triler may be used to express the core of SquishQL[5], a proposed language for querying RDF (with variants such as RDQL). In SquishQL queries, the WHERE clause is a collection of triplets, forming a template for the specified retrieval; this template immediately maps to a Datalog body. SquishQL not closed on triadic relations, however, in that SquishQL query may return tuples over an arbitrary list of attributes. Thus, similar to the construction of $\mathcal{L}$ (Lemma 24), such arbitrary lists of values may be returned in encoded form. Theorem 28 may be used to translate arbitrary SquishQL queries to Triler.

7   Conclusion

This paper has introduced an algebra, Triler, over triadic relations. An essential characteristic of an algebra is closure – that is, all algebraic operations produce results from the same set as the inputs. Other interesting models of RDF queries are not algebras in this strict sense, even when query results are projected down to exactly three-element tuples. This is because all these models require intermediate constructions with more than three active elements[1] for certain queries. Hence their primitive operations do not collectively specify an algebra.

Triler surmounts this problem with a mechanism for encoding triples of values in a single value. This mechanism thus supports a kind of reification. However, if the reified values are treated only as internal values (that is, reified values are not allowed in input or output), the encoding provides no additional query capability beyond other formalisms (RA, Datalog, FOL) suitably restricted to triples. This suggests that reification can be introduced where semantic considerations require it, without concern that this introduction would seriously impact the formalism in other ways.

Triler is fully symmetric, unlike other approaches from databases [5, 2] or logic [6, 1]. Thus interpretation (*e.g.* mapping to labeled graphs) is entirely by convention, rather than being imposed by the algebra and its operators.

This work also illustrates the well-known tradeoff between complexities of representation and manipulation. That is, given suitable constant relations, the only operators necessary are join and relative complement.

Of course most of this work can be replicated in higher degrees. A suitable join operation is

$$\text{njoin}(\mathbf{R}_1, \cdots, \mathbf{R}_k) \stackrel{def}{=} \{(x_1, \cdots, x_k) : \exists y_1, \cdots, y_k [\&_{j=1}^k \mathbf{R}_j(v_{1,j}, \cdots, v_{k,j})]\}$$

where $v_{i,j} = x_j$ if $i = j$ and y_i otherwise.

Acknowledgments. Thanks for valuable comments and suggestions by Richard Martin and Dirk Van Gucht.

References

1. J. Micheael Dunn. A representation of relation algebras using Routly-Meyer frames. In C. Anthony Anderson and M. Zelëny, editors, *Logic, Meaning, and Computation*, pages 77-108. Kluwer Academic Publishers, 2001.
2. Claudion Gutierrez, Carlos Hurtaddo, and Alberto Mendelzon. Foundations of semantic web databases. In *ACM Principles of Database System*, 2004.
3. Frank Harary. *Graph Theory*. Addison-Wesley, 1969.
4. Michael Kifer, Georg Lausen, and James Wu. Logical foundations of object-oriented and frame-based languages, *J. of ACM*, 42(4):741-843, 1995.
5. Libby Miller, Andy Seaborne, and Alberto eggiori. Three implementations of squishql, a simple rdf query language, In *International Semantic Web Conference (ISWC)*, 2002.
6. Charles Sanders Peirce. On the algebra of logic. *Amer. J. of Math.*, pages 180-202, 1885.

---

[1] The notion of "active element" is merely intuitive, roughly corresponding to the minimum number of variables in relational calculus or Datalog.

7. John F. Sowa. *Knowledge Representation: Logical, Philosophical, and Computational Foundations.* Brooks Cole, 2000.
8. Alfred Tarski. On the calculus of relations, *J. of Symbolic Logic*, 6(3):73-89, 1941.
9. Jeffry D.Ullman, *Princ. of Database abd KnowledgeBase Systems*, volume I-Fundamental Concepts, Computer Science Press, New York, 1988.
10. Dirk Van Gucht, Lawrence V. Saxton, and Marc Gyssens. Tagging as an alternative to object creation, In Hohann Chirstoph Freytag, David Maier, and Gottfried Vossen, editors, *Query Processing for Advanced Database Systems*, pages 201-242. Morgan Kaufmann, 1994.
11. W3C. Defining n-ary relations on the semantic web: Use with individuals, 1999. http://www.w3.org/TR/swbp-n-aryRelations.
12. W3C. RDF Model Theory, 2002. www.w3.org/TR/rdf-mt/.
13. Guizhen Yang and Michael Kifer, On the sematntics of anonmous identity and reification. In *DBLP 2002*, volume 2519 of *Lecture Notes in Computer Scinces*, pages 1047-1066. Springer, 2002.
14. Guizhen Yang, Michael Kifer, and Chang Zhao. Flora-2: User's manual, June 2002. http://flora.sourceforge.net.

Semantically Unlocking Database Content Through Ontology-Based Mediation

Pieter Verheyden, Jan De Bo, and Robert Meersman

Vrije Universiteit Brussel - STARLab
Pleinlaan 2, Gebouw G-10, B-1050 Brussels, Belgium
{pverheyd, jdebo, meersman}@vub.ac.be
http://www.starlab.vub.ac.be

Abstract. To make database content available via the internet, its intended shared meaning, i.e. an interpretation is required of the database (schema) symbols in terms of a so-called ontology. Such an ontology specifies not only concepts and their relationships in some language, but also includes the manner in which an application or service is permitted to make use of these concepts. Ontologies therefore also play a key role in making databases interoperate. The DOGMA approach to ontology engineering is specifically adapted to the classical model-theoretic view of (relational) databases. Notably, it rigorously separates an ontology base of elementary lexical fact types called lexons, from the rules and constraints governing the concepts referred to by the lexons in the ontology base. These rules are reified in so-called ontological *commitments* of applications to the ontology base. In this paper we formalise and make precise the structure of this commitment layer by defining Ω-RIDL, a new type of so-called commitment language. Examples derived from its use in a non-trivial case study are provided. We illustrate how some of its key constructs, designed to specify mediators by mapping databases to an ontology base, can conveniently be reused in a conceptual query language, and report on its ongoing implementation.

1 Introduction

Suppose we want to make certain database content meaningfully available for applications on the World Wide Web. In such an open environment applications and application types in general are unknown a priori, including the manner in which they will want to refer to the data, or more precisely, to the concepts and attributes that take their values from the database. Therefore, elements of meaning for the database's underlying domain have to be agreed, and represented explicitly. They will need to be stored, accessed, and maintained externally to the database schema as well as to the intended applications. Computer resources that formally represent a domain's semantics in this external, application-independent way are called (domain-)*ontologies*. In a nutshell, an application system and in particular its database schema can be assigned a formal semantics, also known as (first order) *interpretation*. Such semantics in our

C. Bussler et al. (Eds.): SWDB 2004, LNCS 3372, pp. 109–126, 2005.
© Springer-Verlag Berlin Heidelberg 2005

approach has two separate components, (a) a mapping from the schema's symbols and relationships to a suitable ontology base expressed in lexical terms, and (b) expressions, separate and "ontological", of how database constraints restrict the use of, or precisely *commit to*, the concepts referred by the terms in this ontology base.

In this paper we discuss how elements of a relational database are mapped on elements of an existing domain ontology. We investigate possible difficulties that can be encountered during this non-trivial task. Further, we describe how to translate domain constraints on the database level to semantic constraints on the ontology level. In order to impose these semantic constraints on the terms and relations of the ontology, we developed a new ontological commitment language called *Ω-RIDL*. The above mentioned principles are illustrated and clarified by a practical case study. In this case study we investigate how the relational database of the National Drug Code (NDC) Directory relates to the medical ontology LinKBase®.

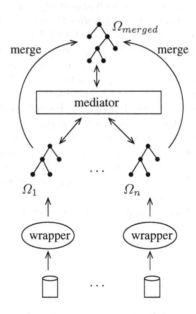

Fig. 1. Mediator approach for data integration

The research in this paper fits in the broader context of data integration because it will be very unlikely that a user's information needs will be satisfied by accessing the data repositories accessible through mappings associated with a single ontology. To support this, ontologies are aligned with each other. The OBSERVER framework [20] proposes an approach to use the inter ontology relationships to translate the original query from terms of the source ontology into terms of another component, also referred to as a target ontology. This kind of query rewriting does not always occur without loss of information. The *Interontology Relationship Manager (IRM)* in the OBSERVER system serves as a pool where all interontology relationships between the different ontologies are made available. For n ontologies involved one has to compute $\frac{n(n-1)}{2}$ sets of interontology relationships. To minimise this effort we have chosen for a *mediator inspired framework*. It is our goal to develop a framework for data integration that is easy to maintain and to extend. Therefore the source ontologies are merged into one global ontology. In a binary merging strategy this requires only $n - 1$ alignments [2]. The only additional steps to be performed are to check for conflicts and to integrate the separate ontologies into a global ontology. The mediator then decomposes the global query into a union of queries on the underlying source ontologies and unifies all resultsets into a global result. The framework is depicted in Figure 1. Each time our framework is extended with a new ontology we only have to merge this ontology with the global ontology and adjust the mediator accordingly. It is obvious that this is less time consuming than having to perform alignments with all present ontologies.

The focus of this paper is to present a new ontological commitment language called Ω-*RIDL*, and not to elaborate further on the mediator framework here proposed. The syntax of the language and its principles are introduced in section 4, and its usage is explained by means of a case study which we describe in section 3. In section 5 we illustrate how ontological commitments are deployed in the mediator framework. We finalise this paper with sections on related work (section 6) and future work (section 7), and present a conclusion in section 8. In section 2 we briefly discuss our DOGMA approach to ontology engineering.

2   The DOGMA Ontology Model

DOGMA[1] is a research initiative of VUB STARLab where various theories, methods, and tools for ontologies are studied and developed. A DOGMA inspired ontology is based on the classical model-theoretic perspective [21] and decomposes an ontology into an *ontology base* and a layer of *ontological commitments* [17, 18]. This is called the principle of *double articulation* [22].

An ontology base holds (multiple) intuitive conceptualisation(s) of a particular domain. Each conceptualisation is simplified to a "representation-less" set of context-specific binary fact types called *lexons*. A lexon is formally described as a 5-tuple $< \gamma \quad term_1 \quad role \quad co-role \quad term_2 >$, where γ is an abstract context identifier, lexically described by a string in some natural language, and is used to group lexons that are logically related to each other in the conceptualisation of the domain. Intuitively, a lexon may be read as: within the context γ, the $term_1$ (also denoted as the *header* term) may have a relation with $term_2$ (also denoted as the *tail* term) in which it plays a *role*, and conversely, in which $term_2$ plays a corresponding *co-role*. Each (context,term)-pair then lexically identifies a unique *concept*. An ontology base can hence be described as a set of plausible elementary fact types that are considered as being true. Any specific (application-dependent) interpretation is moved to a separate layer, i.e. the commitment layer.

---

[1] Developing Ontology-Guided Mediation for Agents

Ontology Base

Context	Header Term	Role	Co−role	Tail Term
MEDICINE	DENTAL DRUG	IS_A		MEDICINAL PRODUCT
MEDICINE	MEDICINAL PRODUCT	HAS−PATH		ROUTE OF ADMINISTRATION
MEDICINE	PER VAGINA	IS_A		ROUTE OF ADMINISTRATION
MEDICINE	MEDICINAL PRODUCT	HAS−INGREDIENT	IS−INGREDIENT−OF	INGREDIENT OF MEDICINAL SUBSTANCE
MEDICINE	MEDICINAL PRODUCT	HAS_ASSOC		MATERIAL ENTITY BY PRESENTATION SHAPE
MEDICINE	LOTION	IS_A		MATERIAL ENTITY BY PRESENTATION SHAPE
MEDICINE	MEDICINAL PRODUCT	HAS_ASSOC		ENTERPRISE
MEDICINE	ENTERPRISE	HAS_ASSOC		COUNTRY − STATE
MEDICINE	CANADA	IS_A		COUNTRY − STATE

Fig. 2. A small extract of the ontology base represented by a simple table format

The commitment layer mediates between the ontology base and its applications. Each such ontological commitment defines *a partial semantic account of an intended conceptualisation* [13]. It consists of a finite set of axioms that specify which lexons of the ontology base are interpreted and how they are *visible* in the committing application, and (domain) rules that semantically constrain this interpretation. Experience shows that it is much harder to reach an agreement on domain rules than one on conceptualisation [19]. E.g., the rule stating that *each patient is a person who suffers from at least one disease* may hold in the Universe of Discourse (UoD) of some application, but may be too strong in the UoD of another application.

3   A Motivating Case Study

In the health care sector, access to correct and precise information in an efficient time frame is a necessity. A Hospital Information System (HIS) is a real-life example of an Information System consisting of several dispersed data sources containing specific information, though interrelated in some way. These data sources can vary from highly structured repositories (e.g., relational databases), structured documents (e.g., electronic patient records), or even free text (e.g., patient discharge notes written in some natural language). VUB STARLab joins hands with Language and Computing (L&C) N.V. [2] in the IWT R&D project SCOP[3] with the aim of finding a suitable solution to integrate such medical data sources through "semantic couplings" to an existing medical ontology. The initial focus was set on medical relational databases.

Throughout the years, L&C has built up, and still maintains, an extensive medical ontology called LinKBase® [12]. Further, The National Drug Code

---

[2] URL: http://www.landcglobal.com
[3] Semantic Connection of Ontologies to Patient data

(NDC) Directory of the U.S. Food And Drug Administration (FDA) was used as a case study. The ontological commitment to a DOGMA ontology base containing ontological knowledge from (a relevant part of) LinKBase® [4] was defined for the NDC Directory. Figure 2 presents a small extract of the ontology base represented by a simple table format.

In the following subsection we give some relevant background information on the NDC Directory and its relational database. Parts of its ontological commitment definition will be used for illustration purposes in section 4.

3.1   The NDC Directory

The National Drug Code (NDC) Directory was originally established as an essential part of an out-of-hospital drug reimbursement program under Medicare, and serves as a universal product identifier for human drugs. The current edition of the NDC is limited to prescription drugs and a few selected over-the-counter (OTC) drug products. The following information about the listed drug products are available: product trade name or catalogue name, National Drug Code (NDC), related firms, dosage form, routes of administration, active ingredient(s), strength, unit, package size and type, and the major drug class.

By federal regulation, NDCs are 10-digit numbers that identify the labeller/vendor, product, and trade package size. NDCs follow one of three different formats: 4-4-2, 5-4-1, or 5-3-2. The first set of digits, the labeller code assigned by the FDA, identifies the labeller (i.e. any firm that manufactures, repacks, or distributes a drug product). The second set of digits, the product code assigned by the firm, identifies a specific strength, dosage form, and formulation for that particular firm. The third set of digits, the package code assigned by the firm, identifies package sizes. Because of the variability of the length of the subcodes within an NDC, almost all governmental and commercial organisations other than the FDA use 11-digit NDCs. In particular, the Centers for Medicare & Medicaid Services (CMS)[5] uses and distributes 11-digit NDCs. These non-standard 11-digit NDCs are created by a system of zero-filling so that each NDC follows a 5-4-2 format (e.g., 00006-4677-00). NDCs may be reused and reassigned to different drugs. So, a given NDC cannot be assumed to be constant over time. If a manufacturer is acquired by another firm, or if a manufacturer sells the production rights of a drug to another entity, there is a good chance that the new manufacturer or re-distributor will change all the NDCs assigned to a particular drug (even though the drug product remains exactly the same in terms of its formulation, preparation, packaging, etc.).

The relational database schema of the NDC Directory is presented by Figure 3. The freely available ASCII data files from which this relational database has

---

[4] Due to some significant differences between both ontology approaches, the exchange of ontological knowledge was not so straightforward. We will not elaborate on this issue because it is less relevant here, but, we can mention that this exchange could be done semi-automatically by using RDFS as communication language between both ontology frameworks.

[5] URL: http://www.cms.hhs.gov

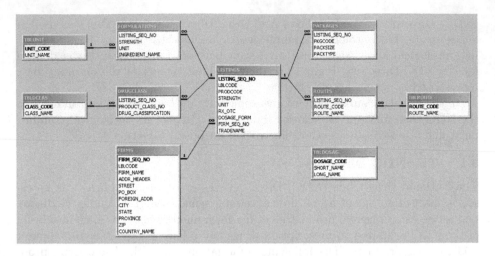

Fig. 3. The relational database schema of the NDC Directory

been constructed, together with detailled descriptions, can be found on the official website of the NDC Directory [6]. We mention following issues that clearly indicate a poor design of the relational database regarding its provided schema and population:

- **Referential Integrity.** We had to manually update the population of some relations to enable a correct linking with other relations (e.g., the linking of the relation "ROUTES" with "TBLROUTE").
- **Normalisation.** Some attributes of the relation "LISTINGS" allow multiple entries as one value. As a result, the relational database schema is not in first normal form (1NF).
- **Data Redundancy.** Some attributes appear in more than one relation, which causes update anomalies (e.g., the attribute "LBLCODE" can be found in the relation "LISTINGS" as well as in the relation "FIRMS").

4   Defining Ontological Commitments in Ω-RIDL

4.1   Historical Background

The main syntactic principles of Ω-RIDL are adopted from RIDL[7], an old conceptual language developed in 1979 by R. Meersman at the Database Management Research Lab (Brussels) of Control Data. It was developed as an integrated formal syntactic support for information and process analysis, semantic specification, constraint definition, and a query/update language at a conceptual level rather than at the logical "flat data" level. The conceptual support for RIDL

---

[6] URL: http://www.fda.gov/cder/ndc/
[7] Reference and IDea Language.

was provided by (the "binary subset" of) the so-called *idea/bridge* model for conceptual schemata developed by Falkenberg and Nijssen. Problem specifications in this model were obtained through a methodology commonly known as NIAM[8] [24], which is the predecessor of ORM[9] [14]. A result of this analysis methodology was (partially) represented by a conceptual data schema graphically depicted by a dedicated diagram notation. In the idea/bridge philosophy, such a conceptual data schema was also denoted as an idea/bridge view of a world (i.e. the UoD on which the analysis is done). A fundamental characteristic was the strict separation between *non-lexical object types* (NOLOTs; "things" that cannot be uttered or written down, e.g., "patient") and *lexical object types* (LOTs; "things" that can be uttered, written down, or otherwise represented, e.g., "date of birth") [25]. A relation (consisting of a role and co-role) between two NOLOTs was called an *idea*; a relation between a NOLOT and a LOT was called a *bridge*. Such relationships are commonly called *fact types*. Further, subtype relations between NOLOTs were also supported. This strict separation between NOLOTs and LOTs was also explicitly respected by RIDL. Since the idea/bridge philosophy was very close the user's understanding of a problem, RIDL also had to be close to a natural formulation of the information description and manipulation [16].

RIDL can be roughly divided into two parts: the constraint definition part (RIDL\cns) and the query/update part (RIDL\qu). These two parts were used by two, in general disjunctive, kind of users: database engineers and end-users. Database engineers used RIDL\cns to formally and naturally express a conceptual data schema and its constraints. At compile time, such a conceptual data schema was (semi-)automatically transformed into a relational database schema, satisfying some normal form which was controlled by the database engineer [10]. The end-user used RIDL\qu, after the generated relational database was populated, to retrieve/update data at runtime through (possibly interactive) conceptual queries on the conceptual data schema, instead of constructing SQL queries on the underlying relational database [16]. During the eighties, dedicated tools were developed and enhanced for the transformation of a conceptual data schema into a relational database schema (RIDL* graphical workbench [10, 11]), and the translation of RIDL queries/updates into correct SQL queries/updates (RIDL Shell).

RIDL was developed at the same time when the first SQL systems appeared on the market and was therefore far ahead of its time. Although none of the commercial RIDL* prototypes found their way to the market, the RIDL* fun-

---

[8] aN/Natural/Nijssen's Information Analysis Method.

[9] Object-Role Modeling (URL: `http://www.orm.net`)

[10] This control included the choice of how a subtype relation from the conceptual data schema should be translated in the relational database schema to be generated. This can be done by, e.g., an "indicator" attribute (e.g., a relation "Person" having an attribute "Sex" only allowing the values "M" or "F"), or by a foreign key (resulting in a decomposition, e.g., the relations "Male" and "Female" with foreign keys to the relation "Person").

damentals still live in today's ORM-based modelling and database design CASE tools. RIDL's conceptual querying part got the attention of Halpin and resulted in ConQuer[11][4], and a successor ConQuer-II [5], a language for building conceptual queries within the ORM context.

Although RIDL was intended for data(base) modelling, its main syntactic principles have been reconsidered to be adopted for the development of an ontological commitment language, simply called Ω-RIDL ("Ω" refers to "ontology base").

4.2   Defining an Ontological Commitment

An ontological commitment defined in Ω-RIDL consists of four distinct parts:

1. a commitment declaration,
2. a lexical interpretation layer,
3. a lexical association layer,
4. a semantic constraint layer.

In the following subsections we will focus on each part separately. It will also be clear that these four parts together define an ontological commitment; they are closely linked with each other and therefore are not to be seen as independent of each other.

To give the reader already an idea of how an ontological commitment definition looks like, a highly trimmed version of the ontological commitment definition corresponding to our case study is therefore given below:

```
define commitment in context MEDICINE with subsumption IS_A/[]
  lexical interpretations
    map FIRMS.COUNTRY_NAME=CANADA
    on  CANADA IS_A "COUNTRY - STATE" [] [HAS_ASSOC] ENTERPRISE
  lexical associations
    assoc FIRMS.COUNTRY_NAME=CHINA with "COUNTRY - STATE"
  semantic constraints
    each ENTERPRISE HAS_ASSOC exactly one "COUNTRY - STATE"
  end
```

In this example, words in upper case are elements of either the committing relational database, either the committed ontology base; words in lower case are keywords of Ω-RIDL. Double quotes are used in the language to denote a terminal consisting of more than one string which are separated from each other by blank spaces. Note how the language aims at defining an ontological commitment close to its natural formulation. As a result, most syntactic expressions can be naturally read and understood by humans.

4.3   Commitment Declaration

The commitment declaration states the context in which the commitment will be defined, referenced by its name from the ontology base, and the ontological rela-

---

[11] CONceptual QUERy.

tion(s) that will be interpreted in the commitment as subsumption relation(s). Such an ontological relation, referenced by resp. its role and co-role labels, must be described by at least one lexon within the declared context. As a result, the specialisation of a "super"-term will play a declared role (e.g., "is a") in the commitment, and the generalisation of a "sub"-term will play a corresponding declared co-role (e.g., "subsumes").

A commitment declaration is syntactically simplified to one sentence, e.g.:

```
define commitment in context MEDICINE with subsumption IS_A/[]
```

Note that this example introduces a so-called *syntactic placeholder*, expressed with "[]", which denotes a non-existing co-role in the ontology base. Such place-holders were introduced in the language because most co-roles are not modelled in LinKBase® [12]. They serve as null values which can be replaced if a corresponding co-role is eventually modelled in the ontology base by an authorised ontology engineer.

4.4 Lexical Interpretation Layer

The lexical interpretation layer contains lexical mappings. A lexical mapping defines a mapping of a formula expressing a path of the relational database (e.g., the attribute expressed by the formula "FIRMS.CITY") on a path in the ontology base.

An ontological path is recursively defined as an ordered sequence of lexons from the ontology base, within the declared context. A minimal ontological path is constructed from one lexon, e.g.:

```
"MEDICINAL PRODUCT" HAS-INGREDIENT "INGREDIENT OF MEDICINAL SUBSTANCE"
```

For reading convenience we do not include the corresponding co-role here. However, in some cases the co-role must be explicitly specified to disambiguate which lexon is interpreted. Let us clarify this with an example. Imagine following lexons being modelled in the ontology base [13]:

```
<MEDICINE,PHYSICIAN,HAS_ASSOC,XXX,PATIENT>
<MEDICINE,PHYSICIAN,HAS_ASSOC,YYY,PATIENT>
```

If the first lexon has to be interpreted, we have to express a (minimal) ontological path as follows:

```
PHYSICIAN HAS_ASSOC [XXX] PATIENT
```

where the co-role of the lexon to be interpreted is explicitly specified between square brackets. In the case of a non-existing co-role, we use the same syntactic placeholder we already introduced earlier, e.g.:

---

[12] An ontology engineer is not allowed to model a relation between a $concept_x$ and a $concept_y$ in LinKBase®, if, according to the real world, that relation does not hold for *each possible instance of $concept_x$*.

[13] Note that these lexons cannot be modelled in LinKBase®.

```
                "COUNTRY - STATE" [] [HAS_ASSOC] ENTERPRISE
```

For understanding convenience we explicitly specify the corresponding role between square brackets.

The next step is then to add a lexon with a common term to a minimal ontological path, e.g.:

```
        CANADA IS_A "COUNTRY - STATE" [] [HAS_ASSOC] ENTERPRISE
```

is constructed from the following two lexons:

```
        <MEDICINE,CANADA,IS_A, ,COUNTRY - STATE>
        <MEDICINE,ENTERPRISE,HAS_ASSOC, ,COUNTRY - STATE>
```

We distinguish two kinds of lexical mappings: *reference* mappings and *relation* mappings. A reference mapping expresses a mapping involving a reference path from the committing relational database. Such a reference path is an attribute or an attribute value, and is expressed by an intuitive formula, e.g., "FIRMS.CITY". The following reference mapping involves an attribute being mapped:

```
map LISTINGS.DOSAGE_FORM
on "MATERIAL ENTITY BY PRESENTATION SHAPE" [] [HAS_ASSOC] "MEDICINAL PRODUCT"
```

and must be read and interpreted as follows: the relation "LISTINGS" contains an attribute "DOSAGE_FORM" that semantically corresponds with "MATERIAL ENTITY BY PRESENTATION SHAPE" that has a relation with role "HAS_ASSOC" with "MEDICINAL PRODUCT" to which "LISTINGS" semantically corresponds. In other words, "LISTINGS" is mapped on "MEDICINAL PRODUCT", the "." is mapped on the relation with role "HAS_ASSOC", and "DOSAGE_FORM" is mapped on "MATERIAL ENTITY BY PRESENTATION SHAPE". Attribute values can reflect ontological knowledge as well, and therefore it is sometimes necessary to define reference mappings at the level of attribute values, e.g:

```
    map FIRMS.COUNTRY_NAME=CANADA
    on  CANADA IS_A "COUNTRY - STATE" [] [HAS_ASSOC] ENTERPRISE
```

In this example, the subsumption relation is to be found between the attribute "COUNTRY_NAME" and its values (e.g., "CANADA").

Some attributes are merely added to the relational database schema as unique tuple identifiers, and therefore reflect no semantics in the application's UoD. Next to that, they are often the result of a decomposition during normalisation, and function as foreign keys. However, a foreign key often semantically corresponds with a (direct or indirect) relation between two terms in the ontology base. Let us clarify this with some examples. In the following relation mapping, a foreign key (expressed by a formula) is mapped on the direct relation between two terms:

```
map (LISTINGS.FIRM_SEQ_NO = FIRMS.FIRM_SEQ_NO)
on  "MEDICINAL PRODUCT" (HAS_ASSOC) ENTERPRISE
```

For understanding convenience we use parenthesis to delimite which element is mapped on which element. In some cases, a combination of foreign keys needs to be mapped. In the following example, the combination of two foreign keys is mapped on the direct relation between two terms:

```
map (LISTINGS.LISTING_SEQ_NO = ROUTES.LISTING_SEQ_NO,
     ROUTES.ROUTE_CODE = TBLROUTE.ROUTE_CODE)
on  "MEDICINAL PRODUCT" (HAS-PATH) "ROUTE OF ADMINISTRATION"
```

4.5 Lexical Association Layer

The lexical association layer contains (possible) lexical associations. A lexical association defines an association between a reference path of the relational database, which is meaningful in the considered UoD, with a term of the ontology base. A reference path is a formula expressing an attribute or attribute value which has not already been mapped by a reference mapping defined in the lexical interpretation layer.

Lexical associations are also to be seen as syntactic placeholders. Let us clarify this by following example:

```
lexical interpretations
  map FIRMS.COUNTRY_NAME=CANADA
  on  CANADA IS_A "COUNTRY - STATE" [] [HAS_ASSOC] ENTERPRISE
lexical associations
  assoc FIRMS.COUNTRY_NAME=CHINA with "COUNTRY - STATE"
```

The attribute value "FIRMS.COUNTRY_NAME=CHINA" could not be mapped because the ontology base does not contain a semantically corresponding term, e.g., "CHINA". Therefore, it is lexically associated with the term "COUNTRY - STATE" in expectation from a corresponding lexon involving the associated term, e.g., the lexon <MEDICINE,CHINA,IS_A, ,COUNTRY - STATE>. If this lexon is eventually modelled in the ontology base by an authorised ontology engineer, the above association can be transformed to a reference mapping, i.e.:

```
map FIRMS.COUNTRY_NAME=CHINA
on  CHINA IS_A "COUNTRY - STATE" [] [HAS_ASSOC] ENTERPRISE
```

4.6 Semantic Constraint Layer

The semantic constraint layer accounts for the intended meaning of the conceptualisation by defining one or more constraint rules on interpreted lexons. These rules reflect (as good as possible) the rules intended by the UoD of the application, e.g., the integrity constraints of the committing relational database. The syntax in which these constraint rules are expressed is adopted from the old RIDL, e.g.:

```
each ENTERPRISE HAS_ASSOC exactly one "COUNTRY - STATE"
```

expresses the rule that each application instance of "ENTERPRISE" must play the role "HAS_ASSOC" with "COUNTRY - STATE" exactly once. This rule constrains a lexon interpreted through a following reference mapping:

```
map FIRMS.COUNTRY_NAME=CANADA
on  CANADA IS_A "COUNTRY - STATE" [] [HAS_ASSOC] ENTERPRISE
```

and reflects the attribute "COUNTRY_NAME" not allowing null values, i.e. each particular firm is located in exactly one country or state (according to the considered UoD).

5   Deploying Ontological Commitments for Mediation

Defining ontological commitments for relational databases (or applications in general) must aim for some practical use. In this section we demonstrate how an ontological commitment (defined in Ω-RIDL) can be deployed for mediation, i.e. the translation of a conceptual query (query on ontology level) into a correct logical query (query on database level).

By adopting the ORM diagram notation we graphically represent an ontological commitment by a tree. Figure 4 presents a part of the ontological commitment of the NDC Directory represented by such a tree. An ontological commitment tree is constructed by connecting the ontological paths from the the lexical interpretation layer of the ontological commitment definition. A dashed ellipse (a LOT in the original NIAM context) represents the start term of an ontological path. Terms other than the start term involved in an ontological path are represented by solid ellipses (NOLOTs in the original NIAM context). Subsumption relations are represented by arrows; other ontological relations are represented by boxes. Boxes highlightened in bold indicate that relation mappings are involved. The combination of the dot and box arrow graphically represents the constraint rule: *each ENTERPRISE HAS_ASSOC exactly one "COUNTRY - STATE"*.

A conceptual query can now be formulated by constructing a subtree of our ontological commitment tree. Let us demonstrate this with an example. A naturally formulated query can be: *list all cities in Germany in which enterprises are located that are related to medicinal products having a nasal route of administration*. By adopting RIDL\qu (the query/update part of the old RIDL) and the syntactic placeholder mechanism of Ω-RIDL, this query can be formally written down as:

```
list CITY [] [HAS_ASSOC] ENTERPRISE
                 (HAS_ASSOC GERMANY
                 and
                 [] [HAS_ASSOC] "MEDICINAL PRODUCT"
                                HAS-PATH "ORAL ROUTE")
```

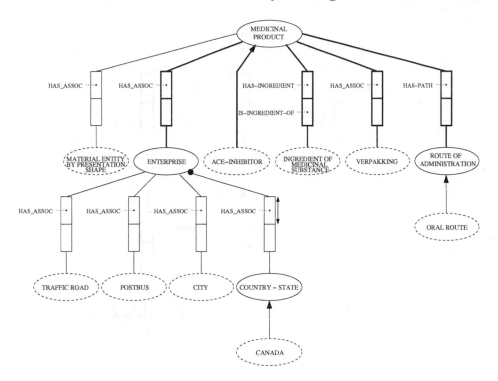

Fig. 4. Part of the ontological commitment of the NDC Directory represented by a tree graphically depicted by adopting the ORM notation

Figure 5 presents the graphical representation of this query as a subtree of the ontological commitment tree of Figure 4. The translation of this conceptual query into a correct logical query is done by a tree traversal:

- the left "selection" branch is traversed buttom-up;
- the middle and right "condition" branches are traversed top-down, connecting them with the logical "and"-operator (as specified by our formulated conceptual query).

During this traversal we deploy the reference and relation mappings defined in the corresponding ontological commitment to decide whether (part of) a branch of the conceptual query tree is visible in the committed relational database and, if so, in what we have to translate it. Figure 6 presents the resulting SQL query. Boxes denote elements from reference mappings; boxes highlightened in bold denote elements from relation mappings. The execution of this SQL query on the relational database of the NDC Directory finally returns us the desired instance data.

Apart from their use in mediation, conceptual queries are also important, as argued in [23], as a convenient way to formally define and specify end-user profiles, intended to customise an individual's interaction with the system. Intuitively, the result of an ontology query, or user profile, is a set of (concept) terms, together with the query formulation itself that implies the intended relationships between the concepts as seen and expected by the end-user.

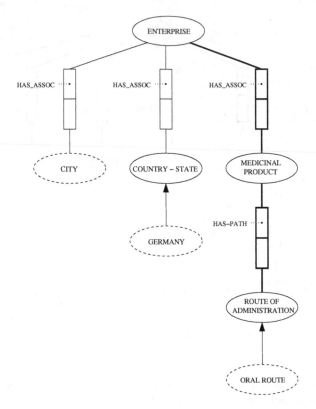

Fig. 5. Example of a conceptual query represented as a subtree of an ontological commitment tree

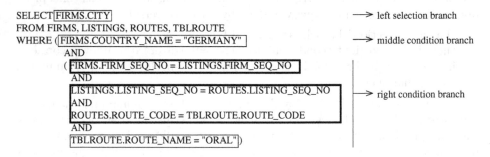

Fig. 6. The SQL query as a result of the conceptual query translation

6   Related Work

Efforts on integration of heterogeneous datasources can be divided into two main categories. A first category of approaches have in common that they build a global conceptual datamodel from different datasources. The second category follows a fundamental different approach in that datasources are mapped to *existing* domain ontologies. The methodology for data integration proposed in this paper is classified under the second category. We will now give a classification of various approaches in the first category.

1. *Schema integration:* In this case, the input of the integration process is a set of source schemata, and the output is a single (target) schema representing the reconciled intentional representation of all input schemata (i.e. a global conceptual schema). The output includes also the specification of how to map source data schemata into portions of the target schema. This kind of schema integration is often referred to as *view integration* in the database research community. View integration is considered as an essential step in database design. A stepwise methodology for schema integration is given in [2].

2. *Virtual data integration:* The input is a set of source data sets, and the output is a specification of how to provide a global and unified access to the sources in order to satisfy certain information needs. The data are kept only in the sources. These sources also remain autonomous throughout the whole process and are queried using views. Database integration [2] appears in distributed databases environments and has as main goal the design of an integrated global schema (often called a virtual view) from local schemata. Virtual data integration is not only restricted to databases but may as well be extended to other kinds of datasources (structured, semi-structured, or not structured at all). In [3] Bergamaschi illustrates how the MOMIS system is built. Briefly summarised, wrappers are responsible for translating the original description languages of any particular source into a common data language and to add all information needed by the mediator, such as the source name and the type. Above the wrappers there is the mediator, which is a software module that has as most important task to build a global conceptual schema. Queries are then formulated against the global schema and are translated into local queries. The query result is then combined by the mediator and presented to the user. The TSIMMIS project [7] is primarily focused on the semi-automatic generation of wrappers, translators, and mediators.

3. *Materialised data integration:* As in the previous case, the input is a set of source data sets, but here the output is a data set representing a reconciled view of the input sources, both at the intentional and the extensional level. The field of data integration with materialised views is the one most closely related to data warehousing.

4. *Data Warehousing:* With the aid of wrappers and mediators a datawarehouse schema is formed of the local source schemata. The datawarehouse itself is responsible for storing the data of the local sources. Source integration in data warehousing identifies three perspectives: *a conceptual perspective, a logical perspective* and a *physical perspective* [15].

The OBSERVER system [20], which belongs to the second category, has already been discussed in section 1. We have argued the differences between our framework and that of OBSERVER. Another important difference which has been described in this paper is the ability we provide to impose semantic domain constraints at the ontology level. This aspect is completely absent in the OBSERVER project. Another project, comparable with OBSERVER, is SIMS [1]. In this system the different information sources are accessed using a system based on Description Logics, Loom. The CARNOT project [8] used the global upper ontology Cyc to describe the whole information system. A key shortcoming with this approach is the difficulty and complexity of managing a large global ontology (more than 50.000 entities and relationships). For this reason we have focused on an approach that involves the use of multiple ontologies as stated in the introduction.

7   Future Work

A prototype of a compiler, called *omegaridlc*, is developed to support the language in the current DOGMA ontology framework. It enables an automatic verification of an ontological commitment definition on syntax and semantics, and the translation to a more machine processable form. This form is currently a markup version of the language, expressed in the popular XML, which enables a more convenient adaptation by existing ontology-based mediation technology, e.g., the MaDBoks[14] system [9] developed by L&C N.V. as an extension to their LinKFactory® Ontology Management System [6]. This adaptation and its implementation is currently being investigated as part of the SCOP project.

8   Conclusion

In this paper we have focused on a new ontological commitment language called Ω-RIDL. This language is developed to naturally describe how elements of a relational database semantically correspond to a (given) domain ontology. One of the novel aspects of this language is the support of imposing semantic domain constraints at the ontology level.

By means of a real-life case study we have explained the principles of the language, and demonstrated how a syntactic placeholder mechanism was introduced to overcome assumed incompleteness of the given domain ontology. Further, we have illustrated how some of its key constructs can conveniently be reused in a conceptual query language. We demonstrated this with an example of how an ontological commitment defined in Ω-RIDL can be deployed for mediation, i.e. the process of translating a conceptual query (query on ontology level) to a correct logical query (query on database level).

Acknowledgments. This work has been funded by the IWT (Institute for the Promotion of Innovation by Science and Technology in Flanders): Pieter

---

[14] MApping DataBases Onto Knowledge Systems

Verheyden is supported in the context of the SCOP project ("Semantische Connectie van Ontologieën aan Patiëntgegevens"; IWT O&O #020020/L&C), while Jan De Bo has received an IWT PhD grant (IWT SB 2002 #21304). We also like to thank Carlo Wouters (La Trobe University; VUB STARLab) and Tom Deray (L&C N.V.) for their valuable comments on earlier drafts of this paper.

References

1. Arens, Y., Knoblock, C. and Shen, W. (1996) Query Reformulation for Dynamic Information Integration. In *Journal of Intelligent Information Systems, 1996 6(2-3), pp. 99-130.*
2. Batini, C., Lenzerini, M. and Navathe, S. (1986) A Comparative Analysis of Methodologies for Database Schema Integration. In *ACM Computing Surveys, 1986 18(4) Dec, pp. 323-364.*
3. Bergamaschi, S., Castano, S., De Capitani di Vimercati, S., Montanari, S. and Vincini, M. (1998) An Intelligent Approach to Information Integration. In *Guarino, N. (ed.), Formal Ontology in Information Systems, Proceedings of the First International Conference (FOIS'98), IOS Press, pp. 253-267.*
4. Bloesch, A., and Halpin, T. (1996) ConQuer: a Conceptual Query Language. In *Proc. ER'96: 15th International Conference on Conceptual Modeling, Springer LNCS, no. 1157, pp. 121-33.*
5. Bloesch, A., and Halpin, T. (1997) Conceptual Queries using ConQuer-II. In *Proc. ER'97: 16th International Conference on Conceptual Modeling, Springer LNCS, no. 1331, pp. 113-26.*
6. Ceusters, W., Martens, P., Dhaen, C. and Terzic, B. (2001) LinKFactory® : an Advanced Formal Ontology Management System. K-CAP 2001, Victoria, Canada, October 2001.
7. Chawathe, S., Garcia-Molina, H., Hammer, J., Ireland, K., Papakonstantinou, Y., Ullman, J. and Widom, J. (1994) The TSIMMIS project: Integration of heterogeneous information sources. In *Proceedings of the 10th Anniversary Meeting of the Information Processing Society of Japan, pp. 7-18.*
8. Collet, C., Huhns, M. and Shen W. (1991) Resource Integration Using a Large Knowledge Base in CARNOT. In *IEEE Computer, 24(12), pp. 55-62.*
9. Deray, T. and Verheyden, P. (2003) Towards a Semantic Integration of Medical Relational Databases by Using Ontologies: a Case Study. In *Meersman, R., Tari, Z. et al. (eds.), On the Move to Meaningful Internet Systems 2003 (OTM 2003) Workshops, LNCS 2889, Springer-Verlag, pp. 137-150.*
10. De Troyer, O., Meersman, R. and Verlinden, P. (1988) RIDL* on the CRIS Case: a Workbench for NIAM. In *Olle, T.W., Verrijn-Stuart, A.A., Bhabuta, L. (eds.), Computerized Assistance during the Information Systems Life Cyle, Elsevier Science Publishers B.V. (North-Holland), pp. 375-459.*
11. De Troyer, O. (1989) RIDL*: A tool for the Computer-Assisted Engineering of Large Databases in the Presence of Integrity Constraints. In *Clifford, J., Lindsay, B., Maier, D. (eds.), Proceedings of the ACM-SIGMOD International Conference on Management of Data, ACM Press, pp. 418-430.*
12. Flett, A., Casella dos Santos, M. and Ceusters, W. (2002) Some Ontology Engineering Processes and Their Supporting Technologies. In *Gómez-Pérez, A., Richard Benjamins, V. (eds.), Knowledge Engineering and Knowledge Management. Ontologies and the Semantic Web, EKAW 2002, LNCS, Springer-Verlag, pp. 154-165.*

13. Guarino, N., and Giaretta, P. (1995) Ontologies and Knowledge Bases: Towards a Terminological Clarification. In *Mars, N. (ed.), Towards Very Large Knowledge Bases: Knowledge Building and Knowledge Sharing, IOS Press, Amsterdam, pp. 25-32.*

14. Halpin, T. (2001) Information Modeling and Relational Databases (From Conceptual Analysis to Logical Design). Morgan Kauffman, 2001.

15. Jarke M., Lenzerini, M., Vassiliou, Y. and Vassiliadis, Y. (1999) Fundamentals of Data Warehouses. Springer-Verlag, 1999.

16. Meersman, R. (1982) The High Level End User. In *Data Base: The 2nd Generation, Infotech State of the Art Report (vol. 10, no. 7), Pergamonn Press, U.K., 1982.*

17. Meersman, R. (1999) The Use of Lexicons and Other Computer-Linguistic Tools in Semantics, Design and Cooperation of Database Systems. In *Zhang, Y., Rusinkiewicz, M., Kambayashi, Y. (eds.), Proceedings of the Conference on Cooperative Database Systems (CODAS 99), Springer-Verlag, pp. 1-14.*

18. Meersman, R. (2001) Ontologies and Databases: More than a Fleeting Resemblance. In *d'Atri, A., Missikoff, M. (eds.), OES/SEO 2001 Rome Workshop, Luiss Publications.*

19. Meersman, R. (2002) Semantic Web and Ontologies: Playtime or Business at the Last Frontier in Computing? In *NSF-EU Workshop on Database and Information Systems Research for Semantic Web and Enterprises, pp. 61-67.*

20. Mena, E., Kashyap, V., Illaramendi, A. and Sheth, A. (1998) Domain Specific Ontologies for Semantic Information Brokering on the Global Information Infrastructure. In *Guarino, N. (ed.), Formal Ontology in Information Systems, Proceedings of the First International Conference (FOIS'98), IOS Press, pp. 269-283.*

21. Reiter, R. (1984) Towards a Logical Reconstruction of Relational Database Theory. In *Brodie, M., Mylopoulos, J., Schmidt, J. (eds.), On Conceptual Modelling, Springer-Verlag, pp. 191-233.*

22. Spyns, P., Meersman, R. and Jarrar, M. (2002) Data Modelling versus Ontology Engineering. *SIGMOD Record: Special Issue on Semantic Web and Data Management, 2002, 31(4), pp. 12-17.*

23. Stuer, P., Meersman, R. and De Bruyne, S. (2001) The HyperMuseum Theme Generator System: Ontology-based Internet support for the active use of digital museum data for teaching and presentation. In *Bearman, D., Trant, J. (eds.), Museums and the web 2001: Selected Papers, pp. 127-137. Archives & Museum Informatics, Pittsburgh, PA, 2001.*
   Available at: http://www.archimuse.com/mw2001/papers/stuer/stuer.html

24. Verheijen, G. and Van Bekkum, J. (1982) NIAM, aN Information Analysis Method. In *Olle, T., Sol, H., Verrijn-Stuart, A. (eds.), IFIP TC-8 Conference on Comparative Review of Information System Methodologies (CRIS-1), North-Holland.*

25. Wintraecken, J.J.V.R. (1985) Informatie-analyse Volgens NIAM. Academic Service, 1985. (English version published by Kluwer Academic Publishers, 1990).

Representation and Reasoning About Changing Semantics in Heterogeneous Data Sources

Hongwei Zhu, Stuart E. Madnick, and Michael D. Siegel

MIT Sloan School of Management,
30 Wadsworth Street, MA, 02142, USA
{mrzhu, smadnick, msiegel}@mit.edu
http://interchange.mit.edu/coin

Abstract. Changes of semantics in data sources further complicate the semantic heterogeneity problem. We identify four types of semantic heterogeneities related to changing semantics and present a solution based on an extension to the Context Interchange (COIN) framework. Changing semantics is represented as multi-valued contextual attributes in a shared ontology; however, only a single value is valid over a certain time interval. A mediator, implemented in abductive constraint logic programming, processes the semantics by solving temporal constraints for single-valued time intervals and automatically applying conversions to resolve semantic differences over these intervals. We also discuss the scalability of the approach and its applicability to the Semantic Web.

1 Introduction

The Web has become a large database, from which obtaining meaningful data is becoming increasingly difficult. As a simple example, try querying historic stock prices for Daimler-Benz from Yahoo. Figure 1 shows what Yahoo returned for the prices at stock exchanges in New York and Frankfurt.

Date	Open	High	Low	Close	Volume	Adj Close*
6-Jan-99	105.25	105.74	103.92	105.13	2,061,200	90.49
5-Jan-99	99.05	103.43	98.93	103.31	2,634,600	88.92
4-Jan-99	99.66	100.69	98.08	98.99	3,441,400	85.20
31-Dec-98	94.49	94.55	93.21	93.51	506,900	80.49
30-Dec-98	94.97	95.34	94.18	94.18	391,300	81.06
29-Dec-98	96.13	96.25	95.64	95.95	1,195,700	82.58
28-Dec-98	95.64	96.43	95.16	95.64	1,707,800	82.32
6-Jan-99	90.10	92.40	89.30	92.30	13,950,500	86.67
5-Jan-99	86.80	88.60	86.10	86.80	12,329,300	81.51
4-Jan-99	83.50	88.50	82.50	87.50	13,680,200	82.16
30-Dec-98	166.30	167.90	164.50	164.50	4,934,820	154.47
29-Dec-98	166.00	166.50	164.50	165.00	5,039,660	154.94
28-Dec-98	159.50	167.80	159.30	166.50	9,748,480	156.34

*Close price adjusted for dividends and splits.

Fig. 1. Stock prices for Daimler-Chrysler from Yahoo. Top: New York; Bottom: Frankfurt

C. Bussler et al. (Eds.): SWDB 2004, LNCS 3372, pp. 127–139, 2005.
© Springer-Verlag Berlin Heidelberg 2005

What conclusions will you draw from the retrieved data? Perhaps you regret that you were not arbitraging the substantial price differences between the exchanges, or feel lucky that you sold the stock in your Frankfurt account at the end of 1998? Both conclusions are wrong. Here, not only are the currencies for stock prices different at the two exchanges, but the currency at Frankfurt exchange also changed from German Marks to Euros at the beginning of 1999 (the New York exchange remained as US dollars). Once the data is transformed into a uniform context, e.g., all prices in US dollars, it can be seen that there is neither significant arbitraging opportunity nor abrupt price plunge for this stock.

The example illustrates the kinds of problems that the Semantic Web aims to solve. We need not wait until the full implementation of the Semantic Web for meaningful data retrieval. Context Interchange (COIN) framework [7, 10, 11], originated from the semantic data integration research tradition, shares this goal with the Semantic Web research. With the recent temporal extension that processes heterogeneous and changing semantics, described in this paper, COIN provides an extensible and scalable solution to the problem of identifying and resolving semantic heterogeneities. COIN is a web-based mediation approach with several distinguishing characteristics:

- Detection and reconciliation of semantic differences are system services and are transparent to users. Thus with COIN, the historic stock prices in the simple example are automatically transformed before they are returned to the user;
- Mediation does not require that semantic differences between each source-receiver pair to be specified a priori, rather, it only needs a declarative description of each source's data semantics and the methods of reconciling possible differences. Semantic differences are detected and automatically reconciled at the time of query. Scalability is achieved by the use of ontology, context inheritance, and parameterization of conversion functions;
- Mediation is implemented in abductive constraint logic programming. As a result, it allows for knowledge level query and can generate *intensional* answers as well as *extensional* answers. Efficient reasoning is achieved by combining abduction with concurrent constraint solving.

In this paper, we will focus on the representation and reasoning of changing semantics in COIN. Since it is an extension to early implementations, it is capable of mediating static semantic heterogeneities as well as those that change over time.

2 Temporal Semantic Heterogeneities

Temporal semantic heterogeneities refer to the situation where the semantics in data sources and/or receivers changes over time. We categorize them into four types, which are described below, then followed by an illustrative example.

2.1 Categories of Temporal Semantic Heterogeneities

Representational heterogeneity. The same concept can be represented differently in different sources and during different time periods. In the stock price example, the same concept of stock price is represented in different currencies, and for the Frankfurt exchange, the currency also changed in the beginning of 1999. This introduces representational temporal heterogeneity when the receiver needs price data in US dollars. Representational heterogeneity often results from the differences in unit of measures, scale factors, and other syntactic characteristics.

Ontological heterogeneity. The same term is often used to refer to slightly different concepts; in the same source the concepts referred to by a term may shift over time, which introduces ontological temporal heterogeneities. For example, *profit* can refer to *gross profit* that includes all taxes collected on behalf of government, or *net profit* that excludes those taxes. The referred concept may shift from one type of profit to another because of change of reporting rules.

Aggregational heterogeneity. When the data of interest is an attribute of an entity that can consist of other entities, aggregational heterogeneity arises if the component entities vary in different situations. A detailed example is presented in [17], where depending on regulatory requirements and purposes, the financial data of corporations may or may not include those from certain branches, subsidiaries, and majority owned foreign joint ventures. These rules and purposes may change over time, which introduces aggregational temporal heterogeneities. We will give a more detailed example of this category later in this section.

There are certain connections between ontological and aggregational heterogeneities. For example, the question *"does profit include taxes"* concerns ontological heterogeneity; while the question *"does profit for corporation x include that of its subsidiaries"* concerns aggregational heterogeneity. The latter can be seen as a more complicated version of the former in that the heterogeneity results from the entity that the data is about, not the data itself. In addition, data aggregation rules are often more complicated than ontological concept definitions. We will use this connection in COIN to encode and process aggregational heterogeneity.

Heterogeneity in temporal entity. The representation and operations for the domain of time vary across systems. As a result, there exist heterogeneities that include, for example, location dependencies such as time zones, differences in representation conventions, calendars, and granularities. Although it is a type of representational heterogeneity, we treat it as a special category because of the complexity of the domain of temporal entity.

2.2 An Illustrative Example

We use the following example to illustrate representational and aggregational heterogeneities. Readers are referred to [17] for a more complicated aggregational example and to [21] for an example of representational and ontological heterogeneities.

The example involves two sources and one receiver[1]. The receiver is interested in the longitudinal economic and environmental changes in the Balkans area, before and after the war in Yugoslavia. As shown in Figure 2, the sources organize the data by sovereign country, while the receiver is interested in data for the region covered by

---

[1] This example has been simplified in this paper to reduce space while maintaining the key details. The actual situation involves many more sources as well as multiple users, each with a potentially different context.

the former Yugoslavia. The sources also make other implicit assumptions for data in terms of currencies and scale factors. We call these assumptions for interpreting the data *contexts* and identify them using context labels, *c_srs* and *c_target*, in Figure 2.

As the web and traditional databases are often used today, the receiver knows what data is available in the sources and wants to query them directly using query Q – but the user may not know about (nor want to deal with) the differences in contexts. Thus, a direct execution of query Q over the sources would bring back wrong answers because the query does not consider context differences, such as those in currency and scale factor. Additionally, in 1992 former Yugoslavia was divided into five sovereign countries, each with its own distinctive currency (See Table 1). Therefore, the results for data after 1992 are also wrong because of unresolved aggregational differences, i.e., the data represents only a sub-area of the entire region expected by the receiver.

Context *c_src*	Context *c_target*
1. *Monetary values* are in official currency of the country, with a scale factor of 1M;	1. *Monetary values* are always in USD, with a scale factor of 1M;
2. *Mass* is a rate of tons/year with a scale factor of 1000;	2. *Mass* is in tons/year;
3. All *other numbers* have a scale factor of 1;	3. *Other numbers* have a scale factor of 1;
4. All values are aggregated by sovereign country.	4. Value for country denoted by 'YUG' is aggregated to the geographic area of former Yugoslavia.

Schema of source 1:
```
Statistics(Country, Year, GDP, Population)
```

Schema of source 2:
```
Emissions(Country, Year, CO2)
```

Query Q^2:
```
Select S.Country,S.Year,GDP,CO2
From Statistics S, Emissions E
Where S.Country=E.Country and
S.Year=E.Year and S.Country='YUG';
```

Fig. 2. Temporal Context Example, with Subtle Changes in Data Semantics

Table 1. Five Countries Resulting from the Division of the Former Yugoslavia

Country	Code	Currency	Currency Code
Yugoslavia[3]	YUG	New Yugoslavian Dinar	YUM
Bosnia and Herzegovia	BIH	Marka	BAM
Croatia	HRV	Kuna	HRK
Macedonia	MKD	Denar	MKD
Slovenia	SVN	Tolar	SIT

Compared to the stock quote example, the semantic changes in this example are more subtle in that there seem to be no semantic changes in the verbal context descriptions in Figure 2, it is the meaning of the country code 'YUG' that changes over time. To account for this change, we need to make it explicit either in the source context or in the receiver context. We choose the latter in the following discussions.

---

[2] For this example and demonstration to follow, the Query Q is expressed in the Structured Query Language (SQL). The basic COIN approach can be applied to any query language.

[3] The Federal Republic of Yugoslavia was renamed Serbia and Montenegro in 2003. We will not encode this change in the example to simplify illustration.

In addition, the aggregational heterogeneity also dynamically introduces new representational heterogeneities, e.g., currency differences will be encountered in aggregating data for each component country. Another interesting characteristic is that in this simple example the two sources share the same context (in reality, there are likely many context differences amongst the diverse sources).

3 COIN Framework and Architecture

The COIN framework consists of a deductive object-oriented data model for knowledge representation and a general purpose mediation service module that detects and resolves semantic conflicts in user queries at run-time (see Figure 3).

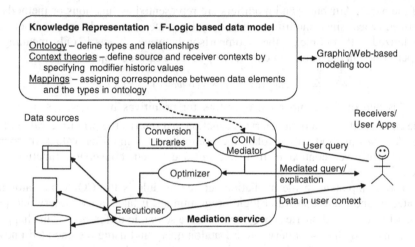

Fig. 3. Architecture of the COIN System

Knowledge representation in COIN consists of three components:

- Ontology – to define the semantic domain using a collection of semantic types and their relationships. A type corresponds to a concept in the problem domain and can be related to another in three ways: 1) as a subtype or super-type (e.g., *profit* is a subtype of *monetary value*; 2) as a named attribute (e.g., *temporal entity* such as year is a temporal attribute of *GDP*); and 3) as a modifier or contextual attribute, whose value is specified in context axioms and can functionally determine the interpretation of instances of the type that has this modifier (e.g., *monetary value* type has a *scale factor* modifier). There is a distinguished type *basic* in the ontology that serves as the super type of all the other types and represents all primitive data types. Objects are instances of the defined types;
- Context theories – to specify the values of modifiers for each source or receiver and the conversions for transforming an object in one context to another. The context of each source or receiver is uniquely identified with a context label, e.g., *c_src* and *c_target* in the example. The value specification for modifiers can be a

simple value assignment or a set of rules that specify how to obtain the value. Conceptually a context can be thought to be a set of <*modifier*, *object*> pairs, where *object* is a singleton in most non-temporal cases; and
– Semantic mappings – to establish correspondences between data elements in sources and the types in the ontology, e.g., *GDP* in the example in Figure 2 corresponds to *monetary value* in the ontology.

These components can be expressed in OWL or F-Logic [15]. Since COIN predates OWL, F-Logic was the language of choice with its rich constructs for describing types and their relationships and has formal semantics for inheritance and overriding. In practice, we translate the F-Logic expressions into a Horn logic program and implement the semantics of inheritance and overriding in the context mediator component described next. For succinctness, we continue to use the F-Logic syntax in the rest of the paper. Attributes and modifiers are represented as functions or methods of the defined types; since modifier values vary by context, methods for modifiers are parameterized with a context label. Comparison between objects is only meaningful when performed in the same context, i.e., suppose x and y are objects,

$$x \overset{c}{\lozenge} y \Leftrightarrow x[value\ (c) \rightarrow u] \wedge y[value\ (c) \rightarrow v] \wedge u \lozenge v.$$

where $\lozenge$ is one of the comparison operators for primitives in $\{ =, \neq, <, \leq, >, \geq, \dots \}$, and the *value* method is a parameterized function that returns the primitive value of an object. A *value* method call invokes the comparison of modifier values in source context and receiver context c, if difference is detected, conversion functions are invoked.

The core component in the mediation service module is the COIN mediator implemented in abductive constraint logic programming. It takes a user query and produces a set of mediated queries ($\mathcal{MQ}s$) that resolve semantic differences. This happens by first translating the user query into a Datalog query and using the encoded knowledge to derive the $\mathcal{MQ}s$ that incorporate necessary conversions from source contexts to receiver context. The query optimizer and processor [2] optimize the $\mathcal{MQ}s$ using a simple cost model and the information on source capabilities, obtain the data, perform the conversions, and return final datasets to the user.

We also developed web-based [16] and graphical [13] tools for data administrators to design ontologies and input context knowledge. As part of ongoing effort of connecting COIN with the Semantic Web, we are also developing OWL and RuleML based representations for the COIN ontology and context knowledge; a prototype is described in [19]. These prototypes also translate the captured knowledge into Prolog syntax required by the current implementation of the mediation service.

4   Representation of Changing Semantics

Like many existing ontologies, previously the ontologies in COIN were based on a snapshot view of the world and lacked the capability of capturing changing semantics. To overcome this limitation, we incorporate in COIN ontologies explicit time concepts such as the ones defined in DAML Time Ontology [12]. *Temporal entity* is the most general concept and can be further specialized into *instant* and *interval*. There is emerging research that aims to systematically temporalize static ontologies [18]; for simple ones, we can manually create a temporal ontology by relating concepts whose value or semantics changes over time to temporal concepts via named attributes. Figure 4 shows a graphical representation of the ontology for the example.

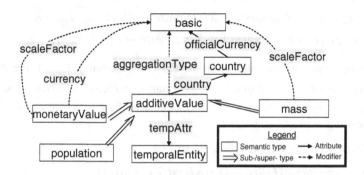

Fig. 4. A graphical representation of the example ontology

We should note that, like other types of conceptual modeling, there could be multiple variants of the example ontology that convey the same ideas in the problem domain, some of which may be even better. We use this one for illustration purposes.

The type *basic* represents system primitives and is the parent of all the other types; this relationship is omitted in the graph to eliminate clutter. The context regarding data aggregation is captured by the modifier *aggregationType* of the semantic type *additiveValue*, which serves as the parent all other types that can be aggregated. Attributes are also added to this parent type to relate to types *country* and *temporalEntity*. Through inheritance and overriding the child types obtain and specialize, if necessary, these relationships and context specifications.

In the following discussion, we assume certain familiarity with the syntax and the semantics of F-Logic. Following Gulog [5], a sub-language of F-Logic, we use $\vdash$ to separate variable type declarations from the rest of a formula. For succinctness we also use non-clausal forms, which eventually will be rewritten in clausal form and translated into equivalent Horn logic clauses.

We represent a named attribute in the ontology as a function and a modifier as a multi-valued method parameterized with context label. For example, the following formula declares that *additiveValue* has *tempAttr* with a return type of *temporalEntity*:

$$additiveValue[tempAttr \Rightarrow temporalEntity].$$

Similarly, the following declares modifier *aggregationType* for *additiveValue*:

$$additiveValue[aggregationType(ctxt) \Rightarrow\Rightarrow basic].$$

The changing semantics is represented by context axioms that specify the entire history of multi-valued modifiers. In the example we have decided to make the semantic change explicit in the receiver context, which means that before the balkanization in 1991, the receiver aggregates data at the country level for Yugoslavia, and for data after 1992, the receiver wants to aggregate at the level of geo-region covered by former Yugoslavia. This is expressed using the following context axiom:

$$\forall X : additiveValue\ \exists Y : basic \vdash$$

$$X[aggregationType(c\_target) \to Y] \wedge X[country \to C] \wedge C \overset{c\_target}{=} 'YUG' \wedge$$
$$(Y[value(c\_target) \to 'country'] \leftarrow X[tempAttr \to T] \wedge T \overset{c\_target}{\in_t} I_{\leq1991}) \wedge \qquad (1)$$
$$(Y[value(c\_target) \to 'georegion'] \leftarrow X[tempAttr \to T] \wedge T \overset{c\_target}{\in_t} I_{1992\leq}).$$

where $I_{\leq1991}$ represents the time interval up to year 1991, similarly $I_{1992\leq}$ is the interval since year 1992, and $\in_t$ is a temporal inclusion relation, which can be translated into a set of comparisons between time points by introducing functions that return the beginning and ending points of an interval:

$$\forall T : temporalEntity, I : temporalEntity \vdash$$
$$T \overset{c}{\in_t} I \Leftrightarrow (begin(I) \overset{c}{\leq} begin(T)) \wedge (end(T) \overset{c}{\leq} end(I)).$$

Conceptually, we can think of temporal context as a set of *<modifier, history>* pairs with *history* being a set of *<object, time_interval>* pairs or a set of time-stamped objects. By abusing syntax, we say the temporal context pertaining to aggregation for the receiver is $< aggregationType, \{<'country', I_{\leq1991}>, <'georegion', I_{1992\leq}>\} >$.

A multi-valued modifier is still single-valued over a certain time interval. Thus, there exist overlapping intervals over which all involved modifiers are single-valued in each context. Within these intervals, the determination and the resolution of context differences are identical to those in a snapshot model. Therefore conversion functions for processing changing semantics are identical to those in snapshot COIN. For the interval after 1992, semantic differences exist between the sources and the receiver in terms of aggregation because the value of *aggregationType* modifier in the sources is 'country', while it is 'georegion' in the receiver context. Conversions are needed to resolve this difference. Conversion functions are defined for the subtypes of *additiveValue*, e.g., for *moentaryValue* we have:

$$X : monetaryValue \vdash$$
$$X[cvt(aggregationType, c\_target) @ c\_src, u \to v] \leftarrow$$
$$X[tempAttr \to T] \wedge statistics\_(C_1, T_1, M_1, \_) \wedge statistics(C_2, T_2, M_2, \_) \wedge$$
$$statistics\_(C_3, T_3, M_3) \wedge statistics\_(C_4, T_4, M_4, \_) \wedge$$
$$C_1 \overset{c\_target}{=} 'BIH' \wedge C_2 \overset{c\_target}{=} 'HIV' \wedge C_3 \overset{c\_target}{=} 'MKD' \wedge C_4 \overset{c\_target}{=} 'SVN' \wedge T_1 \overset{c\_target}{=} T \wedge \qquad (2)$$
$$T_2 \overset{c\_target}{=} T \wedge T_3 \overset{c\_target}{=} T \wedge T_4 \overset{c\_target}{=} T \wedge M_1[value(c\_target) \to m_1] \wedge$$
$$M_2[value(c\_target) \to m_2] \wedge M_3[value(c\_target) \to m_3] \wedge$$
$$M_4[value(c\_target) \to m_4] \wedge v = u + m_1 + m_2 + m_3 + m_4.$$

The function essentially states that to process *aggregationType* semantic difference of a *monetaryValue* object, its value u in c_src context is converted to a value v in c_target context by finding the other *monetaryValue* objects that correspond to the four other countries as indicated by the codes at the same year, convert them into primitive values in c_target, and make v the sum of these primitives. The function for *mass* subtype is similarly defined. Before calling this function, functions that convert for *currency* and *scaleFactor* should have been called to arrive at this interim value u; in calling *value* functions for the four objects C_1-C_4 in the body of the function, conversions for *currency* and *scaleFactor* are dynamically called to ensure that they are summed in the same context. Thus, it is necessary to specify the precedence of modifiers, i.e., the order in which the modifiers should be processed.

This function is not general because of the use of constants in places of context parameters and the references to a semantic relation corresponding to a relation in data source. Using COIN for aggregational heterogeneities is a new research area that we are currently investigating to produce general methodology. For most other types of heterogeneities, though, more general conversions exist and can be utilized in multiple problem domains by collecting them into the conversion library. Generalization is achieved by parameterizing the function with variables for context labels. For example, the following currency conversion function can be used to convert monetary values from any arbitrary context C_1 to any other arbitrary context C_2:

$$
\begin{aligned}
&X : monetaryValue \vdash \\
&\quad X[cvt(currency, C_2) @ C_1, u \to v] \leftarrow \\
&\qquad X[currency(C_1) \to C_f]_{C_2} \wedge X[currency(C_2) \to C_t]_{C_2} \wedge X[tempAttr \to T]_{C_2} \wedge \\
&\qquad olsen\_(A, B, R, D) \wedge C_f = A \wedge C_t = B \wedge T = D \wedge \\
&\qquad R[value(C_2) \to r] \wedge v = u * r.
\end{aligned}
\tag{3}
$$

where *olsen_* corresponds to an external relation that gives exchange rate between two currencies on any specified date.

A recent effort [8] introduced automatic conversion composition based on equational relationships between contexts, e.g., given conversions 1) between base price and tax-included price; and 2) between tax-included price and final price, the conversion between base price and final price can be composed using symbolic equation solvers.

5 Reasoning About Changing Semantics in COIN Mediation

The mediator is to translate a user query that assumes everything is in user context to a set of $\mathcal{MQ}$s that reconcile context differences between each involved source and the user. The following pseudo code sketches the intuition of the procedure:

```
For each source attribute appearing in user query
    Instantiate into object of type in ontology according to mappings
    Find the direct and inherited modifiers
    Order modifiers according to precedence
    For each modifier
        Choose a value and put corresponding temporal constraint in store
        If constraints are consistent
            Compare values in source and receiver
            If different, call conversion function and put abducibls in store
Construct MQ using abducibles
```

We implement this procedure using abductive constraint logic programming (ACLP) [14]. Briefly, ACLP is a triple $<\mathcal{P}, \mathcal{A}, IC>$, where $\mathcal{P}$ is a constraint logic program, $\mathcal{A}$ is a set of abducible predicates different from the constraint predicates, and IC is a set of integrity constraints over the domains of $\mathcal{P}$. Query answering in ACLP is that given a query $q(\vec{X})$, generate a set of abductive hypothesis Δ and a substitution θ so that $\mathcal{P} \cup \Delta$ entails $q(\vec{X})\theta$ and is consistent; Δ consists of abducible predicates and simplified constraints.

The COIN framework can be straightforwardly mapped to ACLP. Knowledge representation in COIN can be translated into an equivalent normal Horn program [1]; or alternatively, the knowledge representation can be directly expressed in first order Horn clauses. This corresponds to $\mathcal{P}$. Predicates and arithmetic operators allowed by the query languages of sources and other callable external functions constitute $\mathcal{A}$. IC consists of integrity constraints in data sources and any constraints introduced in the user query. The user query corresponds to query $q(\vec{X})$ in ACLP; the $\mathcal{MQ}$s are constructed from the set Δ and the substitution θ.

Abductive inference in COIN is a modified SLD-resolution [6] in that literals corresponding to predicates in data sources are abducted without evaluation; constraints are abducted and subsequently propagated/simplified. The constraints include basic arithmetic comparisons, equational relationships among arithmetic operators for conversion composition [8], and temporal relations for processing changing semantics. The mediator is implemented using constraint logic programming environment ECLiPSe [20] with the extension of Constraint Handling Rules (CHR) [9]. Naturally, we use the constraint store to collect the abucibles. At the end of a successful derivation, an $\mathcal{MQ}$ is constructed using the predicates and constraints collected in the constraint store.

As shown earlier, context axioms for multi-valued modifiers contain temporal inclusion comparison, which can be transformed to a conjunction of comparisons of the end points using comparison relation $\leq$. We implement temporal relations as a constraint tle, with $tle(X, Y)$ meaning temporal entity X is *before* (inclusive) Y. Here X and Y are variables of primitive temporal entities in the same context. Similar to semantic relations, we use $tle\_$ for constraint over semantic objects.

In the process of mediation, temporal constraints appearing in a context axiom are abducted into the constraint store after the head of the axiom clause is unified with the goal atom. Applicable CHR rules are triggered immediately after abduction to simply or propagate the constraints. Inconsistency of the constraint store signifies a failure and causes backtracking. The temporal constraints in the consistent store after a successful derivation determine the common interval over which all involved modifiers are single-valued. Suppose the query language in source accepts $\leq$ for temporal entity comparison, the tle constraint in the store is translated back to $\leq$ to construct the $\mathcal{MQ}$s.

The context axiom (2) corresponds to two clauses after it is rewritten in the clausal form; each clause contains temporal constraints corresponding to the interval for pre- or post-balkanization of former Yugoslavia. When the user query in Figure 2 is mediated, each clause posts a temporal constraint into the store and produces a successful derivation. No inconsistency is produced in the example; refer to [21, 22] for an example where inconsistencies occur when multiple modifiers change values at different times. The $\mathcal{MQ}$s in Datalog syntax are a disjunction of two sub-queries; each deals with a time interval in context axiom (2):

```
answer('V8', 'V7', 'V6', 'V5') :-
    'V5' is 'V4' * 1000.0,
    olsen("YUM", "USD", 'V3', 'V7'),
    'Statistics'("YUG", 'V7', 'V2', 'V1'),
    'Emissions'("YUG", 'V7', 'V4'),
    'V7' =< 1991,
    'V6' is 'V2' * 'V3'.
answer('V96', 'V95', 'V94', 'V93') :-
    'V92' is 'V91' * 1000.0, 'V90' is 'V89' * 1000.0,
    'V88' is 'V87' * 1000.0, 'V86' is 'V85' * 1000.0,
    'V84' is 'V83' * 1000.0, 'V82' is 'V90' + 'V92',
    'V81' is 'V88' + 'V82', 'V80' is 'V86' + 'V81',
    'V93' is 'V84' + 'V80', 'V79' is 'V78' * 'V77',
    'V76' is 'V75' * 'V74', 'V73' is 'V72' * 'V71',
    'V70' is 'V69' * 'V68', olsen("SIT", "USD", 'V67', 'V95'),
    Statistics'("SVN", 'V95', 'V66', 'V65'),
    olsen("MKD", "USD", 'V68', 'V95'),
    'Statistics'("MKD", 'V95', 'V69', 'V64'),
    olsen("HRK", "USD", 'V71', 'V95'),
    'Statistics'("HRV", 'V95', 'V72', 'V63'),
    olsen("BAM", "USD", 'V74', 'V95'),
    'Statistics'("BIH", 'V95', 'V75', 'V62'),
    olsen("YUM", "USD", 'V77', 'V95'),
    'Emissions'("SVN", 'V95', 'V83'),
    'Emissions'("MKD", 'V95', 'V85'),
    'Emissions'("HRV", 'V95', 'V87'),
    'Emissions'("BIH", 'V95', 'V89'),
    'Statistics'("YUG", 'V95', 'V78', 'V61'),
    'Emissions'("YUG", 'V95', 'V91'),
    1992 =< 'V95', 'V60' is 'V66' * 'V67',
    'V59' is 'V76' + 'V79', 'V58' is 'V73' + 'V59',
    'V57' is 'V70' + 'V58', 'V94' is 'V60' + 'V57'.
```

The first sub-query corresponds to the pre-balkanization period, when there is no aggregational difference between the sources and the receiver; only representational differences for GDP and CO_2 emissions exist. The second sub-query corresponds to the post-balkanization period, when both aggregational differences for GDP and CO_2 emissions and representational differences exist. Note the currency conversions dynamically introduced in the conversion for aggregational difference have been properly incorporated.

These $\mathcal{MQ}$s are returned to the user as an intensional answer to the original query. With all conversions declaratively defined, these $\mathcal{MQ}$s in fact convey a great deal of useful information to the user. The $\mathcal{MQ}$s are then passed to the optimizer and executioner components that access actual data sources to return final data to the user.

6 Discussion

It is common that data semantics in sources and receivers changes over time. One can draw wrong conclusions when these changes are not adequately represented and properly processed. In this paper, we identified four categories of semantic heterogeneities related to changing semantics. We also presented recent results that extend the COIN framework for representing and processing changing semantics, with a focus on the treatment of aggregational temporal heterogeneities.

As we explained in [21], the COIN framework is applicable to the Semantic Web for several reasons. The use of SQL in the example should not be construed as a limitation. In fact, the data model, the representation language, and the ACLP implementation of COIN mediator are all logic based. Thus, the framework can be applied broadly. To adapt to another query language, we can simply include the logic form of the language constructs as abducibles. More importantly, semantic differences are automatically detected and resolved using declarative descriptions of semantics. This approach is very well in line with the Semantic Web, where each source furnishes a description of its semantics for agents from other contexts to process. In addition, a recent extension to the basic COIN system added an ontology merging capability to allow large applications to be built by merging separate ontologies [7]. This is very similar to how agents work with distributed ontologies on the Semantic Web. Lastly, we are also experimenting with OWL and RuleML based languages for ontology and conversion function representation. These formalisms will allow the COIN mediation service to process other autonomously created ontologies on the Semantic Web.

The COIN framework is also scalable. The number of required conversion functions does not depend on the number of sources/receivers involved; rather, it depends on the variety of contexts, i.e., number of modifiers and their unique values. With context inheritance (e.g., the two sources in the example share the same context, but partial sharing is also possible), parameterization of conversions functions (e.g., the conversion function for currency differences is applicable to any pair of contexts having different currencies), and conversion composition, the number of conversion functions required grows only when the addition of sources introduces new contexts and the existing conversion functions do not handle the conversions for the new contexts. In the illustrative example, suppose we add another two hundred additional sources that have semantic differences with the receiver only in terms of currency and scale factor, the number of conversion functions remains unchanged because the existing conversion functions can process these new contexts. Adding these new sources only involves adding context declarations and semantic mappings, which are declaratively defined.

We acknowledge that the conversion functions for processing aggregational heterogeneities in the illustrative example are not as general. As future research, we plan to investigate ontology modeling techniques and other representational constructs that may help generalize conversion functions of this type. We also note that the heterogeneities in temporal entities are not currently processed in the prototype. As another future research area, we plan to introduce the full Time ontology into knowledge representation and implement conversions as external function calls to web services that specifically handle time zones, calendars, and granularities [3, 4].

Acknowledgements

The work reported herein was supported, in part, by the Singapore-MIT Alliance (SMA) and the Malaysia University of Science and Technology (MUST)-MIT collaboration.

References

1. S. Abiteboul, G. Lausen, H. Uphoff, E. Waller, "Methods and Rules", SIGMOD Rec., 22(2), pp. 32-41, 1993.
2. T. Alatovic, "Capabilities Aware Planner/Optimizer/Executioner for COntext INterchange Project", MS Thesis, MIT, 2002.
3. C. Bettini, "Web services for time granularity reasoning," TIME-ICTL'03, 2003.
4. C. Bettini, S. Jajodia, and X. S. Wang, Time Granularities in Databases, Data Mining, and Temporal Reasoning: Springer, 2000.
5. Dobbie, G., and Topor, R. "On the Declarative and Procedural Semantics of Deductive Object-Oriented Systems," Journal of Intelligent Information Systems (4), 1995, pp 193-219.
6. K. Eshgi, Kowalski, R. "Abduction Compared with Negation as Failure", Proceedings of 6th Intl Conf. on Logic Programming, 1989.
7. Firat, "Information Integration using Contextual Knowledge and Ontology Merging," PhD Thesis, MIT, 2003.
8. A. Firat, S. Madnick, B. Grosof, "Financial information integration in the presence of equational ontological conflicts", WITS, 2002.
9. T. Frühwirth, "Theory and Practice of Constraint Handling Rules," Journal of Logic Programming, 37, pp. 95-138, 1998.
10. C.Goh, "Representing and Reasoning about Semantic Conflicts in Heterogeneous Information Systems", PhD Thesis, MIT, 1997
11. C. Goh, S. Bressan, S. Madnick, and M. Siegel, "Context Interchange: New Features and Formalisms for the Intelligent Integration of Information," ACM TOIS, vol. 17, pp. 270-293, 1999.
12. J. R. Hobbs, "A DAML Ontology of Time," LREC, 2002.
13. S. Jayasena, "Context Mediation Approach to Improved Interoperability amongst Disparate Financial Information Services", MS Thesis, Singapore-MIT Alliance CS Program, 2004.
14. A.C. Kakas, A. Michael, and C. Mourlas, "ACLP: Integrating Abduction and Constraint Solving," Journal of Logic Programming, 44, pp. 129-177, 2000.
15. M. Kiffer, G. Laussen, J. Wu, "Logic Foundations of Object-Oriented and Frame-based Languages", J. ACM, 42(4), pp. 741-843, 1995.
16. P.W. Lee, "Metadata Representation and Management for Context Mediation", MS Thesis, MIT, 2003.
17. S. Madnick, R. Wang, X. Xian, "The Design and Implementation of a Corporate Householding Knowledge Processor to Improve Data Quality", JMIS, 20(3), pp. 41-69, 2004.
18. J. Santos, S. Staab, "FONTE: Factorizing Ontology Engineering Complexity," International Conference On Knowledge Capture, ACM Press, Sanibel Island, FL, USA, 2003, pp. 146-153.
19. P.E.K. Tang, S. Madnick, K.L. Tan "Context Mediation in the Semantic Web: Handling OWL Ontology and Data Disparity through Context Interchange", Second International Workshop on Semantic Web and Databases (in this volume), Toronto, Canada, 2004.
20. M. Wallace, S. Novello, J. Schimpf, " ECLiPSe: A Platform for Constraint Logic Programming", IC-Parc, Imperial College, London, August 1997.
21. H. Zhu, S.E. Madnick, M.D. Siegel, "Reasoning about Temporal Context using Ontology and Abductive Contraint Logic Programming", to appear in Proceedings of Practice and Principles of Semantic Web Reasoning (PPSWR'04), St. Malo, France, September 2004.
22. H. Zhu, S.E. Madnick, M.D. Siegel, "Effective Data Integration in the Presence of Temporal Semantic Conflicts", Proceedings of 11th International Symposium on Temporal Representation and Reasoning (TIME 2004), pp109-114, Normandie, France, July 1-3, 2004.

Context Mediation in the Semantic Web: Handling OWL Ontology and Data Disparity Through Context Interchange

Philip Tan[1], Stuart Madnick[2], and Kian-Lee Tan[3]

[1] Singapore-MIT Alliance, 4 Engineering Drive 3, Singapore 117576
philipt@mit.edu
[2] MIT Sloan School of Management, 50 Memorial Drive, Cambridge, MA 02142, USA
smadnick@mit.edu
[3] Department of Computer Science, National University of Singapore,
3 Science Drive 2, Singapore 117543
tankl@comp.nus.edu.sg

Abstract. The COntext INterchange (COIN) strategy is an approach to solving the problem of interoperability of semantically heterogeneous data sources through context mediation. COIN has used its own notation and syntax for representing ontologies. More recently, the OWL Web Ontology Language is becoming established as the W3C recommended ontology language. We propose the use of the COIN strategy to solve context disparity and ontology interoperability problems in the emerging Semantic Web – both at the ontology level and at the data level. In conjunction with this, we propose a version of the COIN ontology model that uses OWL and the emerging rules interchange language, RuleML.

1 Introduction

The COntext INterchange (COIN) strategy [10] is a mediator-based approach for achieving semantic interoperability among heterogeneous data sources and receivers. As realizations of the strategy, COIN [7] and eCOIN, a recent extension, [6] are two working prototypes that implement the Context Interchange strategy. eCOIN uses FOL/Prolog as the representation and implementation language for the application ontology in the context mediation process. Various sample applications have since been implemented to illustrate its ability to solve semantic interoperability problems in areas such as financial services, weather information, and airfare aggregation and comparison.

One of the core ideas of the Semantic Web is the ability to associate machine understandable meanings to information. A taxonomy, or ontology, is used to enhance the quality of data and information available on the Web, subsequently enhance the functioning of the Web in improving Web searches, relating information by inference rules and complicated query answering [1].

With various active independent ontology development activities around the world, the age-old problem of heterogeneous data interoperability also manifests itself in the

C. Bussler et al. (Eds.): SWDB 2004, LNCS 3372, pp. 140–154, 2005.
© Springer-Verlag Berlin Heidelberg 2005

ontology area. One way to minimize the extent of ontology heterogeneity and disparity is to create a controlled and centralized ontology collection, with the goal to minimize duplication and incompatibility of ontology. However, with decentralized knowledge engineering and ontology development widely implemented in the industry and academic, the problem of ontology disparity is unavoidable. The full potential of ontology and language standardization using OWL will only be realized if they are used in combination with other ontologies in the future to enable data sharing [8].

In fact, W3C recognizes the existence of such problem – "We want simple assertions about class membership to have broad and useful implications. ...It will be challenging to merge a collection of ontologies." [11].

OWL provides a number of standard languages construct that aims at solving a subset of this problem. Ontology mapping constructs such as equivalentClass, equivalentProperty, sameAs, differentFrom and AllDifferent only allows ontology context consolidation at a very limited level. These language constructs are only useful if the consolidation effort requires only disambiguation between ontology. In other words, we can use these facilities to tell that a human in ontology A is the same as person in ontology B, but if they are different, we will not be able to tell how different these two classes are; needless to say that limits interoperability between the two ontologies.

1.1 Our Contribution

Our goal in this paper is to illustrate the novel features of the Context Interchange mediation strategy in solving ontology disparity problem in Semantic Web. Even though this research originated from a long-standing research in the data integration area, the use of this strategy in handling ontology interoperability presented in this paper is new with respect to our previous works and other relevant work in this area. In conjunction with this, we present a new COIN ontology representation model using OWL and RuleML, in alignment to the new and emerging W3C standards.

The rest of the paper is organized as follows. After this introduction, we present a motivational example to highlight the Context Interchange strategy in handling ontology disparity problem. Section 3 describes the building blocks of the Context Interchange strategy. Section 4 details the COIN-OWL ontology model design, design considerations and limitation. The final section presents a summary of our contributions and describes some ongoing research and future research directions.

1.2 Related Work

One relevant effort in the Semantic Web/OWL space is Context OWL (C-OWL) [3], a language whose syntax and semantics have been obtained by extending the OWL syntax and semantics to allow for the representation of contextual ontologies. However, the extension focused on limited context mapping using a set of bridge rules that specify the relationship between contexts as one of the following: equivalent, onto (superset), into (subset), compatible, incompatible. The limited expressiveness of the language fails to address the contextual differences such as those possible with COIN.

On standardization of the COIN ontology representation, Lee [9] has presented a XML-based metadata representation for the COIN framework. The essence of that work lies in modeling and storing of the metadata in RDF format as the base format. A number of intermediate representations of were proposed: RDF, RuleML, RFML and the native Prolog representation used in COIN. The core ontological model of COIN in RDF format is transformed into the aforementioned intermediate representation by applying Extensible Stylesheet Language Transformation (XSLT) on the fly. Context mediation for heterogeneous data is then executed using the ontological model encoded in the COIN language. It is worth noting that the approach proposed in this work primarily deals with a single representation at a time. The intermediate ontological model is represented in RDF, RuleML or RFML individually, but not as a combination of the different formats, which is the approach taken in our approach.

2   Context Interchange in Action

One of the easiest ways to understand the Context Interchange framework is via a concrete example. Consider two financial data sources: Worldscope (worldscope) and Disclosure Corporate Snapshot (disclosure) as shown in Figure 1.

Worldscope provides basic financial information on public companies worldwide, while Disclosure is an information directory on companies publicly traded on U.S. exchanges. Worldscope reports all the financial data information in US dollars, and on the scale factor of 1000, while disclosure reports the financial data information in the local currency of the companies, and on the scale factor of 1.

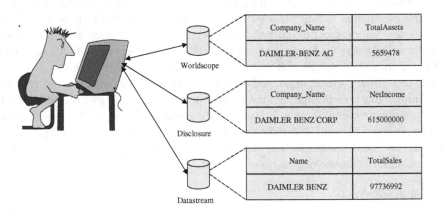

Fig. 1. Multiple databases with similar data, but differing contexts

Using these financial data sources, users are able to post queries on the public companies of interest. For example, to retrieve the asset data of Daimler-Benz AG from the worldscope database, the user may issue the following SQL query:

```
select Worldscope.TotalAssets
from Worldscope
where Worldscope.Company_Name = "DAIMLER-BENZ AG";
```

On the other hand, to retrieve net income data from disclosure, the following SQL query can be used:

```
select Disclosure.Date,Disclosure.NetIncome
from Disclosure
where Disclosure.Company_Name = "DAIMLER BENZ CORP"
and Disclosure.Date = "12/31/93";
```

Although the data can be retrieved from both sources, there are important discrepancies in the data due to the difference in context of the data sources, both in the currencies and the scale factors used (as well as company naming conventions and date formats). Thus, if one wanted to retrieve the TotalAssets from Worldscope and the NetIncome from Disclosure, the results could be confusing since the results would be provided with these context differences.

In a conventional database system, to perform a join table query between Worldscope and Disclosure, these context disparities would have to be resolved manually and encoded in the SQL query. Using COIN, these context discrepancies (different company name format, date format, financial data currency type and scale factor) are mediated automatically and queries such as the following can be used without the user having to know anything about the actual contexts of the sources (the results will be returned to the user in the context defined for the user, independent of the contexts of the sources):

```
select Disclosure.Date, Worldscope.TotalAssets,
Disclosure.NetIncome
from Disclosure, Worldscope
where Disclosure.Company_Name = "DAIMLER BENZ CORP"
and Disclosure.Company_name = Worldscope.Company_Name
and Disclosure.Date = "12/31/93";
```

This automated context reasoning and mediation capability is the essence of the Context Interchange strategy. Using the same context reasoning and mediation engine, ontology interoperability is achieved by defining meta-ontology that describes the disparate ontologies. This is discussed in the subsequent section.

3   Context Interchange Strategy Essentials

The Context Interchange framework employs a hybrid of the loosely- and tightly-coupled approaches in data integration in heterogeneous data environment. The COIN framework was first formalized by Goh et. al in [7] and further realized by Firat [6]. The Framework comprises three major components:

- The domain model, which is a collection of rich types, called semantic types. The domain model provides a lexicon of types, attributes and modifiers to each semantic type. These semantic types together define the application domain corresponding to the data sources which are to be integrated.

– The elevation theory, made up of elevation axioms which define the mapping between the data types of the data source and the semantic types in the domain model. Essentially, this maps the primitive types from the data source to the rich semantic types in the application domain.
– The context theory comprising declarative statements which either provide for the assignment of a value to a context modifier, or identify a conversion function which can be used as the basis for converting the values of objects across different contexts.

These three components form the complete description of the application domain, required for the context mediation procedure as described in [5].

Due to space constraints, we limit the details of the COIN strategy. For detailed theoretic formalism and implementation details, the readers are referred to the literatures [4, 5, 6, 7, 10].

3.1   Context Interchange and Ontology Interoperability

One major perspective the Context Interchange strategy employs is the relational view of the data. Semi-structured data, including information from HTML and XML web pages can be used in the prototype via the Cameleon web wrapper engine [6]. This aspect of the strategy is one distinct area that sets itself apart from the common usage of OWL, where ontology and data are often maintained together in the semi-structured format of OWL.

Intuitively, the use of OWL in COIN can be viewed as the meta-ontology layer on top of OWL, providing an extension to OWL to support context-aware ontology to the current context-oblivious ontology in OWL.

Our approach in solving the ontology interoperability problem is by applying the COntext Interchange strategy at the ontology level, treating disparate ontologies as the subjects to be mediated. This can be done by creating an application meta-ontology describing the contexts of the ontologies. Using this application meta-ontology, the contextual difference can be solved in the same way that the semantic interoperability problem of heterogeneous databases is solved using COIN. With this, we can integrate and interoperate among the disparate ontologies, and subsequently integrate the underlying data represented by these ontologies.

Additionally, the same approach can be used to mediate not only data sources in the Semantic Web, but also traditional relational databases. This is important since it is expected that relational databases will co-exist with the new Semantic Web paradigm. This extension of the Context Interchange strategy will be capable of handling data interoperability within Semantic Web data sources, traditional database sources, as well as interoperability between the Semantic Web data sources and traditional databases.

4   COIN-OWL Ontology Model

Prior to describing the COIN-OWL ontology model design, we explain in brief the OWL Web Ontology Language and Rule Markup Language (RuleML)

4.1   OWL Web Ontology Language

The OWL Web Ontology Language is designed for use by applications that need to process the content of information instead of just presenting information to humans. OWL facilitates greater machine interpretability of Web content than that supported by XML, RDF, and RDF Schema (RDF-S) by providing additional vocabulary along with a formal semantics. OWL has three increasingly-expressive sublanguages: OWL Lite, OWL DL, and OWL Full:

- OWL Lite supports those users primarily needing a classification hierarchy and simple constraints. It should be simpler to provide tool support for OWL Lite than its more expressive relatives, and OWL Lite provides a quick migration path for thesauri and other taxonomies.
- OWL DL supports those users who want the maximum expressiveness while retaining computational completeness (all conclusions are guaranteed to be computable) and decidability (all computations will finish in finite time). OWL DL includes all OWL language constructs, but they can be used only under certain restrictions (for example, while a class may be a subclass of many classes, a class cannot be an instance of another class). OWL DL is so named due to its correspondence with the field of Description Logic.
- OWL Full is meant for users who want maximum expressiveness and the syntactic freedom of RDF with no computational guarantees. OWL Full allows an ontology to augment the meaning of the pre-defined (RDF or OWL) vocabulary. It would be difficult for reasoning software to support complete reasoning for every feature of OWL Full.

A more detailed comparison of the sublanguages is available from [11].

4.2   Rule Markup Language (RuleML)

The RuleML Initiative is a collaboration with the objective of providing a basis for an integrated rule-markup approach. This is achieved by having all participants collaborate in establishing translations between existing tag sets and in converging on a shared rule-markup language. The main goal for the RuleML kernel language is to be utilized as a specification for immediate rule interchange.

Rules can be stated (1) in natural language, (2) in some formal notation, or (3) in a combination of both. Being in the third, 'semiformal' category, the RuleML Initiative is working towards an XML-based markup language that permits Web-based rule storage, interchange, retrieval, and firing/application.

The XML schema definition of RuleML can be viewed as syntactically characterizing certain semantic expressiveness subclasses of the language. As eCOIN represents the ontological model in Prolog, which is in the horn-logic family, our use of RuleML is focused on the datalog and hornlog sublanguage. These two sublanguages provide a comprehensive language facility in describing rules encoded in Prolog. As the application ontologies in COIN may involve complex rules, our design and implementation uses both the datalog and hornlog sublanguages.

4.3   Context Interchange Ontology Model in OWL (COIN-OWL)

Approach. In eCOIN, the FOL/Prolog program formed by the collection of domain model definitions, elevation theories and context theories is used to detect and mediate context disparity and heterogeneity in a query using an abductive procedure defined in [12]. One important principle of our work is to preserve this constraint programming engine in the COIN framework.

We adopt a layered architecture, as shown in Figure 2, in the use of OWL in context interchange framework: (1) the domain ontology will be modeled in OWL (and its extension or relevant technology), (2) the ontology will be transformed to eCOIN FOL/Prolog as the native representation of the domain, and finally, (3) the native program will be taken as input to the abductive engine for context mediation.

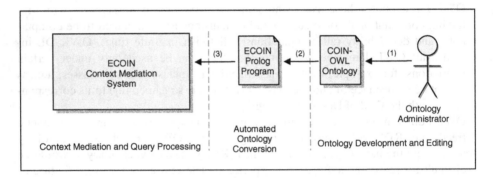

Fig. 2. Three-tier approach for Context Interchange ontology modeling using OWL

The OWL ontology model can be viewed as the front-end of the system, where it is the main interfacing layer to the ontology administrator of the eCOIN system. In the intermediate layer, the transformation from OWL to the native FOL/Prolog program will be transparent and automatic. The transformation process is detailed in the later section of the thesis. With the derived program in its native FOL/Prolog format, the existing mediation engine can be reused in its entirety.

The big win of this approach is that it minimizes re-work: there is little value in re-inventing the wheel, especially when the current functionality of the system provides the total capability currently required. At the same time, the abstraction provided by the middle tier of the architecture shields the ontology administrator from the actual implementation of the COIN context mediator. This componentization fulfills our aim of adoption of OWL in the framework, yet ensuring minimal impact to the existing COIN system.

The conversion from the OWL version of a COIN domain model to its Prolog version is done using Protégé OWL API, while conversion from RuleML to Prolog is done by using XSL Transformation technology, through the use of eXtensible Stylesheet.

OWL and Rule-Based Ontology. One major challenge of the adoption of OWL in the ontology model is that the COIN ontology model encompasses a number of constructs that are not directly available in OWL. Constructs such as Domain Model and Elevation Axioms can be represented in OWL rather easily – conceptually, these constructs describes the relationship among the data types, and can be modeled accordingly using corresponding constructs in OWL that express relationships among classes.

The problem, however, lies in the modeling of context theory, which is the pivotal component in the COIN framework. The collection of context axioms in a context theory is used either to provide for the assignment of a value to a modifier, or identify a conversion function, which can be used as the basis for converting the values of objects across different contexts. Often, the expressiveness of rules is required to define the conversion of a semantic type in the source context to a different context.

In our proposed design, axioms requiring such flexibility are encoded in RuleML. RuleML allows rule-based facts and queries to be expressed in the manner similar to conventional rule language such as Prolog. The concrete representation of RuleML is XML, which fits seamlessly in our effort to standardize the ontology representation in eCOIN.

We chose to use RuleML because it has received significant support and participation from academia and industry in the RuleML working group and it is likely that RuleML may eventually be accepted as part of the W3C standard for Rule-based ontology in Semantic Web. The early adoption of such emerging W3C standard promotes standardization of our effort and allows our work to be re-used by other interested parties in the Semantic Web and data/context integration space.

4.4   COIN-OWL Ontology Model Design

In this section, we examine the modeling of the COIN ontology in OWL with respect to domain model, elevation theory and context theory. The COIN ontology (expressed in OWL) can be used as a base OWL ontology to model disparate data sources for the purpose of data integration by means of context mediation. Where appropriate, the concrete XML presentation of the model is presented to illustrate the proposed implementation of the model.

Domain Model. By definition, the domain model defines the taxonomy of the domain in terms of the available semantic types and modifiers to each semantic types. In addition, the notion of primitive type is used to represent the data types that are native to the source or receiver context.

OWL uses the facilities of XML Schema Datatypes and a subset of the XML Schema datatypes as its standard datatypes (or equivalently, its primitive datatypes). On the other hand, the primitive types in the COIN language consist of string and number. Trivially, the COIN datatypes can be represented using its counterparts in OWL, namely xsd:string and xsd:int, xsd:float or xsd:double.

Source Sets. This COIN concept, the intensional description of the data sources, is not directly available in OWL, as OWL is used as the descriptive language only for semi-structured data on the Web. COIN, on the other hand, is designed to deal with a wide range of data sources, which makes the declarative description of the data sources indispensable for data integration and context mediation.

Context Axioms. A core concept in COIN is the notion of context differences and the ability to interoperate among contexts through context mediation. The fundamental component to context axioms is the definition of context itself.

Context definition: The interpretation of a semantic object value that is decorated by modifiers may vary according to the values taken by the modifier (e.g., the semantic object "TotalAssets" – or the more generic "monetary unit" - might be in US dollars or Euros). The value of the modifier is determined by prior domain knowledge, dependent on the context of the domain. This value can either be static (e.g., monetary units are always US dollar in Worldscope context), or dynamically obtained from other attributes (e.g., monetary units are in the currency of their country). This hierarchical structure translates to the need of modeling a parent ModifierValue class, with two subclasses ModifierStaticValue and ModifierDynamicValue.

Conversion function: A more complex construct available in COIN is the conversion function. In essence, conversion functions enable interoperability of semantic objects across different contexts. This is achieved by defining generic conversion rules for each semantic type that may yield different value under different contexts.

This requirement calls for a language facility that is both flexible and supports rule-based data. However, OWL lacks the ability to model rules in an extensible manner. Therefore, we used RuleML for conversion function modeling. As an example, consider the simple conversion function in eCOIN's Prolog representation, that converts the month expressed as a 3-letter abbreviation into its corresponding numeric value (and vice versa):

```
rule(month("Jan", 01), (true)).
```

This rule can be represented using RuleML as follows:

```
<fact>
  <_head>
    <atom>
      <cterm>
        <_opc><ctor>rule</ctor></_opc>
        <cterm>
          <_opc><ctor>month</ctor></_opc>
          <ind>Jan</ind>
          <ind>01</ind>
        </cterm>
        <ind>true</ind>
      </cterm>
    </atom>
  </_head>
</fact>
```

Elevation Axioms. Elevation axioms are used to describe the functional relationship between data sources and domain model. Intuitively, the elevation axioms can be viewed as the mapping of the primitive relation to its semantic relation. At the lower level, each column and data cell are mapped to their semantic counter part via skolemization.

Complete Ontology Model. Combining the previous individual elements of the ontology model, we present the complete COIN-OWL ontology model in the form of the UML class diagram in Figure 3. Each of the major ontology elements are shaded in gray grouping for clarity.

4.5   Design Considerations

One of the objectives of our design is to adopt emerging W3C standards as the data exchange standard in the Context Interchange project while reusing the established context mediation strategy and implementation in the project. This means that the proposed COIN model in OWL must be able to be translated to FOL/Prolog for actual context mediation and query execution process. This guiding principal is crucial in ensuring the practicality of the proposed model.

Choice of OWL Sublanguage. As introduced in the earlier section, OWL is classified into three language family: OWL Lite, OWL DL and OWL Full. The OWL sub-language used in our design is OWL Lite, as this family of language is sufficiently expressive to represent the COIN ontology model.

With our three-tier architecture, the actual reasoning and context mediation is performed at the backend (see Figure 2). This essentially means that the computation guarantee of OWL Lite and OWL DL is not required. In other words, we have the liberty to use any of these three classes of OWL sublanguages.

However, OWL Lite contains the language constructs that are rich enough for this purpose. One reason for not pushing to use the upper language family of OWL DL and OWL Full is to preserve the computability of the ontology for future. This allows the reasoning and context mediation, should there be a need in the future, to be performed directly at the OWL level without having to first translate the OWL ontology to the native ECOIN Prolog application.

OWL Ontology and Data. As part of the design and operation of COIN, we have a slightly different usage adoption of OWL. In the standard usage of OWL for ontology modeling, the ontology and data are both stored in OWL. Depending on the generality of the taxonomy definition, the ontology and data may co-exist on the same OWL document. In other cases, the ontology is defined and stored in a central OWL ontology library, and referenced in the OWL data document using external namespace reference. An example of such usage is the OWL Wine ontology (at http://www.w3.org/TR/2002/WD-owl-guide-20021104/wine.owl), where both the ontology definition and the individual instantiation (i.e. actual data) are stored in the same OWL document. On the other hand, COIN utilizes the application ontology in a different manner. The COIN-OWL ontology model describes the context semantics of the data sources. Modeled in OWL, this ontology is then used by the context mediation engine to resolve context disparities among the data sources.

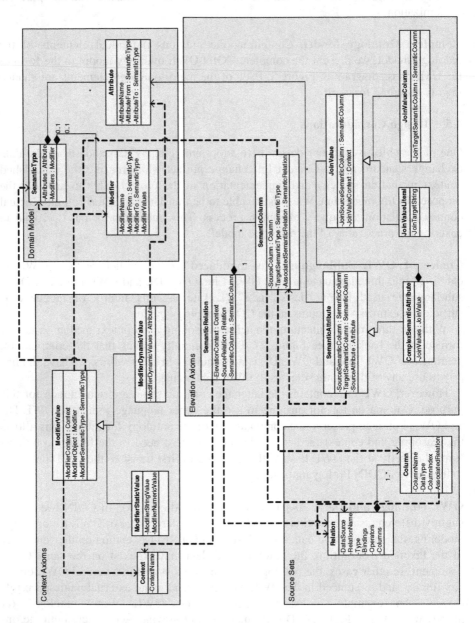

Fig. 3. UML class diagram of the complete COIN-OWL model

While the COIN ontology is modeled in OWL, the actual data may not necessarily be stored in OWL. This is because by design, COIN is architected to solve the heterogeneous data source interoperability problem. This means that the data to be reconciled by COIN will be from disparate data sources, comprising traditional relational databases or traditional semi-structured data sources on the World Wide Web (in XML or HMTL) or even OWL.

Static Type Checking. One of the biggest differences between modeling the ontology in eCOIN and COIN-OWL is the strongly enforced typing facility in OWL. In OWL, all ObjectProperty and DataProperty requires the formal definition of the range of the property, i.e. the type of object that can be specified in property.

As an example, in eCOIN, we model semantic types and modifiers using the following constructs:

```
rule(semanticType(companyName), (true)).
rule(semanticType(companyFinancials), (true)).
rule(modifiers(companyFinancials, [scaleFactor, cur-
rency]), (true)).
```

Here, it is possible for someone to accidentally put companyName as the modifier for companyFinancials:

```
rule(semanticType(companyName), (true)).
rule(semanticType(companyFinancials), (true)).
rule(modifiers(companyFinancials, [companyName]),
(true)).
```

However, as all classes are strongly typed in OWL, the following ontology will yield an error when validated against the COIN ontology:

```
<coin:SemanticType rdf:ID="companyName" />
<coin:SemanticType rdf:ID="companyFinancials">
   <coin:Modifiers rdf:resource="#companyName">
</coin:SemanticType>
```

Functional Property. In all flavors of OWL (OWL Lite, OWL DL and OWL Full), a property P of object X can be tagged as functional such that for objects Y and Z, X.P=Y and X.P=Z implies Y=Z. property P of object X is denoted as X.P.

In other words, object X can functionally determine Y in X.P=Y. Using this language feature, we can enforce a many-to-one relationship between classes. Given the wide array of language features in OWL, this is particularly useful in enforcing syntactically and semantically correct COIN ontology.

As an additional note, such requirements can also be enforced using the owl:cardinality construct. However, it is worth noting that the use of this construct depends on the sublanguage family of OWL. Cardinality expressions with values limited to 0 or 1 are part of OWL Lite. This permits the user to indicate 'at least one', 'no more than one', and 'exactly one'. Positive integer values other than 0 and 1 are permitted in OWL DL. owl:maxCardinality can be used to specify an upper bound. owl:minCardinality can be used to specify a lower bound. In combination, the two can be used to limit the property's cardinality to a numeric interval.

RuleML for Rules Modeling. In the previous work in [9], RDF was used to model the COIN ontology model. However, the work was unable to address the need for a more extensible framework in rules representation. In particular, conversion rules were encoded as raw string in the RDF document:

```
<coin:Ont_ModifierConversionFunction>

convfunc|rule(cvt(companyFinancials, O, currency, Ctxt,
Mvs, Vs, Mvt, Vt), (attr(O, fyEnding, FyDate),
value(FyDate, Ctxt, DateValue), olsen_p(Fc, Tc, Rate,
TxnDate), value(Fc, Ctxt, Mvs), value(Tc, Ctxt, Mvt),
value(TxnDate, Ctxt, DateValue), value(Rate, Ctxt, Rv),
Vt is Vs * Rv)).

        ...

        rule(month("Oct", 10), (true)).

        rule(month("Dec", 12), true)).
|companyFinancials|currency

</coin:Ont_ModifierConversionFunction>
```

These rules were then extracted programmatically from the RDF document and used in context mediation. In comparison, the adoption of RuleML for rules modeling provided a cleaner method for this purpose. In COIN-OWL, these rules are stored as RuleML:

```
<rulebase>
  <!-- rule(month("Apr", 04), (true)). -->
  <fact>
    <_head>
      <atom>
        <cterm>
          <_opc><ctor>rule</ctor></_opc>
          <cterm>
            <_opc><ctor>month</ctor></_opc>
            <ind>Apr</ind>
            <ind>04</ind>
          </cterm>
          <ind>true</ind>
        </cterm>
      </atom>
    </_head>
  </fact>
</rulebase>
```

While this format may look lengthier, this mode of representation adheres to the publicly accepted RuleML language constructs, and thus allow re-use and interchange of rules easily.

Semantic Web Rule Language (SWRL). During the course of our work, a number of relevant emerging standards have branched from RuleML, including RuleML Lite and Semantic Web Rule Language (SWRL). RuleML Lite adopts an integrated concrete syntax of XML and RDF, expanding the language construct available in modeling rules. This opens up the possibility of a tighter integration between the conversion rules in RuleML and the core ontology in OWL. One possibility is to refer to the entities modeled in the OWL ontology using rdf:resource or href attributes, instead of treating the same entity in both documents as individual and disjoint entities in each of the document.

SWRL has been considered but not implemented in this project as the modeling language is still in its very early stage. SWRL is the result of an effort to integrate RuleML into OWL, and hence holds a more holistic view of rules and ontology in the Semantic Web, compared to the use of OWL and RuleML separately.

From the following example, we note that the OWL ontology and RuleML rules are all modeled in one cohesive SWRL document. The rules fragment that expresses x3 hasSex male refers to the OWL class male seamlessly using the owlx:Individual construct:

```
<swrlx:individualPropertyAtom swrlx:property="hasSex">
  <ruleml:var>x3</ruleml:var>
  <owlx:Individual owlx:name="#male" />
</swrlx:individualPropertyAtom>
```

In RuleML 0.8, the RuleML version used in the current COIN-OWL ontology model, such language facility is not available. To refer to an individual defined in the OWL ontology, there are no other ways but to initialize a new individual in the RuleML rules document, hence creating a slight gap between the OWL ontology and RuleML rules.

5 Conclusion

In summary, we have presented an ontology interoperability framework based on the Context Interchange strategy. In conjunction with that, we proposed an ontology modeling approach using OWL and RuleML in conjunction with the Context Interchange strategy. The COIN-OWL ontology model design is built on the building blocks of the OWL Lite sublanguage family and the Rule Markup Language, which are used to model the core ontology and the rule-based metadata in COIN, respectively. In relation to the ontology model, we have highlighted the design considerations, strengths and some of the limitations of the design.

With the growing adoption of OWL and the gradual realization of the Semantic Web vision, this work is instrumental in bridging the gap between COIN and Semantic Web. With this COIN-OWL model, it is hopeful that COIN will be able to reach a larger spectrum of audiences, and hence bringing even more contribution to the database/Semantic Web community in the area of heterogeneous data interoperability and ontology interoperability.

As part of the conclusion of our work, we would like to highlight some of the interesting and promising research areas. The use of the Context Interchange strategy in ontology interoperability and data sharing is an ongoing research work of our group. We are currently working on creating a fully working prototype of the OWL ontology interoperability framework discussed in the paper.

We also noted that in parallel with the development of RuleML, a number of relevant emerging standards have been proposed in the rules interchange community, including RuleML Lite and Semantic Web Rule Language (SWRL). As these standards mature, in particular SWRL, which combines OWL and RuleML, we see that such standards promise a more cohesive rule-based ontology model. One reservation on SWRL, however, is that it is based on the RuleML datalog sublanguage, where as the minimum requirement for our current implementation requires the hornlog sublanguage family for total compatibility with Prolog. These are issues that need further study.

Acknowledgements

The authors acknowledge the help of Aykut Firat and Hongwei Zhu in reviewing drafts of this paper. The research reported herein has been supported, in part, by the Singapore-MIT Alliance (SMA).

References

[1] T. Berners-Lee, J. Hendler, and O. Lassila, "The Semantic Web," in *Scientific American*, vol. 5, 2001, pp. 34-43.

[2] H. Boley, "The Rule Markup Language: RDF-XML Data Model, XML Schema Hierarchy, and XSL Transformations," In Proceedings of the 14th International Conference of Applications of Prolog, 2001.

[3] P. Bouquet, F. Giunchiglia, F. v. Harmelen, L. Serafini, and H. Stuckenschmidt, "C-OWL: Contextualizing Ontologies," In Proceedings of the Second International Semantic Web Conference, 2003.

[4] S. Bressan, K. Fynn, C. H. Goh, S. E. Madnick, T. Pena, and M. D. Siegel, "Overview of a Prolog Implementation of the COntext INterchange Mediator," In Proceedings of the 5th International Conference and Exhibition on The Practical Applications of Prolog., 1997.

[5] S. Bressan, C. H. Goh, T. Lee, S. E. Madnick, and M. Siegel, "A Procedure for Mediation of Queries to Sources in Disparate Contexts," In Proceedings of the International Logic Programming Symposium, Port Jefferson, N.Y., 1997.

[6] A. Firat, "Information Integration Using Contextual Knowledge and Ontology Merging," Ph.D. Thesis, Massachusetts Institute of Technology, Sloan School of Management, 2003.

[7] C. H. Goh, S. Bressan, S. Madnick, and M. Siegel, "Context Interchange: New Features and Formalisms for the Intelligent Integration of Information," *ACM Transactions on Information Systems*, vol. 17, pp. 270-293, 1999.

[8] H. Kim, "Predicting How Ontologies for the semantic Web Will Evolve," *Communications of the ACM*, vol. 45, pp. 48-54, 2002.

[9] P. W. Lee, "Metadata Representation and Management for Context Mediation," Master Thesis, Massachusetts Institute of Technology, Sloan School of Management, 2003.

[10] M. Siegel and S. Madnick, "A Metadata Approach to Resolving Semantic Conflicts," In Proceedings of the 17th Conference on Very Large Data Bases, 1991.

[11] M. K. Smith, C. Welty, and D. L. McGuinness, "OWL Web Ontology Language Guide," 2003. http://www.w3.org/TR/2003/PR-owl-guide-20031215.

HCOME: A Tool-Supported Methodology for Engineering Living Ontologies

Konstantinos Kotis, George A. Vouros, and Jerónimo Padilla Alonso

Dept. of Information & Communications Systems Engineering,
University of the Aegean, Karlovassi, Samos, 83100, Greece
{kkot, georgev, pgeron}@aegean.gr

Abstract. The fast emergent areas of the Semantic Web and knowledge management push researchers to new efforts concerning ontology engineering. The development of ontologies must be seen as a dynamic process that in most of the cases starts with an initial rough ontology that is later revised, refined, enriched, populated and filled in with details. Ontology evolution has to be supported through the entire ontology lifecycle, resulting to a living ontology. The aim of this paper is to present the Human-Centered Ontology Engineering Methodology (HCOME) for the development and evaluation of living ontologies in the context of communities of knowledge workers. The methodology aims to empower knowledge workers to continuously manage their formal conceptualizations in their day-to-day tasks. We conjecture that this methodology can only be effectively supported by eclectic human-centered ontology management environments, such as the HCONE and SharedHCONE.

1 Introduction

Ontologies have been realized as the key technology to shaping and exploiting information for the effective management of knowledge and for the evolution of the Semantic Web and its applications. We consider communities of knowledge workers that are involved in knowledge-intensive tasks within an organization, or World Wide Web users with common interests. Knowledge workers are unfamiliar with knowledge engineering principles and methods, and most of the times have little or no training on using ontology specification tools. In such a distributed setting ontologies establish a common vocabulary for community members to interlink, combine, and communicate knowledge shaped through practice and interaction, binding the knowledge processes of creating, importing, capturing, retrieving, and using knowledge. However, it seems that there will always be the case that community members devise more than one ontologies for the same domain. For community members to explicate, maintain and evaluate the changing conceptualization of a domain, they must get powerful tools that will allow them to edit, review, update and maintain formal ontologies, on their own as well as in collaboration with colleagues [1].

Several methodologies have been proposed for the engineering of ontologies within a knowledge management setting. From the identification of goals and

C. Bussler et al. (Eds.): SWDB 2004, LNCS 3372, pp. 155–166, 2005.
© Springer-Verlag Berlin Heidelberg 2005

requirements' specification, to the implementation, evaluation and maintenance of the conceptualisations, the ontology life cycle must be clearly defined and further supported by ontology development tools [2]. From the methodologies described in [3], [4], [5] and [6], the OnToKnowledge methodology supported by the OntoEdit ontology development tool, being the most well known one, starts from the initial stages of knowledge management projects (feasibility and requirements) and proceeds to the deployment and maintenance of an ontology-based knowledge management system [4], [5]. The OnToKnowledge methodological approach focuses on the application-driven development of ontologies, supporting the introduction of ontology based knowledge management systems [4], [5]. According to this approach, the maintenance of ontologies is primarily an organizational process driven by the knowledge engineer who gathers updates to the ontology and initiates the switchover to a new version of the ontology after thoroughly testing possible effects to the application [4],[5].

In contrast to the methodologies that are centered to the knowledge engineers, we propose the use of a human-centered approach to ontologies management [7], where the active participation of knowledge workers in the ontology life cycle is accentuated. Doing so, ontologies are developed and managed according to knowledge workers' abilities, are developed individually as well as conversationally, and put in the context of workers' experiences and working settings, as an integrated part of knowledge workers' "knowing" process [1], [8]. To leverage the role of knowledge workers by empowering them to participate actively in the ontology lifecycle, the human-centered approach entails the development of tools that provide greater opportunities for workers to manage and interact with their conceptualisations in a direct and continuous mode [7]. Although the final ontology is the product of knowledge worker's collaboration, knowledge engineers must join the discussion in order to further validate the final formal representation of the conceptualizations.

To further support our conjecture for the need of human-centered methodological approaches, let us consider the following ontology management scenarios in a living organization setting:

Scenario No 1: Involved in a knowledge retrieval process, a worker is searching for a specific piece of information about best practices concerning the design of a product type. The retrieval tool exploits the ontology concerning product designs, but the worker can neither find the terms that she thinks to be appropriate for querying the system, nor can she get the needed information by any combination of existing terms. She soon finds out that the definitions of some terms must be changed to reflect the information related to the new case at hand. The information is there, but cannot be reached, since the ontology does not reflect the up-to-date practice of the organization. Imagine now the same case happening for five workers per day in a fast changing domain. We suggest that workers must be empowered to shape their information space, working in collaboration with colleagues and knowledge engineers.

Scenario No 2: In a knowledge use process, a worker browses, recalls existing knowledge items, and process them for further use. During this process the worker may produce derivations that should be captured as new knowledge, indexed by new terms, or by combinations of existing terms. Capturing derived knowledge is very important. Empowering this worker with the proper tools for describing her conceptions formally, incorporating them in organization's information repository, submitting and sharing this information with co-workers readily, accelerates much the knowledge processes.

Scenario No 3: In the day-to-day information creation and import tasks, workers are devising business documents, proposals, product reports, best practices, problem/fault reports, etc. Indexing such information using formal ontological commitments should be done in a seamless way by knowledge workers themselves, during authoring, allowing them to devise, expand and update their shared conceptualizations at the same time.

This paper emphasizes on the methodological implications to ontology engineering of the HCONE and SharedHCONE ontology engineering environments [7] that are oriented to the way people interact and shape their conceptualizations and to the way conceptualizations are formed as part of knowledge workers' day-to-day activities [1].

2 Management of Ontologies

As it is widely argued and shown in the above scenarios, ontologies explicate conceptualizations that are shaped and exploited by humans during *practice*. Being part of knowledge that people possess, ontologies evolve in communities as part of *knowing* [8].

Therefore, ontology management in the context of communities of knowledge workers involves the development, evaluation and exploitation of conceptualizations that emerge as part of practicing in their working contexts. In particular it involves:

- *The development of individual ontologies.* People develop their own conceptualizations that may either explicate (e.g. by formalizing concepts, by taking notes about their meaning or just by naming them) or not (by storing them in the background of their minds). In their day-to-day activities people develop their conceptualizations, either by improvising, by specializing/generalizing/aggregating existing concepts based on their experiences and on interaction with other community members, or by synthesizing existing conceptualizations.
- *The development of commonly agreed group ontologies.* Developing commonly agreed and understandable ontologies is a very difficult and resource-demanding task that requires members of the communities to work synergistically towards shaping the information they exploit. Working synergistically, workers map others' conceptualizations to their own and put them in the context of their own experiences. This leads to a conversation whose back-and-forth, as it is pointed in [8], not only results in exchanging knowledge but also in generating new knowledge.
- *The evaluation and exploitation of ontologies.* Exploitation and evaluation of ontologies as part of the day-to-day practice of communities can be considered only as part of knowing. Conceptualizations are put in practice or in the criticism

of community members who, as already pointed, have to compare them with their own conceptualizations and put them in the context of their own experiences. Evaluation can result in new meanings since concepts are seen under the light on new experiences and evolving contexts.

To empower knowledge workers to participate actively in the ontology engineering process in collaboration with colleagues and knowledge engineers, tools must enable them to improvise, to synthesize ontologies, to produce mappings/alignments between existing ontologies, and to collaboratively develop ontologies with their co-workers, in ways that are natural (according to their cognitive abilities, skills, knowledge, education, context of work and so on) for them, and so that the semantic validity of specifications is assured. Ultimately, this must happen in the background of the day-to-day knowledge intensive activities of workers, seamlessly to their working practices.

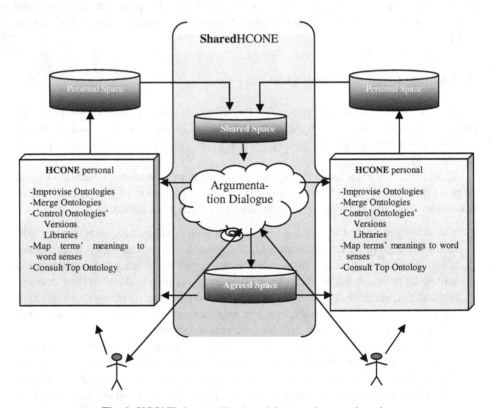

Fig. 1. HCONE decentralized model to ontology engineering

3 HCONE and SharedHCONE

In [7] we extensively describe HCONE and SharedHCONE tools that have been developed to support the above requirements.

HCONE (Human Centered ONtology Environment) follows a decentralized model to ontology engineering that is shown in Fig. 1. According to this model people can create their own ontologies stored in a personal space. Ontologies can be later publicized and shared among groups of workers that jointly contribute to ontologies development, with the aim to reach an agreement in conceptualizing their domain. During this process, workers may evolve ontologies by improvising in their personal space, map and synthesize their conceptualizations with the conceptualizations of their co-workers and discuss their arguments, objections and positions within the group. During collaboration, workers follow a structured argumentation process in which they may raise issues, propose solutions via stating positions, provide arguments for or against a position etc. Agreed ontologies are stored in a virtual space and can be further shared, evolved in workers' personal space and so on.

HCONE (Fig. 2.) is a modular environment, providing access to any integrated tool in any HCONE point. Doing so, workers are free to combine their own method for using the environment, following an eclectic way to ontology engineering. For instance, a worker may construct an ontology in her personal space while receiving comments on a previous version of the same ontology that has shared with co-workers. In the meantime, she is trying to comply with generic ontological commitments that the group has agreed to comply with, while in another slice of her work she is trying to merge her ontology with an ontology issued by a co-worker.

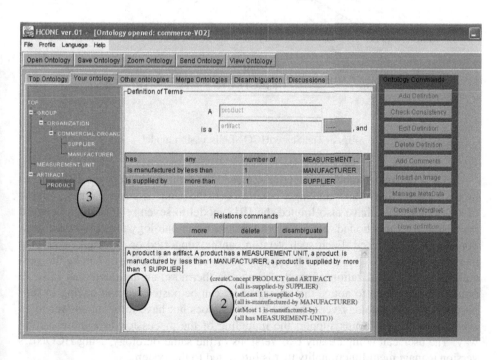

Fig. 2. HCONE support for the specification of the concept "Product": 1) natural language, 2) formal, 3) graphical representation

SharedHCONE (Fig. 4.) supports sharing ontologies to group members and supports group members' participation in structured conversations about conceptualizations. This is a built-in, rather than a patched-on facility, since it has been designed in order to support people to discuss ontological aspects and incorporate their suggestions / positions to specifications, rather than being a generic argumentation or discussion facility. The aim of the system is to support users to discuss upon an ontology and its versions, agree or disagree with a version, post new versions or get others' versions to their private space (HCONE), evaluate and exploit them, and so on. The users are able to post issues, arguments and positions (i.e. ontology versions) following a variation of the IBIS model (Issue-Based Information System), proposed by Kunz and Rittel [10]. Performing dialogue acts, users construct a discourse graph that is presented in the form of a threaded discussion. The discussion is based on three main abstractions, namely *issue*, *position* and *argument*. An issue represents a decision problem, the position is the statement that resolves the issue, and the argument either supports or objects position. These abstractions are related by predefined relationships, as it is shown in Fig. 3.

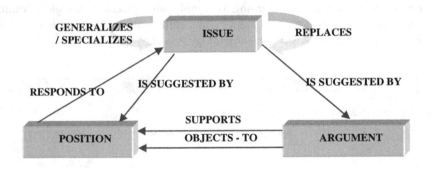

Fig. 3. The SharedHCONE discussion model

For a better understanding, we have replaced the term *position* of the IBIS model by the term *version*: Thus, making a position it is the same as posting a new version of an ontology. We have also limited the IBIS model to seven relationships between the abstractions mentioned: zero or more versions of an ontology may provide a solution for an issue raised. Each such version can be supported or objected by zero or more arguments. Also an issue can suggest a new version, or an issue can be the generalization or specialization of another issue. Furthermore, an argument can raise an issue. It is important to notice that an argument can be posted without having to support or reject an ontology version, and a version does not have to be an answer to an issue. These relationships support the modeling of the discussion in a more natural way. The user can compare any two versions of the same ontology using HCONE's version management functionality that is integrated to the system.

The SharedHCONE functionality:

- Enables criticism, identifying possible opportunities for members' collaboration
  Encourages feedback among community members
- Overcomes deadlocks within problematic situations that arise in ontology specification
- . Supports evaluation of developed ontologies
- Provides an additional ontology versioning mechanism that records motivation behind changes (Fig. 4.)

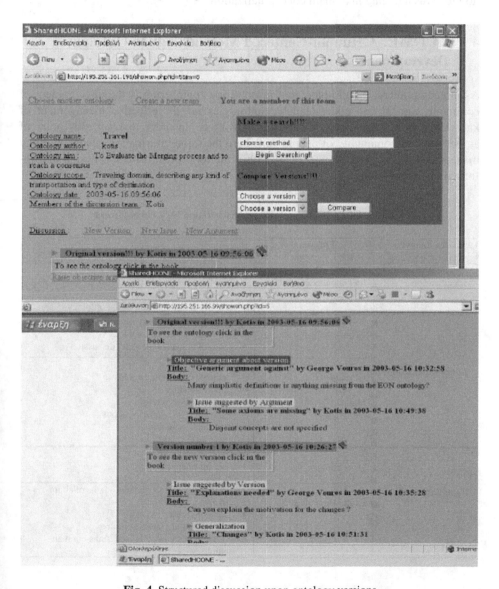

Fig. 4. Structured discussion upon ontology versions

Concluding the above, HCONE and SharedHCONE provides facilities for (a) users to improvise their conceptualizations, (b) consult generic ontologies that provide important semantic distinctions, (c) manage different versions of their ontologies, tracking the differences between the versions, (e) track the generalization/ specialization of an ontology during ontology development, (d) get proper consultation from machine exploitable/ readable lexicons by mapping concepts' meaning to word senses, (e) merge ontologies and further manipulate merged conceptualizations, and (f) share their ontologies with groups of co-workers, following a structured conversation towards agreeing in domain conceptualization.

4   HCOME: A Human-Centered Methodology to Ontology Development

As already pointed, the ultimate goal in ontology engineering is the development of commonly agreed and understandable ontologies for the effective management of knowledge in a community of knowledge workers. In order to reach this point of agreement in a community of people that share the same information needs, ontology management tasks must be integrated within the loop of information design and information exploitation [1].

Table 1. HCOME methodology phases to ontology development

Ontology life-cycle phases	Processes	Tasks
Specification	Define goals and scope, find knowledge sources	▪ discuss requirements (S) ▪ produce documents (S) ▪ identify collaborators, ▪ specify the scope, aim of the ontology (S)
Conceptualization	Acquire knowledge	▪ import from ontology libraries (P) ▪ consult generic top ontology (P) ▪ consult domain experts by discussion (S)
	Develop & Maintain Ontology	▪ improvise (P) ▪ manage conceptualizations (P) ▪ merge versions(P) ▪ compare own versions (P) ▪ generalize/specialize versions (P) ▪ add documentation (P)
Exploitation	Use ontology	▪ browse ontology (P) ▪ exploit in applications
	Evaluate ontology	▪ initiate arguments and criticism collaboratively (S) ▪ compare others' versions (S) ▪ browse/exploit agreed ontologies (S) ▪ manage the recorded discussions upon an ontology (S)

Table 1 summarizes the phases and tasks that knowledge workers perform in the HCOME methodology. These tasks are performed in a loop, until a consensus has been reached between knowledge workers. These tasks are either performed in worker's personal *space* (marked in Table 1 with a P), or they are performed in the *shared space* provided by a collaborative ontology engineering environment such as SharedHCONE (marked in Table 1 with an S). A worker can initiate any task in his personal or shared space, or take part to a shared task that has been initiated by other members of the community.

The initiating tasks of the methodology are included in the "Specification" phase of the ontology lifecycle, and they can be performed within the shared space in collaboration to other community members. The most important tasks are performed in the "Conceptualization" phase. The worker can choose any of the tasks supported by HCONE, or a combination of them, in order to develop an ontology. In the exploitation phase ontologies can be exploited and collaboratively evaluated: Users may raise new issues, form arguments for/against an issue or for/against a specific version of the ontology (i.e. a position) and form new positions (i.e. new ontology versions), feeding again the ontology development loop.

The following paragraphs discuss the major tasks of the HCOME methodological approach to ontology development, starting from the early stages of the ontology lifecycle. It must be strongly emphasized that the approach is iterative and continuous. To devise and maintain living ontologies in evolving domains and open environments, such as the Semantic Web, this iteration is rather necessary to keep on *"for ever"* until the aim for the development of ontologies is obsolete, i.e. until there is not reason for their existence [9].

As it is known, effectiveness and efficiency during the application of methodologies increase significantly through tool support [4]. HCOME is supported by the use of HCONE and SharedHCONE. Specifically, all the tasks of the HCOME phases in both, the personal and shared spaces are supported by the HCONE and the SharedHCONE tools.

4.1 Building Personal Ontologies

During the HCOME specification phase, a team of collaborators can agree on the aim and the scope of a new ontology following an argumentation dialogue in SharedHCONE. Having agreed on that, HCONE supports them to specify their conceptualizations (in their personal spaces), hiding low-level implementation details, enabling them to express subtle ontological distinctions, complying at the same time with formal constraints of specifications [7].

Specifically, HCONE, following the What-You-See-Is-What-You-Meant [11][7] knowledge editing paradigm, supports workers to specify their conceptualizations using the full expressive power of a description logic language, without dealing with low-level implementation details. While users specify the definition of a concept, they get feedback that reflects the definition of the corresponding concept in natural language. Typical tasks that workers may perform when defining a concept include concept and roles mapping to word senses through lexicon consultation, and checking for concepts' definition consistency.

Collaborators can store/manage different versions of their personal ontology, compare any ontology to other ontologies that are considered to be similar and merge relevant/similar ontologies. To support them to perform these tasks, HCONE provides seamless access to advanced services supported by description logics. These services include concepts' mapping to word senses, automatic concepts' classification, concepts' definitions consistency checks (e.g. between a concept and its subsumers) and detection of concepts' definitions differences. Feedback from these reasoning services is constantly provided during ontology development/ management and is of high significance.

Collaborators may also follow a deductive approach to concepts' specifications by elaborating a generic top ontology. In this case, concepts' definitions can be checked for their semantic validity against generic conceptualizations by means of the consistency checking mechanisms provided by the representation and reasoning system. In doing so, the construction of domain specific ontologies is speed-up and guided by the semantic distinctions and ontological principles of the generic ontologies consulted.

Critical to the ontology development process is the lexicons consultation task. Through lexicon consultation, collaborators are guided to the consensual definition of terms, guided to follow well-established norms and practices in the community they are exercising their practice (e.g. by consulting a terminological lexicon or a thesaurus) or in the wider context (e.g. by mapping their conceptions to the appropriate word senses in a lexical database). Lexicon consultation can be supported in any of the following three ways: (a) by mapping concepts definitions to word senses in a machine readable/exploitable lexicon through the concept's meaning mapping process, (b) by formally complying with generic ontological commitments of top level ontologies or (c) by simply consulting lexicons and other ontologies.

4.2 Exploiting and Sharing Ontologies

Having developed their personal ontologies, collaborators may use them within their work setting, and/or share them with colleagues in order to be further discussed, exploited and evaluated. In this context *the exploitation* of an ontology version that has been developed by a colleague is seen as part of the ontology development life-cycle since this process provides feedback for the conceptualizations developed. The need to achieve a common understanding about the working domain, push inevitably ontologies to the shared space [1].

The shared space supports people to devise ontologies conversationally, reaching a consensus on a domain conceptualisation, discuss ontological aspects and incorporate their suggestions into positions about concepts' specifications. The shared space tasks support contextualization of the built ontologies in communities' working practices and experiences, criticism and evaluation of the built artifacts, identification of possible opportunities for community members' collaboration, as well as overcoming deadlocks within problematic situations that arise in ontologies specification.

A shared space contains those ontologies that are conversationally constructed and for which the corresponding group has not reached an agreement. An *agreed space* is part of this shared space and contains those ontologies for which a group has reached an agreement. Any community member can post a new ontology to the shared space, specifying the subject, scope and aim for building this new shared ontology. At the same time, any collaborator can download to her personal space an ontology version developed by other community members, re-specify, change, enrich, compare, merge it with her own, exploit it, and send it back to the shared space, posting new issues, arguments and so forth.

To support the above, the typical process in SharedHCONE goes as follows: Having publicized an ontology, all community members receive a notification by e-mail. The body of this e-mail message provides details about this new ontology and points to the community members that they can become part of the discussion group within a number of days. Being members of the group, it is assumed that community members have already agreed on the importance of the shared ontology, and commit to take part in the upcoming discussion. Any group member can raise issues and arguments concerning the new ontology through an argumentation dialogue. Having all group members agreed on a specific version of the ontology, the ontology "moves" to the agreed space. For the seamless notification of community members about the discourse status, an e-mail notification manager sends each new discourse object to all community members via e-mail.

Users can intervene at any point in the discussion by performing any legal discourse act and can also inspect any ontology version. Inspecting an ontology, users may browse the ontology tree and get the natural language description of any concept. Furthermore, they can inspect the differences between two ontology versions through a formal comparison service. Following the threaded discussion and being able to inspect the differences between the different versions of the same ontology, people can track the rationale behind each version.

5   Conclusion

This paper presents the HCOME decentralized methodology for ontology engineering, which is supported by HCONE and SharedHCONE prototype systems. These systems support the personal and shared tasks of the HCOME ontology engineering methodology, respectively. Tools' key features, functionalities, technical details and screenshots can be found at http://www.samos.aegean.gr/icsd/kkot/HCONEweb and in [7]. Evaluation of the HCONE methodology has been carried out using these prototypes, in comparison to OntoEdit (http://www.ontoprise.de/products/ontoedit) and Protégé-2000 (protege.stanford.edu) supported methodology. The community for performing this evaluation was comprised by graduate students of our department. Their feedback was encouraging to continue our efforts. However, further evaluation of the methodology is needed in different working settings.

References

1. Vouros A. G.: Technological Issues towards Knowledge Powered Organizations. Knowledge Management Journal, Vol 7, No. 1 (2003)
2. Giboin A., Gandon F., Corby O., and Dieng R.: Assessment of Ontology-based Tools: Systemizing the Scenario Approach. In Proceedings of OntoWeb-SIG3 Workshop at the 13th International Conference on Knowledge Engineering and Knowledge Management EKAW 2002, pages 63-73. Siguenza, Spain, 30th September (2002)
3. Fernandez-Lopez M.: Overview of methodologies for building ontologies. Proceedings of the IJCAI-99 Workshop on Ontologies and Problem-Solving Methods (1999)
4. Sure Y.: A Tool-supported Methodology for Ontology-based Knowledge Management. ISMIS 2002, Methodologies for Intelligent Systems (2002)
5. Staab S, Studer R., Schnurr H., and Sure Y.: Knowledge Processes and Ontologies. IEEE Intelligent Systems, pages 26-34, January/February (2001)
6. Fernandez-Lopez M.: A survey on methodologies for developing, maintaining, evaluating and reengineering ontologies. ONTOWEB Consortium for Ontology-based information exchange for knowledge management and electronic commerce. IST-2000-29243, Deliverable 1.4 (2002)
7. Kotis K., Vouros G.: Human Centered Ontology Management with HCONE. Proceedings of the IJCAI-03 Workshop on Ontologies and Distributed Systems (2003)
8. Cook S. D. N., and Brown, J. S.: Bridging epistemologies: The generative dance between organizational knowledge and organizational knowing. Organizational Science, 10:381-400 (1999)
9. Stojanovic L. and Motik B.: Ontology Evolution within Ontology Editors. In Proceedings of OntoWeb-SIG3 Workshop at the 13th International Conference on Knowledge Engineering and Knowledge Management EKAW 2002, pages 53-62. Siguenza, Spain, 30th September (2002)
10. Kunz W. and Rittel H. W. J.: Issues as elements of information systems. Technical Report S-78-2, Institut fur Gundlagen Der Planung I.A, Universitat Stuttgart (1970)
11. Power R., Scott D., and Evans R.: What You See Is What You Meant: direct knowledge editing with natural language feedback. ITRI Technical Report No. 97-03, University of Brighton (1997)

Query Answering by Rewriting in GLAV Data Integration Systems Under Constraints

Andrea Calì

Faculty of Computer Science,
Free University of Bolzano/Bozen,
piazza Domenicani 3 – I-39100 Bolzano, Italy
ac@andreacali.com

Abstract. In the Semantic Web, the goal is offering access to information that is distributed over the Internet. Data integration is highly relevant in this context, since it consists in providing a uniform access to a set of data sources, through a unified representation of the data called *global schema*. Integrity constraints (ICs) are expressed on the global schema in order to better represent the domain of interest, yet such constraints may not be satisfied by the data at the sources. In this paper we address the problem of answering queries posed to a data integration system where the mapping is specified in the so-called GLAV approach, and when tuple-generating dependencies (TGDs) and functional dependencies (FDs) are expressed over the global schema. We extend previous results by first showing that, in the case of TGDs without FDs, known query rewriting techniques can be applied in a more general case, and can take into account also the GLAV mapping in a single rewriting step. Then we introduce FDs with TGDs, identifying a novel class of ICs for which query answering is decidable, and providing a query answering algorithm based on query rewriting also in this case.

1 Introduction

In the Semantic Web [15, 8] the goal is to enrich data accessible on the Web in order to provide semantic knowledge that facilitates users in retrieving and accessing information that is relevant for them. Ideally, the aim is to allow users to pose queries to the Web as if they were querying a single, local knowledge base. Hence, one of the fundamental issues of the Semantic Web is that of integrating the information present in the various sources, and therefore data integration techniques prove to be higly useful for this task. Conceptual modelling formalisms, such as the Entity-Relationship model, have proved to be highly effective for representing intensional information about data, and are now widely accepted means of enriching data with semantic knowledge about the domain of interest. When the data are represented in the relation model, as in the case of this paper, *integrity constraints (ICs)*, like key and foreign key constraints, are able to capture most of the information expressed by conceptual modelling formalisms.

C. Bussler et al. (Eds.): SWDB 2004, LNCS 3372, pp. 167–184, 2005.

A data integration system has the goal of providing a uniform access to a set of heterogeneous data sources, through a unified view of all underlying data, called *global schema*. Once the user issues a query over the global schema, the system carries out the task of suitably accessing the different sources and assemble the retrieved data into the final answer to the query.

In data integration, the specification of the relationship between the global schema and the sources, which is called *mapping* [18], is a significant issue. There are two basic approaches for specifying a mapping in a data integration system [14, 18]. The first one, called *global-as-view (GAV)*, requires that to each element of the global schema a view over the sources is associated. The second approach, called *local-as-view (LAV)*, requires that to each source a view over the global schema is associated. Besides GAV and LAV, a mixed approach, called GLAV [11, 10], consists in associating views over the global schema to views over the sources.

In a data integration system, the global schema is a representation of the domain of interest of the system, therefore there is the need of having a global schema that fits the fragment of real world that is modelled by the system. To this aim, integrity constraints are expressed on the global schema.

It is important to notice that integrity constraints are used to enhance the expressiveness of the global schema, and their presence is not due to constraints on the sources, which in our approach are supposed to be enforced by the systems that manage the local data. Therefore, in general, the data at the sources may not satisfy the constraints on the global schema; in this case a common assumption (which is the one adopted in this paper) is to to consider the sources as *sound*, i.e., they provide a *subset* of the data that satisfy the global schema. Answering queries posed over the global schema in this setting requires to consider a *set* of databases for the global schema, and in particular all those that contain the data provided by the sources through the mapping, and that satisfy the ICs on the global schema. Therefore, query answering requires reasoning on incomplete information.

In this paper we address the problem of query answering in data integration in the relational context, where the mapping is GLAV, and in the presence of *tuple-generating dependencies (TGDs)* and *functional dependencies (FDs)* on the global schema; TGDs and FDs are an extension of two important classes of dependencies in relational database schemata, namely *inclusion dependencies* and *key dependencies* respectively [1, 16].

First we consider TGDs alone: since the query answering under general TGDs is undecidable [17], we solve the problem for a restricted class of TGDs, that we call *cycle-harmless TGDs*, that extends a decidable class known in the literature. Our approach is purely intensional here: we do query answering by *query rewriting*, i.e. by reformulating the query into a new one, which encodes the information about the integrity constraints, and then proceeding as if there were no integrity constraints. The rewriting algorithm used here is the same as in [3]. The form of the TGDs we consider is general enough to consider the GLAV mapping assertion as TGDs over a unified schema constituted by the union of the global schema and the source schema; therefore, we are able to apply the rewriting technique in a single step, taking into account the TGDs and the mapping at the same time.

Then, we address the problem of query answering when also FDs are expressed on the global schema. Even if we consider cycle-harmless TGDs, the presence of FDs causes an interaction that makes query answering again undecidable. We need to consider a new, more restricted class of TGDs, which we call *non-functional-conflicting TGDs*, that do not interact with FDs, and again we present a technique for query answering. In this case, however, we cannot take into account the mapping in an intensional fashion, because it is not realistic to assume that the mapping assertions are non-functional-conflicting TGDs. Therefore, in order to answer queries, we need to construct the *retrieved global database (RGD)* [4], that is the minimum global database that satisfies the mapping. If the RGD satisfies the FDs, we can proceed with the same rewriting technique used for TGDs, simply disregarding the presence of FDs.

The rest of the paper is organised as follows. In Section 2 we present a formal framework for data integration; in Section 3 we address the query answering problem for TGDs alone; in Section 4 we introduce FDs together with TGDs, showing a decidable class of constraints for this case and providing a query answering technique. Section 5 concludes the paper.

2   Framework

In this section we define a logical framework for data integration, based on the relational model with integrity constraints.

2.1   Syntax

We consider to have an infinite, fixed alphabet Γ of constants representing real world objects, and will take into account only databases having Γ as domain.

A *relational schema* $\mathcal{R}$ is a set of first-order predicates, called *relation symbols*, each with an associated arity; a relation symbol R of arity n is denoted by R/n. A *relational database instance* of a schema $\mathcal{R}$ is a set of facts of the form $R(c_1, \ldots, c_n) \leftarrow$, where $R/n \in \mathcal{R}$ and $c_1, \ldots, c_n \in \Gamma$. In the following, for the sake of conciseness, we will use the term "database" instead of "database instance".

Formally, a data integration system $\mathcal{I}$ is a triple $\langle \mathcal{G}, \mathcal{S}, \mathcal{M} \rangle$, where:

1. $\mathcal{G}$ is the *global schema* expressed in the relational model with integrity constraints. In particular:
   (a) $\mathcal{G}$ is constituted by a set of relations, each with an associated arity that indicates the number of its attributes. A relation R of arity n is denoted by R/n.
   (b) A set Σ_T of *tuple-generating dependencies (TGDs)* is expressed over $\mathcal{G}$. A TGD [1, 10] is a first-order formula of the form

$$\forall \boldsymbol{X} (\exists \boldsymbol{Y} \ \chi(\boldsymbol{X}, \boldsymbol{Y}) \ \rightarrow \ \exists \boldsymbol{Z} \ \psi(\boldsymbol{X}, \boldsymbol{Z}))$$

where X, Y, Z are sets of variables or constants of Γ, and χ and ψ are conjunctions of atoms whose predicate symbols are in $\mathcal{G}$. Henceforth, for the sake of conciseness, we will omit the quantifiers in TGDs.

(c) A set Σ_F of *functional dependencies (FDs)* is expressed over $\mathcal{G}$. A FD [1] is written in the form

$$R : \mathbf{A} \rightarrow B$$

where R is a relation symbol, $\mathbf{A}$ is a set of attributes of R, and B is an attribute of R.

2. $\mathcal{S}$ is the *source schema*, constituted by the schemata of the different sources. We assume that the sources are relational, and in particular that each source is represented by a single relation. Assuming sources to be relational is not a restriction, since we may assume that sources that are not relational are suitably accessible in relational form by means of software modules called *wrappers*. Furthermore, we assume that no integrity constraint is expressed on the source schema. This because integrity constraints on the sources are local to the data source, and they are enforced by the source itself.

3. $\mathcal{M}$ is the *mapping* between $\mathcal{G}$ and $\mathcal{S}$, specifying the relationship between the global schema and the source schema. The mapping $\mathcal{M}$ is a set of first-order formulae, which we call *mapping assertions*, of the form

$$\forall \mathbf{X}(\exists \mathbf{Y}\, \varphi_{\mathcal{S}}(\mathbf{X}, \mathbf{Y}) \rightarrow \exists \mathbf{Z}\, \varphi_{\mathcal{G}}(\mathbf{X}, \mathbf{Z}))$$

where X, Y, Z are sets of variables or constants, and $\varphi_{\mathcal{S}}$ and $\varphi_{\mathcal{G}}$ are conjunctions of atoms whose predicate symbols are in $\mathcal{S}$ and $\mathcal{G}$ respectively. Henceforth, we will omit quantifiers in mapping formulae. Note that this kind of mapping assertions is a generalisation of both LAV and GAV assertions; in particular, in a LAV assertion a view (conjunction of atoms) over the global schema is associated to a source relation, while in a GAV assertion a view over the source schema is associated to a relation symbol in $\mathcal{G}$. Henceforth, consistently with [11], we will call *GLAV (global-local-as-view)* this approach.

Example 1 ([19]). Consider a data integration system $\mathcal{I} = \langle \mathcal{G}, \mathcal{S}, \mathcal{M} \rangle$, where the global schema $\mathcal{G}$ consists of the following relations (names of relations and attributes are self-explanatory):

> work(*Person, Project*)
> area(*Project, Field*)
> employed(*Person, Institution*)
> runsProject(*Institution, Project*)

The source schema $\mathcal{S}$ contains the following relations:

> hasjob(*Person, Field*)
> teaches(*Professor, Course*)
> infield(*Course, Field*)
> getgrant(*Researcher, Grant*)
> grantfor(*Grant, Project*)

The GLAV mapping $\mathcal{M}$ is as follows:

$$
\begin{aligned}
\mathsf{hasjob}(R, F) &\rightarrow \mathsf{work}(R, P) \wedge \mathsf{area}(P, F) \\
\mathsf{getgrant}(R, G) \wedge \mathsf{grantfor}(G, P) &\rightarrow \mathsf{work}(R, P) \\
\mathsf{teaches}(R, C) \wedge \mathsf{infield}(C, F) &\rightarrow \mathsf{work}(R, P) \wedge \mathsf{area}(P, F)
\end{aligned}
$$

Note that the first assertion is in fact a LAV assertion, the second one is a GAV one, while the third assertion is a general GLAV assertion.

The set Σ_T of TGDs is constituted by the following TGD:

$$
\mathsf{work}(R, P) \rightarrow \mathsf{employed}(R, I) \wedge \mathsf{runsProject}(I, P)
$$

This TGD imposes that, if a person R works on a project P, he/she needs to be employed in some institution I that is running the project P. ∎

Example 2. Consider a data integration system $\mathcal{I} = \langle \mathcal{G}, \mathcal{S}, \mathcal{M} \rangle$, where the global schema $\mathcal{G}$ is constituted by the relations $R_1/2$ and $R_2/2$, the source schema by relations $S_1/2, S_2/1$. The set of TGDs Σ_T contains the single TGD $\theta : R_1(X, Y) \rightarrow R_1(Y, W) \wedge R_2(Y, X)$. Note that θ introduces a cycle in the dependencies. The mapping $\mathcal{M}$ consists of the assertions $S_1(X, c) \rightarrow R_1(X, Y) \wedge R_2(Y, Z)$ and $S_2(X) \rightarrow R_2(X, Y)$. ∎

Now we come to queries expressed over the global schema; a n-ary *relational query* (relational query of arity n) is a formula that is intended to specify a set of n-tuples of constants in Γ, that constitute the *answer* to the query. In our setting, we assume that queries over the global schema are expressed in the language of *union of conjunctive queries (UCQs)*. A conjunctive query (CQ) of arity n is a formula of the form $q(\mathbf{X}) \leftarrow \omega(\mathbf{X}, \mathbf{Y})$ where $\mathbf{X}$ is a set of variables called *distinguished variables*, $\mathbf{Y}$ is a set of symbols that are either variables (called *non-distinguished*) or constants, q is a predicate symbol not appearing in $\mathcal{G}$ or $\mathcal{S}$, and ω is a conjunction of atoms whose predicate symbols are in $\mathcal{G}$. The atom $q(\mathbf{X})$ is called *head* of the query (denoted $head(q)$), while $\omega(\mathbf{X}, \mathbf{Y})$ is called *body* (denoted $body(q)$). A UCQ of arity n is a set of conjunctive queries Q such that each $q \in Q$ has the same arity n and uses the same predicate symbol in the head.

2.2   Semantics

A *database instance* (or simply *database*) $\mathcal{C}$ for a relational schema $\mathcal{R}$ is a set of facts of the form $R(t)$ where R is a relation of arity n in $\mathcal{R}$ and t is an n-tuple of constants of the alphabet Γ. We denote as $R^{\mathcal{C}}$ the set of tuples of the form $\{t \mid R(t) \in \mathcal{C}\}$.

In the following, we shall often make use of the notion of substitution. A *substitution* of variables σ is a partial function that associates to a variable either a constant or a variable, and to each constant the constant itself. In the following, given a first-order formula F, we will denote with $\sigma(F)$ the formula obtained by replacing in F each variable (or constant) x with $\sigma(x)$. Given an atomic formula $R(x_1, \ldots, x_n)$, where R is a n-ary predicate and $x_1, \ldots, x_n$ are variables or constants, we say that a substitution σ sends $R(x_1, \ldots, x_n)$ to the fact $\sigma(R(x_1, \ldots, x_n))$, that we denote with $R(\sigma(x_1), \ldots, \sigma(x_n)) \leftarrow$. Moreover, given a conjunction $C = A_1 \wedge \ldots \wedge a_m$ of atomic formulae, we will say that a substitution σ sends C to the set of facts $\{\sigma(A_1), \ldots, \sigma(A_m)\}$.

Given a CQ q of arity n and a database instance $\mathcal{C}$, we denote as $q^{\mathcal{C}}$ the evaluation of q over $\mathcal{C}$, i.e., the set of n-tuples $\bar{t}$ of constants of Γ such that there exists a substitution that sends the atoms of q to facts of $\mathcal{C}$ and the head to $q(\bar{t})$. Moreover, given a UCQ Q, we define the evaluation of Q over $\mathcal{C}$ as $Q^{\mathcal{C}} = \bigcup_{q \in Q} q^{\mathcal{C}}$

Now we come to the semantics of a data integration system $\mathcal{I} = \langle \mathcal{G}, \mathcal{S}, \mathcal{M} \rangle$. Such a semantics is defined by first considering a *source database* for $\mathcal{I}$, i.e., a database $\mathcal{D}$ for the source schema $\mathcal{S}$. We call *global database* for $\mathcal{I}$ any database for $\mathcal{G}$. Given a source database $\mathcal{D}$ for $\mathcal{I} = \langle \mathcal{G}, \mathcal{S}, \mathcal{M} \rangle$, the semantics $sem(\mathcal{I}, \mathcal{D})$ of $\mathcal{I}$ w.r.t. $\mathcal{D}$ is the set of global databases $\mathcal{B}$ for $\mathcal{I}$ such that:

1. $\mathcal{B}$ satisfies the ICs Σ_T and Σ_F (TGDs and FDs) in $\mathcal{G}$. In particular:
   - $\mathcal{B}$ satisfies a TGD $\chi(\boldsymbol{X}, \boldsymbol{Y}) \to \psi(\boldsymbol{X}, \boldsymbol{Z})$ when, if there exists a substitution σ that sends $\chi(\boldsymbol{X}, \boldsymbol{Y})$ to a set of facts of $\mathcal{B}$, then there exists another substitution σ' that sends $\psi(\boldsymbol{X}, \boldsymbol{Z})$ to $\sigma(\chi(\boldsymbol{X}, \boldsymbol{Y}))$ and those of $\chi(\boldsymbol{X}, \boldsymbol{Y})$ to sets of facts of $\mathcal{B}$. In other words, σ' is an extension of σ that sends the atoms of $\psi(\boldsymbol{X}, \boldsymbol{Z})$ to sets of facts of $\mathcal{B}$.
   - $\mathcal{B}$ satisfies a FD $R : \boldsymbol{A} \to B$ if there are no two tuples $t_1, t_2 \in R^{\mathcal{B}}$ such that $t_1[\boldsymbol{A}] = t_2[\boldsymbol{A}]$ and $t_1[B] \neq t_2[B]$.
2. $\mathcal{B}$ satisfies $\mathcal{M}$ w.r.t. $\mathcal{D}$. In particular, $\mathcal{B}$ satisfies a GLAV mapping $\mathcal{M}$ w.r.t. $\mathcal{D}$ if for each mapping formula $\varphi_{\mathcal{S}}(\boldsymbol{X}, \boldsymbol{Y}) \to \varphi_{\mathcal{G}}(\boldsymbol{X}, \boldsymbol{Z})$ we have that, if there exists a substitution σ that sends $\varphi_{\mathcal{S}}(\boldsymbol{X}, \boldsymbol{Y})$ to a set of facts of $\mathcal{D}$, then there exists an extension σ' of σ that sends $\varphi_{\mathcal{G}}(\boldsymbol{X}, \boldsymbol{Z})$ to a set of facts of $\mathcal{B}$. Note that the above definition amounts to consider the mapping as *sound* but not necessarily complete; intuitively, for each mapping formula, the data retrievable at the sources by means of the conjunctive query in the left-hand side are a *subset* of the global data that satisfy the conjunctive query on the right-hand side.

We now give the semantics of queries. Formally, given a source database $\mathcal{D}$ for $\mathcal{I}$ we call *certain answers* to a query q of arity n w.r.t. $\mathcal{I}$ and $\mathcal{D}$, the set

$$cert(Q, \mathcal{I}, \mathcal{D}) = \{\bar{t} \mid \bar{t} \in Q^{\mathcal{B}} \text{ for each } \mathcal{B} \in sem(\mathcal{I}, \mathcal{D})\}$$

or, equivalently, $cert(Q, \mathcal{I}, \mathcal{D}) = \bigcap_{\mathcal{B} \in sem(\mathcal{I}, \mathcal{D})} Q^{\mathcal{B}}$.

3   Query Rewriting Under Tuple-Generating Dependencies Alone

In this section we present a technique for query answering based on query rewriting, in the case of a GLAV data integration system where only TGDs are expressed over the global schema. We show that such technique, first presented in [3], is applicable to a more general class of constraints, so that it can take into account the GLAV mapping together with the dependencies on the global schema.

We first introduce the concept of *retrieved global database (RGD)*. Given a source database $\mathcal{D}$ for a data integration system $\langle \mathcal{G}, \mathcal{S}, \mathcal{M} \rangle$, the RGD is the "minimum" global database that satisfies the mapping. Intuitively, the RGD is obtained by "filtering" the data from the sources through the mapping, thus populating the global schema.

Definition 1 ([3]). *Let* $\mathcal{I} = \langle \mathcal{G}, \mathcal{S}, \mathcal{M} \rangle$ *be a GLAV data integration system, and* $\mathcal{D}$ *a source database for* $\mathcal{I}$*. The* retrieved global database $ret(\mathcal{I}, \mathcal{D})$ *is defined constructively as follows. For every mapping assertion* $\varphi_{\mathcal{S}}(\boldsymbol{X}, \boldsymbol{Y}) \rightarrow \varphi_{\mathcal{G}}(\boldsymbol{X}, \boldsymbol{Z})$*, and for each set H of facts of $\mathcal{D}$ such that there exists a substitution σ that sends the atoms of $\varphi_{\mathcal{S}}(\boldsymbol{X}, \boldsymbol{Y})$ to H: (i) we first define a substitution σ' such that* $\sigma'(X_i) = \sigma(X_i)$ *for each X_i in $\boldsymbol{X}$, and $\sigma'(Z_j) = z_j$ for each Z_j in $\boldsymbol{Z}$, where z_j is a fresh constant, not introduced before and not appearing in $\mathcal{D}$; (ii) we add to* $ret(\mathcal{I}, \mathcal{D})$ *the set of facts that are in* $\sigma'(\varphi_{\mathcal{G}}(\boldsymbol{X}, \boldsymbol{Z}))$*.*

Note that, given a a data integration system and a source database $\mathcal{D}$, the RGD is unique, since it is constructed by evaluating the left-hand side of every mapping assertion on $\mathcal{D}$, and by adding suitable tuples according to the right-hand side of the mapping assertion, regardless of the already added tuples and of the other mapping assertions. However, differently from the case of GAV mappings, the RGD is not strictly minimal, since in some cases it is possible to have redundant tuples that can be eliminated while preserving all the properties of the RGD. Minimisation of the RGD is not a significant issue, therefore we will not consider it in the following.

When no constraints are expressed over the global schema, the RGD is a representative of all global databases that satisfy the mapping (and therefore of all databases in $sem(\mathcal{I}, \mathcal{D})$): in fact in this case it can be proved that, for every query Q posed over the global schema, $Q^{ret(\mathcal{I}, \mathcal{D})} = cert(Q, \mathcal{I}, \mathcal{D})$.

Now we come to integrity constraints. Given a data integration system $\mathcal{I} = \langle \mathcal{G}, \mathcal{S}, \mathcal{M} \rangle$ and a source database $\mathcal{D}$, since sources are autonomous and in general do not know each other, the retrieved global database $ret(\mathcal{I}, \mathcal{D})$ does not satisfy the integrity constraints (TGDs in this case) on the global schema. In this case we may think of *repairing* the RGD so as to make it satisfy Σ_T; intuitively, the adoption of the *sound* semantics for the mapping $\mathcal{M}$ allows us to repair the violations of TGDs by adding suitable tuples to the RGD. This is done by building the *chase* [4, 10, 3] of $ret(\mathcal{I}, \mathcal{D})$, a database that we denote with $chase_{\Sigma_T}(ret(\mathcal{I}, \mathcal{D}))$, and that is built by repeatedly applying, as long as it is applicable, the *TGD chase rule*.

TGD CHASE RULE [3]. Consider a database $\mathcal{B}$ for a schema Ψ, and a TGD θ of the form $\chi(\boldsymbol{X}, \boldsymbol{Y}) \rightarrow \psi(\boldsymbol{X}, \boldsymbol{Z})$. The TGD θ is *applicable* to $\mathcal{B}$ if there is a substitution σ that sends the atoms of $\chi(\boldsymbol{X}, \boldsymbol{Y})$ to tuples of $\mathcal{B}$, and there does not exist a substitution $\bar{\sigma}$ that sends the atoms of $\chi(\boldsymbol{X}, \boldsymbol{Y})$ to $\sigma(\chi(\boldsymbol{X}, \boldsymbol{Y}))$, and the atoms of $\psi(\boldsymbol{X}, \boldsymbol{Z})$ to tuples of $\mathcal{B}$. In this case: *(i)* we define a substitution σ' such that $\sigma'(X_i) = \sigma(X_i)$ for each X_i in $\boldsymbol{X}$, and $\sigma'(Z_j) = z_j$ for each Z_j in $\boldsymbol{Z}$, where z_j is a fresh constant of Γ, not already introduced in the construction and not appearing in $\mathcal{B}$; *(ii)* we add to $\mathcal{B}$ the facts of $\sigma'(\varphi_{\mathcal{G}}(\boldsymbol{X}, \boldsymbol{Z}))$ that are not already in $\mathcal{B}$.

Note that in the case of cyclic TGDs, the chase may be infinite.

Example 3. Consider Example 2, and let $\mathcal{B}$ be a RGD constituted by a single fact $R_1(a, b)$. Let us construct $chase_{\Sigma_T}(\mathcal{B})$: at the first step we add the facts $R_1(b, z_1), R_2(b, a)$; at the second step the facts $R_1(z_1, z_2), R_2(z_1, b)$, and so on; note that in this case the construction process is infinite.   ∎

In [3] it is proved that the chase of the RGD, constructed according to the TGDs, is a representative of all databases in $sem(\mathcal{I}, \mathcal{D})$: in particular, for every global query Q we have that $Q^{chase_{\Sigma_T}(ret(\mathcal{I}, \mathcal{D}))} = cert(Q, \mathcal{I}, \mathcal{D})$. Unfortunately the chase of the RGD may be of infinite size, and therefore building it is not only impractical, but sometimes even impossible. In [3], along the lines of [6], the problem is solved in an intensional fashion: query answering is done by query rewriting, i.e., the global query Q is reformulated into another query Q_R that, evaluated over the RGD, returns the certain answers to Q. The function that reformulates Q is denoted as TGDrewrite, and takes as input $\mathcal{G}$, the set of TGDs Σ_T and Q. Formally, we have that

$$\mathsf{TGDrewrite}(\mathcal{G}, \Sigma_T, Q)^{ret(\mathcal{I}, \mathcal{D})} = Q^{chase_{\Sigma_T}(ret(\mathcal{I}, \mathcal{D}))} = cert(Q, \mathcal{I}, \mathcal{D})$$

Such technique avoids the construction of the RGD. The technique is applicable for a restricted class of TGDs, namely the *weakly-joined TGDs (WJTGDs)*; in fact, it is known that query answering under general TGDs is undecidable [17]. WJTGDs are defined as follows.

Definition 2 ([3]). *A TGD of the form* $\chi(\boldsymbol{X}, \boldsymbol{Y}) \rightarrow \psi(\boldsymbol{X}, \boldsymbol{Z})$ *is a weakly-joined TGD (WJTGD) if each* $Y_i \in \boldsymbol{Y}$ *appears at most once in it.*

We give a description of how the algorithm TGDrewrite works. The idea is that the algorithm repeatedly executes a basic rewriting step (together with a minimisation step that we will not see in detail), until there are no more CQs to be added to the rewritten query. In the basic rewriting step, TGDrewrite verifies (besides some other conditions) whether there is a substitution σ that sends a subset of the atoms of the right-hand side of some TGD θ to a subset G of the atoms of the body of some CQ q in Q. If this happens, a new CQ is added to Q, obtained by replacing in q the set of atoms G with the left-hand side of θ, where substitution σ has been applied.

Example 4. Consider Example 2 and a CQ $q(X_1) \leftarrow R_1(X_1, X_2), R_2(X_1, X_3)$, represented as $q(X_1) \leftarrow R_1(X_1, \star), R_2(X_1, \star)$, where (similarly to the Logic Programming notation, where the symbol "_" is used) we indicate with $\star$ the variables appearing only once in the query. The WJTGD θ is applicable to $G = \{R_1(X_1, \star), R_2(X_1, \star)\}$, because the substitution $\sigma = \{X \rightarrow X_3, Y \rightarrow$

$X_1, W \rightarrow X_2\}$ sends the right-hand side of θ to G. Therefore, we apply the basic rewriting step by replacing G with the left-hand side of θ and by applying σ to the obtained query. The result is the CQ $q(X_1) \leftarrow R_1(X_3, X_1)$, which we represent as $q(X_1) \leftarrow R_1(\star, X_1)$.

Suppose there is another WJTGD θ_1 on $\mathcal{G}$, of the form $R_2(Y, W) \rightarrow R_1(X, Y)$. Though there is a substitution sending the right-hand side of θ to $G_1 = \{R_1(X_1, X_2)\}$, the basic rewriting step cannot be executed because the variable X_1 would "disappear", and this is not allowed since X_1 appears outside G_1 (in particular, both in the $head(q)$ and in another atom of $body(q)$).   ∎

In [3] the mapping $\mathcal{M}$ is taken into account in a separate step, by first transforming the GLAV system into a GAV system; query answering in GAV systems is then done by a traditional rewriting technique called *unfolding* [18]. However, the form of the GLAV mapping assertions, similar to TGDs, suggests that the algorithm TGDrewrite can be used for the mapping as well.

Now we introduce a more general class of constraints that will allow us to deal with the mapping assertions together with the constraints on the global schema. First, we consider the global schema $\mathcal{G}$ and the source schema $\mathcal{S}$ as a single database schema, on which are expressed the TGDs in Σ_T, plus the assertions in $\mathcal{M}$, that now we can see as TGDs on $\mathcal{G} \cup \mathcal{S}$, and that we denote with $\Sigma_{\mathcal{M}}$. The TGDs in $\Sigma_{\mathcal{M}}$ are in general not WJTGDs, but the following results, extending those of [3], allows us to deal with a more general class of constraints. We give some preliminary definitions.

Definition 3. *Given a set Σ_T of TGDs expressed over a global schema $\mathcal{G}$, the TGD-graph G_{Σ_T} associated to it is defined as follows:*

- *the set of nodes is the set of relation symbols in $\mathcal{G}$;*
- *an arc (R_1, R_2) exists if R_1 and R_2 appear respectively in the left-hand and right-hand side of some TGD in Σ_T.*

Definition 4. *Given a set Σ_T of TGDs expressed over a global schema $\mathcal{G}$, and the corresponding TGD-graph G_{Σ_T}, a TGD θ is said to be* cycle-harmless *w.r.t. Σ_T if at least one of the following conditions holds:*

1. *for any two relation symbols R_1, R_2 appearing in the body and in the head of θ respectively, the arc (R_1, R_2) is not part of any cycle in G_{Σ_T}, or*
2. *θ is a WJTGD.*

Now we come to the results.

Lemma 1. *Let B be a relational database for a schema $\mathcal{R}$, and Σ_T a set of cycle-harmless TGDs expressed over $\mathcal{R}$. Then for every query Q on $\mathcal{R}$, expressed in UCQs, we have that* $\mathsf{TGDrewrite}(\mathcal{R}, \Sigma_T, Q)^B = Q^{chase_{\Sigma_T}(B)}$.

Proof (sketch). We want to prove that, being n the arity of Q, for any n-tuple t of constants of Γ, we have

$$t \in \mathsf{TGDrewrite}(\mathcal{R}, \Sigma_T, Q)^B \text{ iff } t \in Q^{chase_{\Sigma_T}(B)}$$

"⇐"The proof is by induction on the number of applications of the TGD chase rule. By hypothesis, there is a CQ q in Q such that there exists a query homomorphism ψ (see [16]) that sends the body of q to tuples of $chase_{\Sigma_T}(\mathcal{B})$ and the head of q to t. At the base step, ψ sends the body of q to tuples of $\mathcal{B}$, and since q is part of TGDrewrite($\mathcal{R}, \Sigma_T, Q$), the thesis follows. As for the inductive step, suppose that the result holds when ψ sends the body of q to tuples of the chase (that we briefly denote as $\psi(q)$) that are generated after k applications of the chase rule. It is possible to show that, denoting by H the set of tuples from which $\psi(q)$ is generated (and that are therefore generated from $\mathcal{B}$ with $k-1$ applications of the chase rule), there exists a query homomorphism ψ_1 that sends the body of q_1 to tuples in H and the head of q_1 to t, where q_1 is obtained from q by application of the basic rewriting step of TGDrewrite.

"⇒"The proof is analogous to the previous one, by induction on the number of applications of the basic rewriting rule of TGDrewrite.

Lemma 2. *Let $\mathcal{I} = \langle \mathcal{G}, \mathcal{S}, \mathcal{M} \rangle$ be a data integration system; let Σ_T be a set of TGDs expressed over $\mathcal{G}$. If for every TGD θ in Σ_T it holds that θ is a cycle-harmless TGD w.r.t. Σ_T, then for every source database $\mathcal{D}$ and for every global query Q we have*

$$Q^{chase_{\Sigma_T}(ret(\mathcal{I},\mathcal{D}))} = cert(Q, \mathcal{I}, \mathcal{D})$$

Proof (sketch). Analogously to what is done in [4] for the chase in the presence of inclusion dependencies, it is possible to prove that, for every global database $\mathcal{B}$ that is in $sem(\mathcal{I}, \mathcal{D})$, there exists a homomorphism λ that sends tuples of $chase_{\Sigma_T}(ret(\mathcal{I}, \mathcal{D}))$ to those of $\mathcal{B}$.

We now prove that, being n the arity of Q, for every n-tuple of constants of Γ,

$$t \in Q^{chase_{\Sigma_T}(ret(\mathcal{I},\mathcal{D}))} \text{ iff } t \in cert(Q, \mathcal{I}, \mathcal{D})$$

"⇐"If $t \notin Q^{chase_{\Sigma_T}(ret(\mathcal{I},\mathcal{D}))}$, since the chase is a database in $sem(\mathcal{I}, \mathcal{D})$ because it satisfies both the mapping and the ICs, we immediately deduce that $t \in cert(Q, \mathcal{I}, \mathcal{D})$.

"⇒"By hypothesis, there exists a query homomorphism μ that sends the body of some CQ q in Q to tuples of $chase_{\Sigma_T}(ret(\mathcal{I}, \mathcal{D}))$. Recalling the existence of the homomorphism λ for any global database $\mathcal{B}$ in $sem(\mathcal{I}, \mathcal{D})$, we consider the composition $\mu \circ \lambda$. The existence of such homomorphism for any $\mathcal{B}$ in $sem(\mathcal{I}, \mathcal{D})$ guarantees that $t \in Q^{\mathcal{B}}$ for every $\mathcal{B} \in sem(\mathcal{I}, \mathcal{D})$, and therefore $t \in cert(Q, \mathcal{I}, \mathcal{D})$. ∎

Theorem 1. *Let $\mathcal{I} = \langle \mathcal{G}, \mathcal{S}, \mathcal{M} \rangle$ be a data integration system; let Σ_T be a set of TGDs expressed over $\mathcal{G}$. If for every TGD θ in Σ_T it holds that θ is a cycle-harmless TGD w.r.t. Σ_T, then for every source database $\mathcal{D}$ and for every global query Q we have*

$$\text{TGDrewrite}(\mathcal{G}, \Sigma_T, Q)^{ret(\mathcal{I},\mathcal{D})} = cert(Q, \mathcal{I}, \mathcal{D})$$

Proof. By Lemma 2 we have TGDrewrite($\mathcal{G}, \Sigma_T, Q$)$^{ret(\mathcal{I},\mathcal{D})} = Q^{chase_{\Sigma_T}(ret(\mathcal{I},\mathcal{D}))}$. The thesis follows immediately from Lemma 2. ∎

The following theorem, directly derived from Theorem 1, allows us to take the mapping into account in a single step with the algorithm TGDrewrite.

Theorem 2. *Let $\mathcal{I} = \langle \mathcal{G}, \mathcal{S}, \mathcal{M} \rangle$ be a data integration system; let Σ_T be a set of TGDs expressed over $\mathcal{G}$ and $\Sigma_{\mathcal{M}}$ the TGDs that constitute $\mathcal{M}$. If for every TGD θ in Σ_T it holds that θ is cycle-harmless w.r.t. Σ_T, then for every source database $\mathcal{D}$ and for every global query Q we have*

$$\mathsf{TGDrewrite}(\mathcal{G}, \Sigma_T \cup \Sigma_{\mathcal{M}}, Q)^{\mathcal{D}} = cert(Q, \mathcal{I}, \mathcal{D})$$

Proof. The proof is done by observing that $chase_{\Sigma_{\mathcal{M}}}(\mathcal{D}) = ret(\mathcal{I}, \mathcal{D})$, and that $chase_{\Sigma_T}(ret(\mathcal{I}, \mathcal{D})) = chase_{\Sigma_T \cup \Sigma_{\mathcal{M}}}(\mathcal{D})$. Note that all TGDs in $\Sigma_{\mathcal{M}}$ are cycle-harmless by construction. By Lemma 1 we have

$$\mathsf{TGDrewrite}(\mathcal{G}, \Sigma_T \cup \Sigma_{\mathcal{M}}, Q)^{\mathcal{D}} = Q^{chase_{\Sigma_T \cup \Sigma_{\mathcal{M}}}(\mathcal{D})}$$

and therefore

$$\mathsf{TGDrewrite}(\mathcal{G}, \Sigma_T \cup \Sigma_{\mathcal{M}}, Q)^{\mathcal{D}} = Q^{chase_{\Sigma_T}(chase_{\Sigma_{\mathcal{M}}}(\mathcal{D}))} = Q^{chase_{\Sigma_T}(ret(\mathcal{I}, \mathcal{D}))}$$

The thesis follows immediately from Lemma 2. ∎

Note that we have in some way abused the notation in the statement of the previous theorem; in fact we are evaluating TGDrewrite, which in general is formulated over $\mathcal{G} \cup \mathcal{S}$, over a source database $\mathcal{D}$ that is a database for $\mathcal{S}$. However, we can consider $\mathcal{D}$ as a database for $\mathcal{G} \cup \mathcal{S}$ where for each $g \in \mathcal{G}$ we have $g^{\mathcal{D}} = \emptyset$. Indeed, this observation leads us to the obvious conclusion that, once $\mathsf{TGDrewrite}(\mathcal{G}, \Sigma_T \cup \Sigma_{\mathcal{M}}, Q)$ is computed, in its evaluation over $\mathcal{D}$ we can omit to consider all the CQs in which at least one atom with a relation symbol of $\mathcal{G}$ appears. This can save computation time in the query rewriting phase.

Example 5. Recall Example 1. Suppose the source database $\mathcal{D}$ contains a single fact hasjob($anne, maths$) ←. Consider the global query

$$Q(X) \leftarrow \mathsf{employed}(X, Y) \wedge \mathsf{runsProject}(Y, Z)$$

asking for persons employed in institutions that run some project. A rewriting step, according to the single TGD expressed on $\mathcal{G}$, will produce the CQ

$$Q_1(X) \leftarrow \mathsf{work}(X, Z)$$

Applying the mapping assertions as rewriting rules, we obtain the following CQs:

$$Q_2(X) \leftarrow \mathsf{hasjob}(X, W_1)$$
$$Q_3(X) \leftarrow \mathsf{getgrant}(X, W_2) \wedge \mathsf{grantfor}(W_2, Z)$$
$$Q_4(X) \leftarrow \mathsf{teaches}(X, W_3) \wedge \mathsf{infield}(W_3, W_4)$$

The final rewriting is $Q_R = Q \vee Q_1 \vee Q_2 \vee Q_3 \vee Q_4$ (however, Q and Q_1 will not be considered since they contain relation names not appearing in $\mathcal{S}$). The evaluation of the rewriting over the source database $\mathcal{D}$ returns the answer $Q_R^{\mathcal{D}} = \{(anne)\}$. ∎

4 Query Rewriting Under Tuple-Generating Dependencies and Functional Dependencies

In this section we address the problem of query answering in GLAV systems where two sets of TGDs and FDs, that we will denote with Σ_T and Σ_F respectively, are expressed over the global schema. In this case, even if we restrict to TGDs that are either cycle-harmless w.r.t. Σ_T, the problem of query answering is undecidable.

Theorem 3. *Let $\mathcal{I} = \langle \mathcal{G}, \mathcal{S}, \mathcal{M} \rangle$ be a data integration system, where two sets of TGDs and FDs, Σ_T and Σ_F respectively, are expressed over $\mathcal{G}$; let Σ_T be a set of cycle-harmless TGDs w.r.t. Σ_T itself. We have that the problem of query answering is undecidable.*

Proof. The proof is derived from the undecidability result for query answering in the presence of inclusion dependencies and key dependencies [5], which is clearly a particular case of the one considered here. Note that inclusion dependencies are cycle-harmless TGDs, since they cannot have joins in the left-hand side. In turn, the result of [5] is derived from the undecidability result about implication of functional and inclusion dependencies [7]. ∎

Here we consider a slightly restricted class of TGDs and FDs: in particular, similarly to what is done in [5], we consider a class of TGDs that "does not conflict" with the FDs, and for which query answering is decidable. In the following we will make use of the notion of *freezing* a formula; given a conjunction C of atomic formulae, freezing C consists in defining a substitution σ that sends each distinct variable to a distinct constant; the frozen formula $\sigma(C)$ is a set of facts.

Definition 5. *Given a set of FDs Σ_F over a relational schema $\mathcal{R}$, a TGD θ of the form*

$$\chi(\boldsymbol{X}, \boldsymbol{Y}) \rightarrow \psi(\boldsymbol{X}, \boldsymbol{Z})$$

is a non-functional-conflicting TGD (NFCTGD) *w.r.t. Σ_F if the following conditions hold:*

1. *the database constructed by "freezing" the variables of $\psi(\boldsymbol{X}, \boldsymbol{Z})$ and considering the the obtained facts satisfies Σ_F;*
2. *for each atom $R(\boldsymbol{X}, \boldsymbol{Z})$ in ψ, and for every FD of the form $R : \boldsymbol{A} \rightarrow B$ in Σ_F defined on R, the symbols that are either constants or are in $\boldsymbol{X}$ (we recall that the symbols in $\boldsymbol{X}$ appear both sides of the TGD) are placed in a set of attributes of R that is not a superset of $\boldsymbol{A}$.*

Example 6. Consider a relational schema $\mathcal{R} = \{R_1/3, R_2/1, R_3/2\}$, let Σ_F a set of FDs over $\mathcal{R}$, constituted by a single FD ϕ of the form $R_1 : 1 \rightarrow 2$ (we have indicated the attributes of R_1 with integer numbers). The TGD $\theta : R_3(X,Y) \rightarrow R_1(X,Y,Z), R_2(Y)$ is not a NFCTGD w.r.t. Σ_F because in the first two attributes of the atom $R_1(X,Y,Z)$ are covering a superset of the left-hand-side of ϕ, and X and Y appear in the left-hand side of θ. Moreover, the TGD $\theta_1 : R_3(Z, Y) \rightarrow R_1(X, Y, Z), R_1(X, b, W)$ (where b is a constant) is not a NFCTGD w.r.t. Σ_F because if we freeze its right-hand side we obtain two facts $R_1(c_X, c_Y, c_Z) \leftarrow$ and $R_1(c_X, b, c_W) \leftarrow$ that violate ϕ.

Non-functional-conflicting TGDs are a generalisation of *non-key-conflicting inclusion dependencies (NKCIDs)* [5]; similarly to NKCIDs, the NFCTGDs enjoy the following property.

Proposition 1. *Consider a relational database $\mathcal{B}$ on which a set Σ_F of FDs and a set Σ_T of NFCTGDs w.r.t. Σ_F are defined. If $\mathcal{B} \models \Sigma_F$ then $chase_{\Sigma_T}(\mathcal{B}) \models \Sigma_F$.*

Proof. The proof is by induction on the structure of $chase_{\Sigma_T}(\mathcal{B})$. At the base step, $\mathcal{B}$ satisfies Σ_F, that is true by hypothesis. As for the inductive step, consider the addition of a set of facts $f_1, \ldots, f_n$, due to the application of the TGD chase rule. By Condition 1 of Definition 5, it is straightforward to see that the facts $f_1, \ldots, f_n$ are such that no two facts f_i, f_j ($1 \leq i, j \leq n$) that violate a FD in Σ_F. Moreover, none of the facts in $f_1, \ldots, f_n$ will violate a FD ϕ in Σ_F together with another fact f_1 already present in the segment of $chase_{\Sigma_T}(\mathcal{B})$ until the insertion of $f_1, \ldots, f_n$. In fact, let f and f_1 be of the form $R(c_1, \ldots, c_m) \leftarrow$ and $R(d_1, \ldots, d_m) \leftarrow$ respectively; by Condition 2 of Definition 5, for any FD ϕ in Σ_F of the form $R : \mathbf{A} \rightarrow B$, f and f_1 will never have the same values in the attributes of $\mathbf{A}$. This ends the proof of the claim.

Intuitively, from the previous property follows that, if a global database satisfies the set Σ_F FDs, and the TGDs are all non-functional-conflicting, we can ignore Σ_F w.r.t. to query answering, since the chase is indifferent to the presence of FDs.

At this point, we come to the problem of query answering in a data integration system $\mathcal{I} = \langle \mathcal{G}, \mathcal{S}, \mathcal{M} \rangle$. Recalling Theorem 2 and assuming that both Σ_T and Σ_M contain only NFCTGDs that are also cycle-harmless, we have that the source database $\mathcal{D}$ satisfies Σ_F by construction, since the FDs are defined only on $\mathcal{G}$. Therefore, given a global query Q, we may think of applying the algorithm TGDrewrite to Q under the set of TGDs $\Sigma_T \cup \Sigma_M$, thus solving immediately the problem of query answering by means of rewriting. Unfortunately, while assuming that the TGDs in Σ_T are NFCTGDs is reasonable in practical cases, assuming the same for the dependencies in Σ_M is not. Nevertheless, the TGDs in Σ_M are the only ones having source relations appearing in them (in the left-hand side); such property ensures that we are still in luck when they are not non-functional conflicting. In fact, the problem of query answering is still decidable when TGDs in Σ_T are cycle-harmless and NFCTGDs, and those in Σ_M are cycle-harmless (this is by construction) but in general not non-functional-conflicting. The query answering technique, in this case, requires the construction of the RGD; in particular the algorithm for query answering, given a data integration system $\mathcal{I} = \langle \mathcal{G}, \mathcal{S}, \mathcal{M} \rangle$, a source database $\mathcal{D}$ and a global query Q, consists of the following steps:

1. We build the RGD $ret(\mathcal{I}, \mathcal{D})$.
2. We check whether $ret(\mathcal{I}, \mathcal{D}) \models \Sigma_F$; if $ret(\mathcal{I}, \mathcal{D}) \not\models \Sigma_F$ we are done: in this case there is no global database satisfying both the constraints and the mapping, so $sem(\mathcal{I}, \mathcal{D}) = \emptyset$ (see e.g. [18]); therefore, query answering is trivial, since every tuple of the same arity of Q is in $cert(Q, \mathcal{I}, \mathcal{D})$. If, on the contrary, $ret(\mathcal{I}, \mathcal{D}) \models \Sigma_F$, we proceed with the following steps.
3. We calculate $\mathsf{TGDrewrite}(\mathcal{G}, \Sigma_T, Q)$.
4. We evaluate $\mathsf{TGDrewrite}(\mathcal{G}, \Sigma_T, Q)$ over $ret(\mathcal{I}, \mathcal{D})$: the result is $cert(Q, \mathcal{I}, \mathcal{D})$.

In the presence of FDs on the global schema, the construction of the retrieved global database cannot be done independently of the FDs; in fact, some of the violations of the FDs that occur during the construction of the RGD are not "real" violations; instead, they lead to the inference of equalities among newly introduced constants and constants already present in the part of the RGD constructed in previous steps. The following example illustrates this issue.

Example 7. Consider again Example 1, and suppose that the following FD is expressed over $\mathcal{G}$:

$$\mathsf{work} : 1 \to 2$$

Such FD imposes that a person can work at most on one project. Now, suppose to have a source database $\mathcal{D}$ with the following facts:

$$\begin{aligned}
&\mathsf{hasjob}(anne, maths) \leftarrow \\
&\mathsf{teaches}(anne, databases) \leftarrow \\
&\mathsf{infield}(databases, compScience) \leftarrow
\end{aligned}$$

According to $\mathcal{M}$, The RGD will contain the following facts:

$$\begin{aligned}
&\mathsf{work}(anne, p_1) \leftarrow \\
&\mathsf{area}(p_1, maths) \leftarrow \\
&\mathsf{work}(anne, p_2) \leftarrow \\
&\mathsf{area}(p_2, compScience) \leftarrow
\end{aligned}$$

where p_1 and p_2 are fresh constants introduced in the construction. Note that the facts $\mathsf{work}(anne, p_1) \leftarrow$ and $\mathsf{work}(anne, p_2) \leftarrow$ violate the above FD. In this case, however, the violation is due to the two fresh constants p_1 and p_2: therefore, instead of concluding that $sem(\mathcal{I}, \mathcal{D}) = \emptyset$, we instead infer $p_1 = p_2$. Now suppose that also the following facts are in $\mathcal{D}$:

$$\begin{aligned}
&\mathsf{getgrant}(anne, eu123) \leftarrow \\
&\mathsf{grantfor}(eu123, venus) \leftarrow
\end{aligned}$$

Now the RGD will have the additional fact

$$\mathsf{work}(anne, venus) \leftarrow$$

asserting that *anne* works on project *venus*; here we have another violation, but again we do not conclude that $sem(\mathcal{I}, \mathcal{D}) = \emptyset$: instead, the new facts make us infer that the project on which Anne is working is *venus*. Therefore, we have $p_1 = p_2 = venus$. All occurrencies of p_1 and p_2 in the part of $ret(\mathcal{I}, \mathcal{D})$ constructed so far need to be replaced by *venus*. ∎

Now we present a technique for constructing the RGD in the case of GLAV mapping, in the presence of FDs on the global schema.

Definition 6. *Let $\mathcal{I} = \langle \mathcal{G}, \mathcal{S}, \mathcal{M} \rangle$ be a GLAV data integration system, where a set Σ_F of FDs is defined on $\mathcal{G}$, and $\mathcal{D}$ a source database for $\mathcal{I}$. The retrieved global database $ret(\mathcal{I}, \mathcal{D})$ is defined constructively as follows. Consider a mapping assertion $\varphi_S(\boldsymbol{X}, \boldsymbol{Y}) \to \varphi_{\mathcal{G}}(\boldsymbol{X}, \boldsymbol{Z})$. For each set H of facts of $\mathcal{D}$ such that there exists a substitution σ that sends the atoms of $\varphi_S(\boldsymbol{X}, \boldsymbol{Y})$ to H: (i) we first define a substitution σ' such that $\sigma'(X_i) = \sigma(X_i)$ for each X_i in $\boldsymbol{X}$, and $\sigma'(Z_j) = z_j$ for each Z_j in $\boldsymbol{Z}$, where z_j is a fresh constant, not introduced before and not appearing in $\mathcal{D}$; (ii) we add to $ret(\mathcal{I}, \mathcal{D})$ the set of facts that are in $\sigma'(\varphi_{\mathcal{G}}(\boldsymbol{X}, \boldsymbol{Z}))$. Now, suppose that one of the added facts, say $R(t) \leftarrow$, violates a FD ϕ because of the presence of another fact $R(t_0) \leftarrow$ in the part of the RGD that has been constructed in the previous steps (t and t_0 are tuples of constants). Formally, being ϕ of the form*

$$R : \boldsymbol{A} \to B$$

we have $t[\boldsymbol{A}] = t_0[\boldsymbol{A}]$ and $t[B] \neq t_0[B]$. Let $t[B] = c$ and $t_0[B] = c_0$; there are different cases, that we enumerate as follows:

1. *c is a fresh constant, not appearing in $\mathcal{D}$: in this case we substitute c with c_0 (which can be either a fresh constant or a constant of $\mathcal{D}$) and proceed;*
2. *c is a constant of $\mathcal{D}$ and c_0 is a fresh constant: in this case we replace c_0 with c in all the part of the RGD that has been constructed in the previous steps and proceed.*
3. *c and c_0 are both constants appearing in $\mathcal{D}$: in this case we have sem$(\mathcal{I}, \mathcal{D}) = \emptyset$ and we stop the construction.*

Note that the construction of the RGD in this case can be done in time polynomial in the size of the source database $\mathcal{D}$: in fact, though the replacement can involve all the data in the RGD retrieved at a certain point, we have that the replacement of case 2 can be performed at most once on each constant.

The following theorem states the correctness and completeness of the above technique.

Theorem 4. *Let $\mathcal{I} = \langle \mathcal{G}, \mathcal{S}, \mathcal{M} \rangle$ be a data integration system; let Σ_T and Σ_F two sets of TGDs and FDs defined on $\mathcal{G}$ respectively, where all TGDs in Σ_T are cycle-harmless w.r.t. Σ_T and NFCTFDs w.r.t. Σ_F. If $ret(\mathcal{I}, \mathcal{D}) \models \Sigma_F$, then we have that $\mathsf{TGDrewrite}(\mathcal{G}, \Sigma_T, Q)^{ret(\mathcal{I}, \mathcal{D})} = cert(Q, \mathcal{I}, \mathcal{D})$.*

Proof (sketch). The result follows straightforwardly from Proposition 1; since $ret(\mathcal{I}, \mathcal{D}) \models \Sigma_F$, we can proceed by applying Theorem 1 as if $\Sigma_F = \emptyset$.   ∎'

5   Discussion

In this paper we have addressed the problem of query answering in GLAV data integration systems, in the presence of tuple-generating dependencies and functional dependencies.

Several works in the literature address the problem of query answering under integrity constraints, both in a single database context [5, 2, 12] and in data integration [9, 20, 13, 17, 10, 6, 4]. In particular, [17] presents a technique, well supported by experimental results and theoretical foundations, for query rewriting under *conjunctive inclusion dependencies (CINDs)*; CINDs are analogous to TGDs, but in [17] a syntactic restriction on CINDs imposes that CINDs are *acyclic*, so that the problem of having a chase of infinite size (and therefore the problem of the termination of the rewriting algorithm) is not relevant. Another interesting paper about repair of database dependencies is [10]; this paper addresses the problem of integrity constraints in *data exchange*, so in this case data are to be materialised in a target schema, as well as their chase, and not accessed on-the-fly as in our virtual data integration approach. Due to the need of materialising the target schema, the class of ICs considered, namely the *weakly-acyclic* TGDs together with *equality-generating dependencies*, though certainly quite general, is such that the chase is always finite. Therefore, such class of constraints is not comparable with the one considered in our paper.

In this paper we have first addressed the problem of query answering in the presence of TGDs alone; we have recalled the algorithm TGDrewrite, introduced in [3], showing that it can be applied to a more general class of TGDs, namely the *cycle-harmless TGDs*. The result about the introduced class of TGDs allowed us to use TGDrewrite for rewriting global queries according not only to the TGDs, but also according to the mapping, that can be seen as a set of TGDs over a unified schema including both the global schema and the source schema. The rewriting algorithm can be used, of course, also in particular cases, e.g., when there are no constraints; in such a case, when the mapping is LAV instead of GLAV, our technique is similar to the algorithm MiniCon [21], which incorporates effective optimisation techniques not present in TGDrewrite; however, TGDrewrite is more general, being able to deal with GLAV mappings.

Then, we have introduced functional dependencies together with TGDs, defining a class of ICs for which the query answering problem is decidable, and providing a query answering technique based on the algorithm TGDrewrite. In this case the mapping cannot be dealt with at once, together with the ICs on the global schema; instead, the construction of the retrieved global database is required. After that, if the RGD satisfies the FDs, the form of the constraints is such that we can proceed as if there were no FDs.

As for the computational complexity, we focus our attention on the *data complexity*, i.e. the complexity w.r.t. the size of the data residing at the sources. This is the usual way of considering complexity in a database context, since the size of schemata and constraints is usually negligible with respect to the size of the data. In our case, since we solve the problem of query answering in an intensional fashion, the only phases where the data are involved are the evaluation of the reformulated query over the source database, and the construction of the RGD (only in the presence of FDs). Both such operations can be done in time polynomial w.r.t. the size of the data.

Acknowledgements. This work was partially supported by the project MAIS, funded by the Italian Ministry of Education, University and Research. The author wishes to thank Diego Calvanese, Maurizio Lenzerini, Riccardo Rosati and Domenico Lembo for their insightful comments about this material.

References

1. Serge Abiteboul, Richard Hull, and Victor Vianu. *Foundations of Databases.* Addison Wesley Publ. Co., Reading, Massachussetts, 1995.
2. Marcelo Arenas, Leopoldo E. Bertossi, and Jan Chomicki. Consistent query answers in inconsistent databases. In *Proc. of the 18th ACM SIGACT SIGMOD SIGART Symp. on Principles of Database Systems (PODS'99)*, pages 68–79.
3. Andrea Calì. Reasoning in data integration systems: why LAV and GAV are siblings. In *Proc. of the 14th Int. Symp. on Methodologies for Intelligent Systems (ISMIS 2003)*, pages 562–571, 2003.
4. Andrea Calì, Diego Calvanese, Giuseppe De Giacomo, and Maurizio Lenzerini. Data integration under integrity constraints. *Information Systems*, 29:147–163, 2004.
5. Andrea Calì, Domenico Lembo, and Riccardo Rosati. On the decidability and complexity of query answering over inconsistent and incomplete databases. In *Proc. of the 22nd ACM SIGACT SIGMOD SIGART Symp. on Principles of Database Systems (PODS 2003)*, pages 260–271, 2003.
6. Andrea Calì, Domenico Lembo, and Riccardo Rosati. Query rewriting and answering under constraints in data integration systems. In *Proc. of the 18th Int. Joint Conf. on Artificial Intelligence (IJCAI 2003)*, pages 16–21, 2003.
7. Ashok K. Chandra and Moshe Y. Vardi. The implication problem for functional and inclusion dependencies is undecidable. *SIAM J. on Computing*, 14(3):671–677, 1985.
8. Isabel Cruz, Stefan Decker, Jérôme Euzenat, and Deborah McGuinness, editors. *The Emerging Semantic Web — Selected Papers from the First Semantic Web Working Symposium.* IOS Press, 2002.
9. Oliver M. Duschka and Michael R. Genesereth. Answering recursive queries using views. In *Proc. of the 16th ACM SIGACT SIGMOD SIGART Symp. on Principles of Database Systems (PODS'97)*, pages 109–116.
10. Ronald Fagin, Phokion Kolaitis, Renee J. Miller, and Lucian Popa. Data exchange: Semantics and query answering. In *Proc. of the 9th Int. Conf. on Database Theory (ICDT 2003)*, pages 207–224.
11. Marc Friedman, Alon Levy, and Todd Millstein. Navigational plans for data integration. In *Proc. of the 16th Nat. Conf. on Artificial Intelligence (AAAI'99)*, pages 67–73, 1999.
12. Gianluigi Greco, Sergio Greco, and Ester Zumpano. A logic programming approach to the integration, repairing and querying of inconsistent databases. In *Proc. of the 17th Int. Conf. on Logic Programming (ICLP'01)*, volume 2237 of *Lecture Notes in Artificial Intelligence*, pages 348–364. Springer.

13. Jarek Gryz. Query rewriting using views in the presence of functional and inclusion dependencies. *Information Systems*, 24(7):597–612, 1999.
14. Alon Y. Halevy. Answering queries using views: A survey. *Very Large Database J.*, 10(4):270–294, 2001.
15. Jeff Heflin and James Hendler. A portrait of the semantic web in action. *IEEE Intelligent Systems*, 16(2):54–59, 2001.
16. David S. Johnson and Anthony C. Klug. Testing containment of conjunctive queries under functional and inclusion dependencies. *J. of Computer and System Sciences*, 28(1):167–189, 1984.
17. Christoph Koch. Query rewriting with symmetric constraints. In *Proc. of the 2nd Int. Symp. on Foundations of Information and Knowledge Systems (FoIKS 2002)*, volume 2284 of *Lecture Notes in Computer Science*, pages 130–147. Springer, 2002.
18. Maurizio Lenzerini. Data integration: A theoretical perspective. In *Proc. of the 21st ACM SIGACT SIGMOD SIGART Symp. on Principles of Database Systems (PODS 2002)*, pages 233–246, 2002.
19. Maurizio Lenzerini, 2004. Personal communication.
20. Jinxin Lin and Alberto O. Mendelzon. Merging databases under constraints. *Int. J. of Cooperative Information Systems*, 7(1):55–76, 1998.
21. Rachel Pottinger and Alon Y. Levy. A scalable algorithm for answering queries using views. In *Proc. of the 26th Int. Conf. on Very Large Data Bases (VLDB 2000)*, pages 484–495, 2000.

Utilizing Resource Importance for Ranking Semantic Web Query Results

Bhuvan Bamba and Sougata Mukherjea

IBM India Research Lab,
New Delhi, India
{bhubamba, smukherj}@in.ibm.com

Abstract. To realize the vision of the Semantic Web, effective techniques of Information Retrieval need to be developed. Ranking the results of a search is one of the main challenges of an Information Retrieval system. In this paper we present a technique for ranking the results of a Semantic Web query. The ranking is based on various factors including the Semantic Web resource importance. We have modified a World-wide Web link analysis technique that has been effectively used to identify important Web pages to calculate the importance of Semantic Web resources. Our ranking technique has been utilized for ranking the query results of a Biomedical Patent Semantic Web.

1 Introduction

The Semantic Web [1] is a vision of the next generation World-wide Web in which data is described with rich semantics thereby enabling software agents to understand the data and perform complex tasks on behalf of humans. To achieve this vision, researchers have developed languages for specifying the meaning of concepts, relating them with custom ontologies for different domains and reasoning about the concepts. The most well-known languages are Resource Description Format (RDF) [2] and RDF Schema (RDFS) [3] which together provide a unique format for the description and exchange of the semantics of Web content. To realize the full potential of the Semantic Web, effective techniques for information retrieval need to be developed.

Generally, to answer queries linking the properties specified by one or more *RDF* triples, SQL-type declarative query languages are utilized. In a real world Semantic Web, for many queries a large number of results will be retrieved. Since users tend to consider only the first few results, effective techniques for ranking the results are required. In traditional Information Retrieval the ranking is mainly dependent on the number of query keywords that are present in the result documents. On the other hand, for World-wide Web search engines, the ranking is also dependent on the importance of the retrieved Web pages which is determined by the number of pages linking to it and the importance of the linking pages. In the Semantic Web the information space is complex since it contains resources, the relations between them as well as ontologies. Therefore,

C. Bussler et al. (Eds.): SWDB 2004, LNCS 3372, pp. 185–198, 2005.
© Springer-Verlag Berlin Heidelberg 2005

the ranking should be dependent on several factors including the number of triples related to the results as well as the importance of the Semantic Web resources corresponding to the results.

We have developed a technique to determine the importance of the Semantic Web resources based on a WWW link-analysis algorithm to identify important Web pages. In [4] we discuss how the importance score can be used to rank the results of a keyword search in a Semantic Web. However, for RDF queries, the ranking should be dependent not only on the Semantic Web resource importance but other factors also. In this paper we explain our technique for ranking the results of a Semantic Web query. The paper is organized as follows. Section 2 cites related work. Section 3 explains our method for determining Semantic Web resource importance and Section 4 discusses our technique for ranking RDF query results. Finally, section 5 concludes the paper.

1.1   Example Semantic Web

Our technique has been implemented in the **BioPatentMiner** system [4]. The system provides several techniques for querying a Semantic Web of Biomedical patents. In this Semantic Web there are resources for the patents, the inventors and assignees of the patents as well as the biological terms present in the patents. Moreover, there are 4 properties connecting the resources:

- $<patentA$ **refers_to** $patentB>$ (patentA refers to patentB)
- $<inventorC$ **invented** $patentD>$ (inventorC has invented patentD)
- $<assigneeE$ **assigned** $patentF>$ (patentF is assigned to assigneeE)
- $<patentG$ **has_term** $bioTermH>$ (patentG has the biological concept bioTermH)

The property *has_term* links the patents to the biological concepts they refer to. These concepts are derived from the Unified Medical Language System (UMLS) [5]. UMLS is a consolidated repository of medical terms and their relationships, spread across multiple languages and disciplines (chemistry, biology, etc). An essential section of UMLS is a **Semantic Network** which has 135 biomedical semantic classes like *Gene or Genome* and *Amino Acid, Peptide, or Protein*. The semantic classes are linked by a set of 54 semantic relationships (like *prevents*, *causes*). The UMLS biological concepts are associated with one or more semantic classes. For example, the concept *blood cancer* has the semantic class *Neoplastic Process*. We created RDFS classes for all the Semantic Network classes and RDF Properties for all Semantic Network relationships except *isa*. A RDF statement is created to represent each relationship among the classes. The *isa* relationship is represented by *RDFS:subClassOf* relationship if it is between classes and *RDFS:subPropertyOf* relationship if it is between properties. The biological concepts are represented as RDF resources. They are named by their UMLS concept ids and the various names associated with a concept are stored as RDFS labels.

2   Related Work

2.1   Building and Querying the Semantic Web

In recent times tools like Jena [6] have been developed that facilitate the development and representation of Semantic Webs. The development of effective information retrieval techniques for the Semantic Web has become an important research problem. There are a number of proposed techniques for querying RDF data including RQL [7], TRIPLE [8] and RDQL [9]. Most of these query languages use a SQL-like declarative syntax to query a Semantic Web as a set of RDF triples. They also incorporate inference as part of query answering. However, none of these systems propose any strategy to rank the query results.

2.2   Determining WWW Page Importance

In this paper we introduce a technique to determine the importance of resources in a Semantic Web. This has been influenced by the extensive research in recent years to determine the importance of World-wide Web pages. The most well-known technique is *Page Rank* [10] which calculates the importance of Web pages based on the pages that point to them.

Another technique for finding the important pages in a WWW collection has been developed by Kleinberg [11] who defined two types of scores for Web pages which pertain to a certain topic: *authority* and *hub* scores. Documents with high authority scores are authorities on a topic and therefore have many links pointing to them. On the other hand, documents with high hub scores are resource lists - they do not directly contain information about the topic, but rather point to many authoritative sites. Transitively, a document that points to many good authorities is an even better hub, and similarly a document pointed to by many good hubs is an even better authority. Kleinberg's algorithm has been refined in CLEVER [12] and Topic Distillation [13]. Both of these algorithms augment Kleinberg's link analysis with textual analysis. A slightly different approach to find hubs and authorities is SALSA [14]. A good overview of various link analysis techniques to find hubs and authorities and suggestions for improvements are presented in [15].

2.3   Ranking Search Results

Ranking of search result is an important research area in Information Retrieval [16]. Since a WWW search returns a large number of results for most queries, effective ranking of the results is critical for the success of a Web search engine. The popularity of the Google Web search engine is mainly because it has used Page Rank very effectively for ranking. [17] presents a technique to rank keyword search over XML documents using a technique derived from Page Rank. Since RDF queries are different, the previous approaches may not be appropriate for the Semantic Web.

[18] is the only previous research on ranking the results of Semantic Web queries. The system defines two metrics:

- *Ambiguity of a Term in a Relation Instance*: This is determined by the number of triples with the same term and property. So for example, suppose there is a triple *(I1 invented P1)*. If *I1* has 3 patents and *P1* has 2 inventors, Ambiguity of *I1* with respect to the *invented* property is 3 and the Ambiguity of *P1* with respect to the *invented* property is 2.
- *Specificity of a Relation Instance*: This is the reciprocal of Ambiguity of each term. Thus the Specificity of the above relation instance will be $\frac{1}{3} * \frac{1}{2} = \frac{1}{6}$.

Overall, the relevance is based on Specificity of all the relation instances and is determined from a *AND-OR tree*.

There are two main limitations of this approach. Firstly, the a-priori importance of a resource based on the overall information space is not considered during the ranking. Thus, the importance of an inventor or a patent will not be considered when ranking these resources. As Google has shown, the ranking of the search results should not be determined just by the specific query but by the importance of the results in the overall information space. Secondly, according to the above ranking based on the Specificity, an inventor with more patents will have a lower rank!

An interesting Semantic Web querying technique is *Semantic Associations* between Semantic Web resources [19] which can be utilized to identify complex relationships between two resources. [20] discusses strategies to rank these complex relationships. Some of these strategies can also be applied for RDF querying.

3   Semantic Web Resource Importance

In this section we will discuss how we can customize the link analysis algorithms for the World-wide Web to determine the importance of Semantic Web resources.

3.1   Graphical Representation of the Information Space

To fully capture the richness of a Semantic Web, a graphical representation of the information space is required. Let us define a Semantic Web as (C, P, NC) where C are the classes, P are the properties and NC are the normal resources (neither classes nor properties) that are defined for the Semantic Web. For creating the graphs we ignore classes and properties that are not defined in the local namespace (for example *RDF:Resource, RDFS:subClassOf*, etc.) We represent the information space using two graphs: isaGraph and propertyGraph.

IsaGraph. The isaGraph is a directed graph whose vertices represent C, the classes of the Semantic Web. For all triples *(c1 RDFS:subClassOf c2)* defined in the Semantic Web, an edge $(c2, c1)$ is created in the isaGraph. Thus, the isaGraph represents the class hierarchy (*subClassOf* relation) of the Semantic

Web. We ignore triples formed by inference while creating this graph. Note that the *subClassOf* relation cannot be represented as a tree, since a class can have more than one parent.

PropertyGraph. Let P_r be a subset of P, containing only properties whose objects are resources; (that is we ignore properties whose objects are literals). Let R be a subset of $(C \cup NC)$ satisfying the condition:
$\forall (r \in R) \exists (p_r \in P_r)$ such that r is a subject or object of a triple whose predicate is p_r or r is the domain or range of p_r.
The propertyGraph is a directed graph representing the properties defined in the local namespace. Its vertex set is R, the resources that are related to other resources by local properties. An edge from r_1 to r_2 exists in the propertyGraph if any one of the conditions hold:

- A triple (r_1, p_r, r_2) exists in the Semantic Web for any $(p_r \in P_r)$. In other words, an edge is created between two resources in the propertyGraph if they are the subject and object of a triple.
- $(p_r, RDFS:domain, r_1)$ and $(p_r, RDFS:range, r_2)$ exist in the Semantic Web for any $(p_r \in P_r)$. In other words, an edge is created between two resources (classes) in the property graph if they are the domain and range of a local property (and are thus related).

Note that we ignore triples formed by inference while creating this graph.

3.2   Subjectivity and Objectivity Scores

A resource that has relationships with many other resources in the Semantic Web can be considered to be important since it is an important aspect of the overall semantics; the meaning of many other resources of the Semantic Web have to be defined with respect to that resource. In the context of the propertyGraph, vertices that have a high in-degree or out-degree should be considered important.

Kleinberg's hub and authority scores give a good indication about the connectivity of nodes in the WWW graph. It not only considers the number of links to and from a node but also the importance of the linked nodes. If a node is pointed to by a node with high hub score, its authority score is increased. Similarly, if a node points to a node with high authority score, its hub score is increased. Therefore, we calculate scores similar to the hub and authority scores of the propertyGraph to get an estimate of the importance of the resources in the Semantic Web. These scores are called **Subjectivity** and **Objectivity** scores corresponding to hub and authority scores. A node with high subjectivity/objectivity score is the subject/object of many RDF triples.

In the WWW all links are similar and can be considered to be equally important while calculating the hub and authority scores. On the other hand in a Semantic Web links in the propertyGraph represent properties which may not be equally important. For example, consider the property *refers_to* in the example Patent Semantic Web which links a patent to the patents it refers to. The importance of the patent should not be dependent on the number of patents it refers to. However, the importance should increase if it is referred to by many patents. On the other hand, consider the property *invented* in the Semantic Web which links an inventor to a patent. The importance of a patent should not increase if it has many inventors. However, the importance of an inventor is obviously dependent on her patents. Therefore for each property we have pre-defined subjectivity and objectivity weights which determine the importance of the subject/object of the property. By default these scores are 1.0. Properties like *refers_to* will have a lower subjectivity weight while properties like *invented* will have a lower objectivity weight.

We have modified Kleinberg's algorithm to calculate the Subjectivity and Objectivity scores of Semantic Web resources as follows:

1. Let N be the set of nodes and E be the set of edges in the propertyGraph.
2. For every resource n in N, let $S[n]$ be its subjectivity score and $O[n]$ be its objectivity score
3. Initialize $S[n]$ and $O[n]$ to 1 for all r in R.
4. While the vectors S and O have not converged:
   (a) For all n in N, $O[n] = \sum_{(n1,n)\in E} S[n1] * objWt(e)$ where $objWt$ is the objectivity weight of the property representing the edge
   (b) For all n in N, $S[n] = \sum_{(n,n1)\in E} O[n1] * subWt(e)$ where $subWt$ is the subjectivity weight of the property representing the edge
   (c) Normalize the S and O vectors

Our modification is that while determining the subjectivity and objectivity scores of a vertex we multiply the scores of the adjacent vertex by the subjectivity/objectivity weights of the corresponding link. This will ensure that the scores of the resources are not influenced by unimportant properties. For example, a low objectivity weight for the *invented* property will ensure that the objectivity scores of patents are not increased by the number of inventors for that patent. Note that Kleinberg had proved that the algorithm will terminate, that is the vectors will converge, for the WWW graph. It can be also proved that our modified algorithm will converge for any Semantic Web graph.

An important observation is that there is no "preferred direction" for a property. For example instead of the *invented* property we can have the *invented_by* property for which a patent is the subject and the inventor is the object. Thus, depending on the schema, a resource could equally well be a subject or an object. That is, the Subjectivity and Objectivity scores will be affected by the schema. However, the combined Subjectivity and Objectivity scores will be independent of the schema.

3.3   Determining Class Importance

The importance of a Semantic Web class is determined by how well it is connected to other classes. Obviously, this will be dependent on its subjectivity and objectivity scores. If c_1 is a subclass of c_2, all the properties of c_2 should be inherited by c_1. Therefore, the importance of a class should also be influenced by its parents. Because of the transitive property of the *subClassOf* relation, the importance of a class should actually be dependent on all its ancestors. However, we believe that a class should only marginally influence a distant descendent much lower in the *isa* hierarchy. Based on these beliefs, we calculate the importance of a class as:

1. Let *parentWt*, *subWt*, *objWt* be predefined constants that determine the importance attached to the parents, subjectivity and objectivity scores while calculating the importance.
   $parentWt + subWt + objWt = 1.0$
2. If there are no links between class and non-class resources, filter the propertyGraph to include only the classes and the links between them. (In other words, we remove all data resources and their related properties from the propertyGraph). If there are links between the schema and data resources the filtering is not necessary.
3. Calculate the Subjectivity and Objectivity scores of the classes from this graph.
4. Let C be the set of nodes and E be the set of edges in the isaGraph. (Obviously C contains the classes of the Semantic Web).
5. For every class c in C, let $S[c]$, $O[c]$, $PI[c]$ and $I[c]$ be its subjectivity, objectivity, parent importance and importance scores respectively.
6. $PI[c] = \frac{\sum_{(c1,c) \in E} I[c1]}{indegree(c)}$
7. $I[c] = PI[c] * parentWt + S[c] * subjWt + O[c] * objWt$

Thus, the importance of a class is determined by its subjectivity and objectivity scores and the importance of its parents. If $(c_1, subClassOf, c_2)$ and $(c_2, subClassOf, c_3)$, then $I(c_2)$ will be influenced by $I(c_3)$. Since $I(c_1)$ is influenced by $I(c_2)$, it is also influenced by $I(c_3)$. However, the influence of an ancestor on a node is inversely proportional to its distance from the node. It should be noted that we ignore RDF and RDFS vocabulary elements like RDF:Resource while calculating the Class Importance because we are only interested in the classes defined in the local namespace.

In many Semantic Webs, there will be no links connecting the schema (Class) and non-class (Data) resources. Thus there will be two separate subgraphs. If one of these subgraphs is more densely connected compared to the other subgraph, the importance scores of the vertices in the sparsely connected subgraph will be insignificant. To prevent this scenario, if there are no links between class and non-class resources, we filter non-class resources from the propertyGraph while calculating the Subjectivity and Objectivity scores of classes.

3.4   Determining Resource Importance

We believe that the importance of a Semantic Web non-class resource should be determined by how well it is connected to other resources. We also believe that it should be influenced by the importance of the classes it belongs to. Therefore we calculate the importance of a non-class resource as follows:

1. Let *classWt*, *subWt*, *objWt* be predefined constants that determine the importance attached to the classes, subjectivity and objectivity scores while calculating the importance.
   $classWt + subWt + objWt = 1.0$

2. If there are no links between class and non-class resources, filter the propertyGraph to only include the non-class resources in the Semantic Web and the links between them. (In other words, we remove all schema resources and their related properties from the propertyGraph).

3. Calculate the Subjectivity and Objectivity scores from this graph.

4. Let NC be the non-class resources in the Semantic Web. For every resource n in NC, let $S[n]$, $O[n]$, $CI[n]$ and $I[n]$ be its subjectivity, objectivity, class importance and importance scores respectively.

5. Let $noClass[n]$ be the number of triples in the Semantic Web where n is the subject and *RDF:type* is the predicate.

6. $CI[n] = \frac{\sum_{(n, RDF:type, c) \in SemanticWeb} I[c]}{noClass[n]}$

7. $I[n] = CI[n] * classWt + S[n] * subWt + O[n] * objWt$

Thus the importance of a resource r is determined by its subjectivity and objectivity scores as well as the importance of all classes for which the triple $(r, RDF : type, c)$ is defined explicitly in the Semantic Web. Note that the *subWt* and *objWt* constants for calculating the Class and Resource importance are different.

4   Ranking RDF Query Results

Let us now discuss our technique to rank the results retrieved by querying the RDF triples of a Semantic Web. We assume that we are using RDQL [9] as the Semantic Web query language. It should be noted our ranking technique is applicable to other RDF query languages like RQL [7] and TRIPLE [8] also.

As an example, let us assume that for the BioMedical Patent Semantic Web we want to find inventor and assignee pairs who have a patent which has a term belonging to the UMLS class *Molecular_Function*. The RDQL query will be:

```
SELECT ?inventor, ?assignee,
WHERE (?inventor,invented,?patent),
      (?assignee,assigned,?patent),
      (?patent,has_term,?bioTerm),
      (?bioTerm,rdf:type,Molecular_Function)
```

RDQL returns sets of variable bindings matching the query parameters. Each unique set of values for the parameters in the SELECT clause will form a result. Graphs are formed from the triples matching the query criteria for each result. Thus, for our example query, each unique pair of inventors and assignees will be a result and graphs are formed from the triples matching the 4 query criteria for these results. For example, if inventor $I1$ and assignee $A1$ match the query

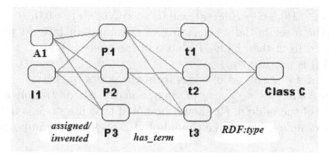

Fig. 1. An example graph for the triples corresponding to one of the results of the example RDF query

criteria, we will form a graph for $I1$, $A1$ as well as the patents invented/assigned to them that have biological terms of type *Molecular_Function*. The Semantic Web resources for the biological terms as well as the Semantic Web Class for *Molecular_Function* will also be included in the graph. Let us assume that Figure 1 is the resultant graph. It shows that the inventor and the assignee pair of $I1$ and $A1$ has invented 3 patents which have terms which belong to the required class. Note that in most cases the graphs will not be very large since users generally specify queries with a few criteria.

We believe that the relevance of the result to the query is dependent on the following factors:

- *Importance of the nodes*: If an inventor or assignee has a high importance in the overall Semantic graph their ranking should be higher. In fact the ranking should be dependent on the importance of all the nodes of the graph. However, if the user is interested in inventors (as determined from the SELECT clause of the query) their importance should be given more weight. We believe that as the distance of a node from the node of interest increases, it should be given less weight.
- *Size of the graph*: If the inventor, assignee pair has more patents the number of nodes and edges in the graph will increase as well as its relevance. So the size of the graph is important to determine relevance.
- *Inverse Property Frequency*: We believe that if a property is very common in the Semantic Web, its corresponding edge should be given less weight. This is similar to the notion of *Inverse Document Frequency* in traditional Information Retrieval which ensures that keywords that are very common in the document collection are given less weight. Therefore for each property we calculate its *Inverse Property Frequency* as:
$log(\frac{N}{n})$ where N is the total number of triples in the Semantic Web and n is the number of triples with that property.

Based on these beliefs, for each result r we calculate two scores $scoreNode(r)$ and $scoreEdge(r)$ from the graph consisting of the triples corresponding to the result as follows:

- Let $decay = 1.0$, $scoreEdge(r) = 0.0$, $scoreNode(r) = 0.0$
- Let Adj be a set initially consisting of the nodes of interest to the user as determined from the SELECT clause of the query.
- While Adj is not Empty
  - Let $Edges$ be the set of edges from the nodes in Adj.
  - $scoreNode(r)+ = \sum_{n \in Adj} Imp[n] * decay$ where $Imp[n]$ is the importance of the node n. (It should be noted that if a node is not a resource, for example a literal like the label of a resource, its importance will be 0).
  - $scoreEdge(r)+ = \sum_{e \in Edges} IPF[e] * decay$ where $IPF[e]$ is the Inverse Property Frequency of the edge e in the $Edges$ set.
  - $decay* = decayFactor$ where $decayFactor$ is a constant less than 1.0.
  - Reinitialize Adj to all the nodes that have not yet been visited and are adjacent to the previous nodes in the set.

Thus for the graph in Figure 1:

$$scoreNode(r) = Imp(I1) + Imp(A1) +$$
$$[Imp(P1) + Imp(P2) + Imp(P3)] * decayFactor +$$
$$[Imp(t1) + Imp(t2) + Imp(t3)] * decayFactor^2 + \dots$$
$$scoreEdge(r) = IPF(invented) * 3 + IPF(has\_term) * 6 * decayFactor + \dots$$

After the scores of all the results are determined, they are normalized and the ranking is dependent on a final score which is calculated as:
$NormalizedScoreNode(r) * nodeWt + NormalizedScoreEdge(r) * edgeWt$
where $nodeWt$ and $edgeWt$ are constants determining the importance attached to the Node score and Edge score and $nodeWt + edgeWt = 1$.

4.1   Effect of Inference

Although RDQL is data-oriented and does not support inference, triples can be created during querying using inference. For example, if the triples *(Genetic_Function RDFS:subClassOf Molecular_Function)* and *(r1 RDF:type Genetic_Function)* are present, it can be automatically inferred that *(r1 RDF:type Molecular_Function)* also exists. Now consider a simple query:

```
SELECT ?bioTerm
WHERE (?bioTerm,rdf:type,Molecular_Function)
```

Various UMLS concepts will be retrieved including *C0017952 (glycolysis)* and *C0040669 (transfection)*. One can argue that the first term is more relevant because the triple *(C0017952,rdf:type,Molecular_Function)* exists in the Semantic Web and no inference is required to retrieve this term during query answering. One can also argue that the second term is more relevant because it is of type *Genetic_Function* which is a subclass of *Molecular_Function* and thus has a more specific meaning.

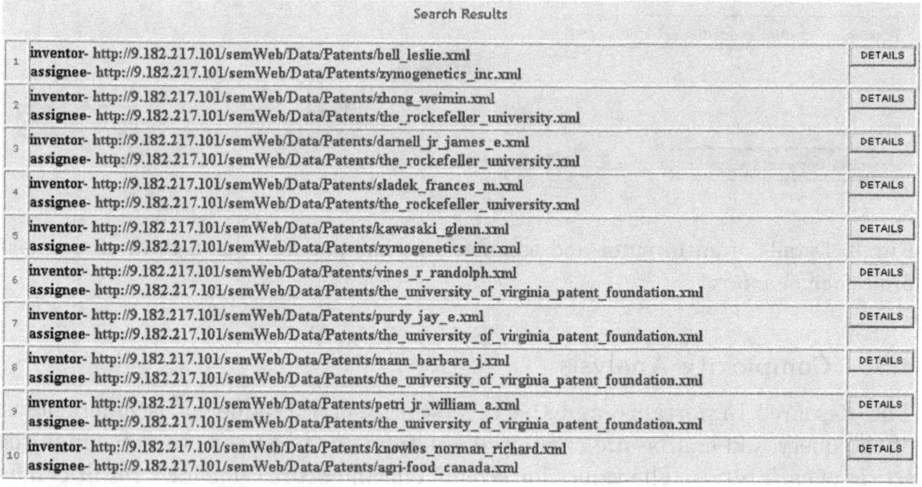

Fig. 2. Results of a search using RDQL ranked by our technique in the BioPatentMiner system

We believe that the effect of inference on the ranking should be determined by the knowledge administrator of the Semantic Web or the user of the system. Our technique allows the inference factor to be rewarded, penalized or ignored. By default the inference factor is penalized and the importance of the node is divided by a constant $inferenceWt$ (> 1). Thus for the result $C0017952$, $scoreNode$ will be:

$$Imp(C0017952) + Imp(Molecular\_Function) * decayFactor$$

while for $C0040669$ it will be:

$$Imp(C0040669) + \frac{Imp(Molecular\_Function)*decayFactor}{inferenceWt*inferenceLevel}$$

where $inferenceLevel$ is the number of inferences required to form the relevant triple. For $C0040669$, $inferenceLevel$ is 1 since $Genetic\_Function$ is a direct subclass of $Molecular\_Function$. However, if the query was to determine all terms of type $Biologic\_Function$, $inferenceLevel$ for $C0040669$ will be 2, since $Biologic\_Function$ is the parent of $Molecular\_Function$.

4.2   Implementation

Our ranking strategy has been implemented in the BioPatentMiner system [4]. For example, Figure 2 shows the results retrieved by our first example query on a collection of United States patents related to *glycolysis*. The resultant inventors and patents that have a patent with terms of class *Molecular_Function* are ranked based on our technique. The user can see the details for any result. For example Figure 3 shows the triples associated with one of the results. It shows that the inventor and assignee pair has two patents which has a term $C0017952$ of class *Molecular_Function*.

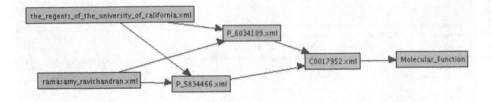

Fig. 3. Details of an inventor and assignee who has patents with a term of the class *Molecular_Function*

4.3 Complexity Analysis

The Resource Importance and the Inverse Property Frequency is independent of the query and can be pre-computed. At run-time one needs to determine the scores of each result. The values for *scoreNode* and *scoreEdge* for a result can be calculated by traversing the corresponding graph of related triples in $O(n + e)$ where n and e is the number of nodes and edges in the graph respectively. Therefore the overall complexity is $O(n + e)R$ where R is the total number of results. Since for most graphs n and e will be small, the overall running time would not be significant. In fact for the BioPatentMiner system, our ranking technique added insignificant overhead to the overall performance of querying using RDQL.

4.4 Example from Another Domain

Let us now determine whether our technique is applicable to a University Semantic Web (similar to the Motivating Example of [18]). Suppose that in this Semantic Web there are classes for *Researcher, Professor, PhdStudent, Project and Topic. Professor* and *PhdStudent* are subclasses of *Researcher*. Moreover, there are 4 properties connecting the resources:

- $<projectA$ **hasTopic** $topicB>$
- $<topicC$ **subTopicOf** $topicD>$
- $<researcherE$ **researchIn** $topicF>$
- $<researcherG$ **worksIn** $projectH>$

Let us also assume that there are the following rules (in addition to RDFS rules):

- $\forall r, p_1, t_2 \ (r, worksIn, p_1) \wedge (p_1, hasTopic, t_2) \Longrightarrow (r, researchIn, t_2)$
- $\forall r, t_1, t_2 \ (r, researchIn, t_1) \wedge (t_1, subTopicOf, t_2) \Longrightarrow (r, researchIn, t_2)$

Now suppose the user is interested in finding all researchers who *researchIn Knowledge Management (KM)*. Let us discuss the relevance of several possible researchers who match the query condition (as discusses in [18]):

- If *ysu* works on just one project in KM and *rst* works in 3 projects all in KM, the graph for *rst* will be larger and thus *rst* most probably will have a higher relevance. (The relevance will also depend on their importance).

- If *gst* is a Professor and *nst* is a PhD student who both work in KM, most probably *gst* will have more relevance since her overall importance may be higher in the Semantic Web (the connectivity of a Professor will generally be higher than a PhDStudent).
- If *nst* works on one project on KM and *meh* works on one project in TextMining which is a subTopicOf KM, *nst* will have more relevance based on our inference factor.
- Now suppose *ysu* works on just one project in KM and *gst* works on 3 projects of which only one is in KM. In our technique most probably *gst* will have a higher relevance since her overall importance may be higher in the Semantic Web (since she works on 3 projects). [18] argues that *ysu* should be ranked higher since she dedicates herself only to KM. Actually, it is very difficult to determine which result should be ranked higher.

Overall, our ranking technique seems to be appropriate for this domain also.

5   Conclusions

In this paper we have introduced a technique to rank the results of a Semantic Web query. The ranking is dependent on a number of parameters like the number of triples relevant to the result, the importance of the Semantic Web resources in the triples, the Inverse Property Frequency of the properties in the triples as well as the effect of inference. Our system has been implemented in the BioPatentMiner system which includes a Semantic Web of Biomedical Patents.

A formal evaluation of the ranking techniques is difficult since there is no standard corpus available for testing. Therefore, we plan to conduct user studies with domain experts to validate the effectiveness of the various techniques to facilitate information retrieval for biomedical patents that are available in the BioPatentMiner. We are collaborating with a Pharmaceutical company for this purpose. We also plan to apply and evaluate our ranking technique to Semantic Webs in other domains.

References

1. Berners-Lee, T., Hendler, H., Lasilla, O.: The Semantic Web. Scientific American (2001)
2. Resource Description Format: http://www.w3.org/1999/02/22-rdf-syntax-ns.
3. Resource Description Format Schema: http://www.w3.org/2000/01/rdf-schema.
4. Mukherjea, S., Bamba, B.: BioPatentMiner: An Information Retrieval System for BioMedical Patents. In the Proceedings of the Very Large Databases (VLDB) Conference, Toronto, Canada (2004)
5. UMLS: http://umlsks.nlm.nih.gov.
6. JENA: http://www.hpl.hp.com/semweb/jena2.htm.
7. Karvounarakis, S., Alexaki, S., Christophides, V., Plexousakis, D., Scholl, M.: RQL: A Declarative Query Language for RDF. In Proceedings of the Eleventh International World-Wide Web Conference, Honolulu, Hawaii (2002)

8. Sintek, M., Decker, S.: TRIPLE A Query, Inference and Transformation Language for the Semantic Web. In the Proceedings of the 1st Semantic Web Conference, Sardinia, Italy (2002)

9. Seaborne, A.: RDQL: A Data Oriented Query Language for RDF Models http://www.hpl.hp.com/semweb/rdql-grammar.html.

10. Brin, S., Page, L.: The Anatomy of a Large-scale Hypertextual Web Search Engine. Computer Networks and ISDN Systems. Special Issue on the Seventh International World-Wide Web Conference, Brisbane, Australia **30** (1998) 107–117

11. Kleinberg, J.: Authorative Sources in a Hyperlinked Environment. In Proceedings of the 9th ACM-SIAM Symposium on Discrete Algorithms. (1998)

12. Chakrabarti, S., Dom, B., Gibson, D., Kleinberg, J., Raghavan, P., Rajagopalan, S.: Automatic Resource Compilation by Analyzing Hyperlink Structure and Associated Text. Computer Networks and ISDN Systems. Special Issue on the Seventh International World-Wide Web Conference, Brisbane, Australia **30** (1998) 65–74

13. Bharat, K., Henzinger, M.: Improved Algorithms for Topic Distillation in a Hyperlinked Environment. In Proceedings of the ACM SIGIR '98 Conference on Research and Development in Information Retrieval, Melbourne, Australia (1998) 104–111

14. Lempel, R., Moran, S.: The Stochastic Approach for Link-structure Analysis (SALSA) and the TKC effect. In Proceedings of the Ninth International World-Wide Web Conference, Amsterdam, Netherlands (2000) 387–401

15. Borodin, A., Roberts, G., Rosenthal, J., Tsaparas, P.: Finding Authorities and Hubs from Link Structures on the World Wide Web. In Proceedings of the Tenth International World-Wide Web Conference, Hong Kong (2001) 415–429

16. Van-Rijsbergen, C.: Information Retrieval. Butterworths (1979)

17. Guo, L., Shao, F., Botev, C., Shanmugasundaram, J.: XRANK: Ranked Keyword Search over XML Documents. In the Proceedings of the ACM SIGMOD Conference, San Diego, Ca (2003)

18. Stojanovic, N., Studer, R., Stojanovic, L.: An Approach for the Ranking of Query Results in the Semantic Web. In the Proceedings of the Second International Semantic Web Conference, Sanibel Island, Florida (2003)

19. Anyanwu, K., Sheth, A.: ρ-Queries: Enabling Querying for Semantic Associations on the Semantic Web. In Proceedings of the Twelfth International World-Wide Web Conference, Budapest, Hungary (2003)

20. Aleman-Meza, B., Halaschek, C., Arpinar, L., Sheth, A.: Context-Aware Semantic Association Ranking. In Proceedings of the Workshop on Semantic Web and Databases, Berlin, Germany (2003)

Querying Faceted Databases

Kenneth A. Ross* and Angel Janevski

Columbia University
{kar, aj311}@cs.columbia.edu

Abstract. Faceted classification allows one to model applications with complex classification hierarchies using orthogonal dimensions. Recent work has examined the use of faceted classification for browsing and search. In this paper, we go further by developing a general query language, called the entity algebra, for hierarchically classified data. The entity algebra is compositional, with query inputs and outputs being sets of entities. Our language has linear data complexity in terms of space and quadratic data complexity in terms of time. We compare the expressive power of the entity algebra with relational algebra. We also describe an end-to-end query system based on the language in the context of an archeological database.

1 Introduction

A number of application domains require the modeling of complex entities within classification hierarchies. For many of these domains, the hierarchy is where the main complexity of the domain is concentrated, with other features of the domain, such as relationships between entities, being relatively simple. We aim to develop a data model and a query language appropriate for such domains.

A *monolithic* concept hierarchy is one in which a single large classification tree is used to represent the application domain. Monolithic hierarchies have been criticized for "rigid hierarchical and excessively enumerative subdivision that resulted in the assignment of fixed 'pigeonholes' for subjects that happened to be known or were foreseen when a system was designed but often left no room for future developments and made no provision for the expression of complex relationships and their subsequent retrieval." [21]

A *faceted* classification, on the other hand, "does not assign fixed slots to subjects in sequence, but uses clearly defined, mutually exclusive, and collectively exhaustive aspects, properties, or characteristics of a class or specific subject. Such aspects, properties, or characteristics are called facets of a class or subject, a term introduced into classification theory and given this new meaning by the Indian librarian and classificationist S.R. Ranganathan and first used in his Colon Classification in the early 1930s." [21]

Computers can make faceted classifications work for search [7, 8]. Once a domain has been classified into a number of orthogonal facets, users can select

---

* This research was supported by NSF grant IIS-0121239.

values for one of more facets independently. As the search progresses, the candidate set of answers shrinks. The computer can give feedback to the user on the current size of the candidate answer set, and can update the search so that categories with no answer candidates in them are not displayed. The user is relieved of knowing the exact classification system used, and can find an object by describing its properties. Systems implementing document search for such data models include Flamenco [4] and FacetMap [3]. A user study of Flamenco is presented in [23]. The use of faceted hierarchies is common among e-commerce sites on the World Wide Web [6]. Faceted classification is a good match for the Semantic Web because it allows access to data using multiple orthogonal dimensions, and because it allows the incremental construction of new facets after the initial schema design, something much more difficult to achieve with monolithic hierarchies.

Our aim is to go beyond a simple search facility for faceted hierarchies, and to provide a *query language* for the formulation of more sophisticated queries.

Relational query languages do not provide built-in facilities for manipulating hierarchies. Hierarchies must be simulated, in ways that are often cumbersome. In a sense, the relational model uses one construct, i.e., the relation, to represent both relationships of entities to one another, as well as the structure of the entities themselves. In domains where the entity structure is the dominant source of complexity, it is natural to make a different design choice, namely to make the "set of entities" the basic data structure. Related formalisms that also focus on sets of entities are described in Section 2.10.

Our Approach

We start with faceted classification as our basis. A domain expert provides the schema, i.e., a collection of orthogonal classifications of the application domain into moderately-sized hierarchies. Our fundamental notion is the "entity set," a collection of (possibly heterogeneous) entities from various classes in the hierarchy.

A query in our "entity algebra" takes entity-sets as input, and produces an entity-set as output. We thus achieve *compositionality*, meaning that the inputs to a query and the output from a query are of the same type, so that complex queries can be build by composing simpler pieces. Since entities of different classes may coexist in such an entity set, the system must determine, from a query expression and from the schema (but not from the data; see Section 2.10), which attributes are available in all entities in the result of a query expression.

We are aiming for a language that, while allowing most queries typical of our target domain, possesses *low data complexity*. A benefit of our approach is that we guarantee linear space complexity and quadratic time complexity for all expressible queries. In contrast, the relational model admits queries that can take polynomial time and space, where the exponent of the polynomial can be proportional to the number of operators in the query.

The capacity of our system to write queries whose answers represent general relationships is limited. This is a deliberate choice. Our primary goal is to make the data model and query language conceptually simple and understandable to users. Being able to represent complex relationships as well as complex entity hierarchies would create a much higher conceptual burden on users, as well as a higher data complexity.

The system informs the user of all attributes that are available for querying. This can require some calculation in a faceted hierarchy, because (a) attributes are inherited from multiple sources, and (b) constraints may imply membership in a more specific class whose attributes then become available. From the user's point of view, this process is transparent: the user is presented with the set of available attributes for each query or subquery.

We compare the expressive power of the entity algebra with the relational algebra. In general, the expressiveness of the two algebras is incomparable. If we focus on "flat" schemas and relational queries that return just entity-IDs, we can quantify exactly what kinds of relational queries we are forgoing in order to get our complexity results. The answer (projections, and joins with cyclic hypergraphs) is reassuring, since such constructs are typically not crucial for queries on complex hierarchies.

Our design has been implemented in two prototype systems. One system supports an archeological database of finds that are organized into a variety of categories. A second system supports a database of human anatomy, that is classified into hierarchies in various ways. Both systems share a common infrastructure corresponding to the model described here. They differ in the definition of the hierarchies (i.e., the schema) and in the actual data stored. Additional domains could easily .be incorporated given a schema and the corresponding data.

In Section 2, we describe our framework, introduce the entity algebra, and assess its complexity and expressiveness. In Section 3 we describe an implementation of our framework. We conclude in Section 4.

2   Framework

2.1   Domain Model

The units of operation for our query language are *sets of entities*. Each query operates on one or more sets of entities and always returns a set of entities. In the archaeology domain, for example, all excavation finds are entities in the database. Each find has many attributes and one of the attributes is the entity type, which can be *object*, i.e., an artifact, or *context*, i.e., a characteristic region of the excavation site.

Entity sets that have explicitly stored entities in them are called *classes*. A schema defines a finite set of classes. Classes have *attributes* associated with them. An attribute has a name and a data type. Each entity in a class must have a *value* of the appropriate type for each attribute. An entity may belong to multiple classes. For example, an object can belong to the class "Pots" and the class "My-Favorite-Objects" simultaneously. Such an object provides values for all attributes of all classes it belongs to. Note that we do not require the

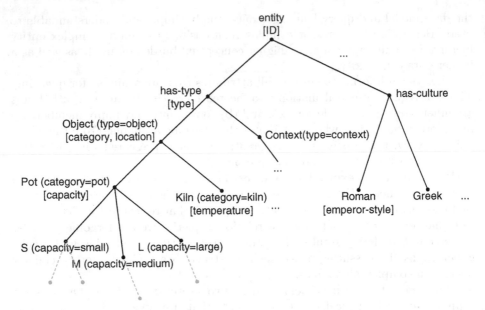

Fig. 1. A Partial Archeology Schema

creation of a subclass "My-Favorite-Pots" to store favorite objects that happen
to be pots. This modeling style is what makes faceted classification different from
traditional object-oriented models of hierarchies. If we did require such classes,
there would be too many of them, as each class could be intersected with an
arbitrary set of other classes. Figure 1 shows a class hierarchy based on our
archeology application. Attributes are shown in square brackets.

Classes may also have *constraints* attached to them. For example, the class
"Big-Pots" might have a constraint on the *capacity* attribute of the pots which
can belong to that class. Note that these are integrity constraints in the traditional sense, and not view definitions. There may be large pots in the database
that, for some reason, do not belong to the "Big-Pots" class. Additional examples
of constraints appear in round brackets in Figure 1. The constraints imply that
Pots and Kilns are disjoint, while an entity may have both Greek and Roman
culture.

Classes are organized into a *hierarchy*. We write $C_1 < C_2$ to mean that C_1 is
a subclass of C_2. This is graphically represented by drawing a line with C_2 above
C_1. The transitive closure $\preceq$ of the subclass relationship is a partial order with
a single maximal element E, which denotes the class of all entities. If $C_1 \preceq C_2$
then all attributes of C_2 are also attributes of C_1. Similarly, all constraints on
entities in C_2 also apply to entities in C_1. The maximal class E has a single
attribute called "ID". All values of the ID attribute are unique. If an entity in
class "Pots" has ID 123, and an entity in class "Roman objects" has ID 123,
then they refer to the same real-world artifact, namely a Roman pot.

Since different classes may use the same name for semantically different attributes, we disambiguate attributes by providing as a prefix the name of the class in the hierarchy from which a class inherited the attribute. So, if both C_1 and C_2 have an attribute *style*, and $C_3 \preceq C_1$ and $C_3 \preceq C_2$, then C_3 has two attributes $C_1::style$ and $C_2::style$. In principle, C_3 could also define its own distinct attribute $C_3::style$. There is no over-riding of attributes. Also, an attribute that is inherited from a single class on multiple paths is not replicated.

While we have not explicitly represented relationships, we note that general relationships can be simulated by thinking of tuples as entities. This is the dual of the relational model, in which entities are modeled as relations.

2.2   Constraints

We assume that a constraint language CL is given. A typical constraint language may allow equalities and inequalities over integers, reals, and strings. Formulas in CL may use as free variables expressions of the form $S.A$ where S is an entity set, and A is an attribute of S. The domain of $S.A$ corresponds to the type of A in S. We assume that CL includes logical conjunction "$\wedge$" and disjunction "$\vee$".

Integrity constraints from CL may be placed on classes. We use the same constraint language to define operators such as selection; see Section 2.3.

We will say that a constraint language CL is *decidable* if the satisfiability of sentences in CL is decidable. Constraint language implementations may benefit from the use of a constraint solving system [15].

2.3   Operators and Queries

A query is formed by applying operators to entity sets to form new entity sets. The user starts with a collection of entity sets defined by the classes in the schema. During a query session, the user can refer to a previously defined entity set as a subexpression. The language defined by the operators below is called the *entity algebra*.

If C is a class, then the query expression C denotes all entities that are members of a class C' where $C' \preceq C$. We allow the following operators where E and E' are entity sets, θ is a constraint with free variables ranging over attributes of E, and θ' is a constraint from CL with free variables ranging over attributes of E and E'.

- $\sigma_\theta(E)$ returns all entities from E that satisfy the condition θ.
- $E \bowtie_{\theta'} E'$ returns all entities e from E for which there is some entity e' in E' such that (e, e') satisfies θ'.
- $E \cup E'$ returns all entities that are in either E or E'; duplicates are omitted.
- $E \cap E'$ returns all entities that are in both E and E'.
- $E - E'$ returns all entities that are in E but not in E'.

This definition of our operators is not quite complete. If E is a class, then it is clear which attributes are available for the conditions θ and θ' above. However, if E is itself an expression, we have not yet explained how to determine the attributes available from E. For example, we need to know how to determine which attributes are available from the expression $C_1 \cup C_2$ which admits entities belonging to two different classes. This issue is addressed in Section 2.4.

We remark that having entities from different classes poses no structural problem in our model. A set of entities can contain entities from many classes, and each entity can have its own set of defined attributes. When one wants to display the entities in the result of a query, each entity can be displayed in a way that is appropriate to its attributes and their type(s). For our application domains, this kind of result structure is much more convenient than a relation. In order to show all attributes of all result entities, a relation would need to have an attribute for each possible attribute of any entity in the result set, with most attribute values being null.

2.4   Attributes of Expressions

The determination of which attributes are available from query expressions is not trivial. We can state a semantic correctness criterion informally as follows: An attribute A is *correct* for a query expression E if and only if, for every possible database instance, every entity in the result of E possesses attribute A. This criterion needs to be slightly refined to allow for the possibility that a query expression is not well-formed. As a result, we formulate a recursive formal definition.

Definition 1. *If an entity set E is a class, then the correct set of attributes for E is the set of attributes defined for that class in the schema.*

Let F be an operator on entity-sets $E_1, \ldots, E_n$, and suppose that the correct set of attributes for $E_1, \ldots, E_n$ has been determined. Suppose that F is well-formed, i.e., that conditions in F refer only to attributes that are correct for $E_1, \ldots, E_n$. Then an attribute A is correct *for the query expression $F(E_1, \ldots, E_n)$ if and only if, for every possible database instance, every entity in the result of the query possesses attribute A.*

Given this semantic correctness criterion, we wish to determine syntactic methods for obtaining the correct set of attributes. We emphasize that it is up to the system, and not the user, to determine the correct set of attributes. As the user incrementally formulates each subquery, the system gives the user feedback about which attributes are available. We illustrate some of the subtleties of determining the correct set of attributes in the examples below.

Example 1. If E is an expression such as $C - C$ or $\sigma_{\text{false}}(C)$ that is guaranteed to be empty, then all attributes are correct for E. Thus, in order to determine the correct attributes for $\sigma_\theta(C)$ we need to know whether θ is satisfiable. Similarly, to determine the correct attributes for $C - \sigma_\theta(C)$ we need to know whether θ is a tautology. If class C has an integrity constraint ϕ, then the above statements apply to $\theta \wedge \phi$ rather than just θ.

Example 2. If C_1 and C_2 are classes, then $C_1 \cap C_2$ should include all attributes from both C_1 and C_2. On the other hand, $C_1 \cup C_2$ should include only attributes that are common to both C_1 and C_2, i.e., attributes that are inherited from a common ancestor in the hierarchy. Note that there may be more than one "least" ancestor, because the hierarchy is not necessarily a tree. A common ancestor is guaranteed by the presence of the class E.

Example 3. In this example we show that correct attribute sets cannot be computed for each subexpression separately, and unioned or intersected incrementally.

Consider three classes S, M, and L representing "small," "medium" and "large" pots, respectively. Suppose that each such class is a subclass of the class Pot, which has an attribute "capacity". Each subclass has a constraint on capacity. For example, class S would have the constraint capacity=small. For the sake of argument, suppose that each of S, M, and L has its own additional attributes.

Consider the expression $(S \cup M) \cap (M \cup L)$. The correct attributes of $(S \cup M)$ would be the attributes of class Pot. The same reasoning applies to $(M \cup L)$. So it would seem that the attributes of Pot are precisely the correct attributes of the whole expression. This reasoning is fallacious. To see why, let us rewrite the original expression as the equivalent expression $(S \cap M) \cup (S \cap L) \cup (M \cap M) \cup (M \cap L)$. The constraints on each subclass mean that the only nonempty term in the union is $(M \cap M) = M$. Thus, the correct set of attributes are those of M, which is a strict superset of those belonging to class Pot.

Example 3 shows that we cannot compute the complete attribute sets via a function g with $g(X \cap Y) = g(X) \cup g(Y)$.

We now describe our initial typing algorithm for queries involving selections, unions and intersections.

Algorithm 1. *We are given an entity algebra query Q, using just selections, intersections and unions. Compute an equivalent query T by (a) pushing the selection conditions down to classes, using the fact that selections distribute over unions and intersections, and then (b) rewriting the result in disjunctive normal form so that T is a union of conjunctive queries. Replace instances of $\sigma_\theta(\sigma_\phi(E))$ by $\sigma_{\theta \wedge \phi}(E)$. Suppose that $T = T_1 \cup \ldots \cup T_n$, where each T_i is a conjunctive query.*

For each T_i, do the following. Suppose that $T_i = \sigma_{\theta_1} C_1 \wedge \ldots \wedge \sigma_{\theta_m} C_m$, where each C_j is a class and each θ_j is a (possibly trivial) condition. If the constraints on the respective classes are $\phi_1, \ldots, \phi_m$, then determine whether $\phi_1 \wedge \ldots \wedge \phi_m \wedge \theta_1 \wedge \ldots \wedge \theta_m$ is satisfiable. If so, compute the attribute set A_i as the union of all attributes in $C_1, \ldots, C_m$.

Return the intersection of all computed attribute sets A_i. If there were no such sets computed, return the universal set of all attributes.

Lemma 1. *Suppose that the constraint language is decidable. Then Algorithm 1 terminates, and computes exactly the correct set of attributes for query Q.*

Proof. *Given the decidability of the constraint language, all steps of the algorithm terminate. To show that the algorithm is sound, suppose that attribute A is output by the algorithm. Then attribute A is possessed by some class in* each term T_i that is satisfiable. Thus, every entity satisfying Q has attribute A. To show completeness, suppose that some correct attribute A was not output by the algorithm. Then for some satisfiable term T_i, no class in T_i has attribute A. Since T_i is satisfiable, there exists a database instance in which there is an entity belonging to all classes in T_i and satisfying the selection conditions of T_i, thus satisfying Q. However, this entity does not possess attribute A, contradicting the assumption that A was correct for Q.

We can extend the algorithm to queries with semijoins.

Definition 2. *Consider a query $E_1 \ltimes_\theta E_2$ where E_1 and E_2 contain just selections, unions and intersections. Using the construction of Algorithm 1, we can obtain a query Q_2 equivalent to E_2 in disjunctive normal form. We abstract Q_2 into a logical formula by forming a logical disjunction of terms, one per conjunctive term in Q_2. Each term consists of the conjunction of the θ and ϕ expressions described in the construction. Let us call the complete formula F_2. We can then "abstract" the semijoin, treating it as if it were a selection $\sigma_{\theta'}(E_1)$, where θ' is defined as $\theta \wedge F_2$. In this formula, free variables from E_2 are assumed to be existentially quantified.*

The abstracted semijoin removes the requirement that matching tuples *actually* exist in E_2, and replaces it with the broader criterion of whether matching tuples *could possibly* exist in E_2. The transformation may introduce extra conjunctions, disjunctions, and free variables, but the decidability of satisfiability in the constraint language is not compromised.

Example 4. Let class C_1 have an attribute X, and suppose classes C_2 and C_3 both have attributes Y and Z. Suppose that C_2 has an integrity constraint stating that $Y = Z$. Then

$$C_1 \ltimes_{X=Y} (C_2 \cap \sigma_{Z<3}(C_3))$$

can be abstracted as $\sigma_\theta(C_1)$, where θ is

$$\exists Y, Z : (X = Y) \wedge (Y = Z) \wedge (Z < 3)$$

which can be simplified to $X < 3$.

Lemma 2. *A semijoin query is satisfiable only if its abstracted semijoin query is satisfiable.*

Proof. *Suppose the semijoin query $E_1 \ltimes_\theta E_2$ is satisfied by tuples e_1 and e_2 in E_1 and E_2 respectively in some database instance. Then e_1 satisfies the abstracted query, with e_2 providing the satisfying values for the existentially quantified variables.*

The converse of Lemma 2 does not hold. To see this, consider the query $(S \cup M) \ltimes_{ID=ID} M$, where S and M represent classes of small and medium-sized pots respectively. The query is equivalent to M, since S and M are disjoint.

All attributes of M are correct. However, the abstracted query does not "notice" that the existence of a tuple in M excludes that tuple from S.

Algorithm 1 is extended by first applying the transformation of Definition 2 to each semijoin in the query in a bottom-up order. The transformed query contains only unions, intersections and selections, and can be processed through Algorithm 1 as before. The soundness argument is a simple extension of Lemma 1 using Lemma 2. Because of examples like those mentioned above, the extended algorithm is no longer complete.

Subtraction seems intrinsically harder than the other operations, due to its nonmonotonicity. A corresponding abstraction process requires a constraint language CL that is closed under negation and universal quantification. Further, we cannot analyze subexpressions of a query independently, because one subexpression might require the *absence* of a certain tuple for satisfiability, while another might require its *presence*.

For subtraction we use a sound, but not necessarily complete method for determining the attribute set. For a query Q that includes subtraction, we form a query Q' by eliminating all subtractions from Q. Every subexpression of the form $E_1 - E_2$ in Q is replaced simply by E_1 in Q'. We then compute the attributes of Q' as above.

The worst-case query complexity of Algorithm 1 is at least exponential in the size of the query, since it has to perform a transformation into disjunctive normal form. The complexity of satisfiability checking in CL also has obvious implications for the complexity of Algorithm 1.[1] Nevertheless, we expect queries to be short, and Algorithm 1 to be useful in practice. In Section 2.5 we show that the language has low data complexity.

Example 5. Consider the schema of Figure 1 and suppose we wish to find all kilns located within a certain distance t of any medium-sized Roman pot. This kind of query cannot be answered by using a conventional search facility; a query language is required. In the entity algebra, we could express this query as

$$Kiln \bowtie_\theta \left(\sigma_{capacity=medium}(Pot \cap Roman) \right)$$

where θ is "$d(Kiln.location, Pot.location) < t$." All attributes of both Pot and $Roman$ are available for use in the selection and semijoin conditions.

The use of a sound but not necessarily complete algorithm for determining the correct set of attributes (for queries with semijoins and/or difference) is deliberate. Our choice allows us to reason solely in the constraint language, without having to perform more elaborate reasoning about the entity algebra itself. This is a more practical short-term goal, given our intention to implement this reasoning mechanism in a functional query interpreter, described later. When the algorithm is not complete, entities in a query result Q may share an attribute A

---

[1] In the event that CL is not decidable, then we are forced to settle for sound but incomplete satisfiability testing in Algorithm 1.

that the system does not perceive is shared. There is a simple way for users to make this attribute available for other queries, namely to intersect Q with the class defining A. Thus, in practice, users are not prevented from writing certain queries.

On the other hand, reasoning solely within the constraint language does not allow the attribute-determining algorithm to take into account constraints (such as foreign key constraints for relationships) that can be expressed only within the entity algebra. Developing algorithms that allow complete reasoning about entity algebra expressions is an interesting direction for future work.

2.5   Data Complexity

One of our initial goals was to choose a language with low data complexity. In this section we demonstrate that all entity algebra queries can be answered in linear space complexity (with constant of proportionality 1), and quadratic time complexity.

Lemma 3. *Entity algebra queries generate output that is no larger than the total size of the union of the input classes.*

Proof. *By induction, the output must be a subset of the union of all inputs.*

Lemma 4. *Union-free entity-algebra queries generate output that is a subset of at least one of the input classes.*

Proof. *By induction; this is a property of all operators other than union.*

Lemma 5. *All entity algebra queries can be computed in time at most quadratic in the total size of the input.*

Proof. *Selection can be computed in linear time. Union, intersection and difference can be computed in $O(n \log n)$ time, where n is the total size of the inputs. Semijoins can be computed in $O(n^2)$ time by simply comparing all pairs of tuples. Given that the size of the output of a subexpression is bounded by the size of its inputs (Lemma 3), the whole query takes at most quadratic time.*

2.6   Language Extensions

Because one of our initial goals was to obtain low data complexity, we do not consider desirable language extensions that increase the data complexity. Similarly, our model is centered around the notion of always returning a set of entities in response to a query. An extension that broadened the types of results, such as to return pairs of entities, would *weaken* the model. We believe that the uniformity and simplicity of input and outputs makes the conceptualization task easier for the user.

We discuss two language extensions that retain the spirit of the entity algebra. The first is the capacity to define new attributes as *views*. For example, suppose that each member of class object has a recorded (x, y, z) position at which it was discovered, in a local coordinate system. We could define new global position attributes (gx, gy, gz) derived from (x, y, z) and the reference point entity coordinates. (Formally, this feature would entail a generalization of the semi-join operator.) These new attributes would be available for all members of class object, including members of its subclasses. If the view was registered in the database schema, then the set of available attributes for entities in each class would be extended appropriately.

The second extension is a form of aggregation. The idea is to allow a limited form of aggregation that corresponds (in relational terms) to grouping by the entity-ID. Thus we could define, for each person working on the site, the number of discoveries made by that person. The result would be represented as a view attribute on class person. To achieve this functionality, we again extend the semijoin operation to allow an optional aggregate computation over the records of the second entity set matching each entity in the first entity set. Neither of these extensions change the asymptotic space or time complexity of the language. They also preserve the central theme of inputs and outputs being entity sets.

2.7   Expressive Power

The expressive power of the entity algebra is incomparable with relational algebra. Relational algebra is capable of expressing queries that return tuples of entities, which the entity algebra cannot. Its space complexity and time complexity are polynomial, as opposed to the linear space and quadratic time complexity of the entity algebra. On the other hand, relational algebra (without nulls) is not capable of expressing a query analogous to Example 3 in which the attributes of class M are available in the result.

Nevertheless, we can compare the expressive power of the two languages in the context of a *flat* hierarchy. Imagine each class as a relation, and consider a query expressed in relational algebra over those flat relations. For comparability, suppose we limit ourselves to relational queries that return a single column of entity-IDs. Under what circumstances can such a query be expressed in our language? The answer to this question will give us a sense of what kinds of relational queries we are giving up in order to obtain our more limited language.

Lemma 6. *Let S be a relational schema in which every relation has a column named ID that is known to be a key. Let Q be a relational algebra query that involves only joins, and suppose $R.ID$ is a column of the output of Q, where R is a relation in S. Then $\pi_{R.ID}(Q)$ is expressible in the entity algebra if the join hypergraph [20] for Q is acyclic.*

Proof. *This result uses a result of Yannakakis [22] (see also [20]). The joins can be ordered so that "ears" [20] of the join hypergraph are removed one by one, ending with R. Because of the special form of the projection (one attribute from relation R), no attributes from an inner subexpression are needed in an outer subexpression, and joins can be replaced with semijoins.*

Lemma 6 suggests that the entity algebra cannot express cyclic joins. The intuition is given in Example 6. Since queries with cyclic hypergraphs are rare, this loss of power does not seem like a major sacrifice.

Example 6. Consider the relational query

$$\pi_{R.ID}(R \bowtie_{(R.A=S.B)\wedge(R.C>T.D)} (S \bowtie_{S.F=T.G} T)).$$

The join hypergraph is cyclic. There is no way to express this query using only semijoins, because no matter which pair of relations we semijoin first, we need attributes from both in the remainder of the query. If we include two semijoins, (e.g., $S \ltimes T$ and $T \ltimes S$) then we lose the association between the S and T tuples.

Theorem 1. *The entity algebra can express any relational query that can be written as a combination, via the set operations union, intersection, and difference, and via local selections, of queries satisfying the conditions of Lemma 6.*

Proof. *Local selections can be pushed down to base relations. Each component query can then be expressed via semijoins as shown in Lemma 6. The set operations operate on just IDs, and can be simulated by corresponding set operations in the entity algebra.*

Since set operations distribute over joins, the class of queries that can be written as described in Theorem 1 is fairly broad. Conspicuously absent from Theorem 1 is the projection operator. Example 7 shows an example where the entity algebra cannot express a relational query involving projection.

Example 7. Consider the relational query

$$\pi_{R.ID}(R \bowtie_{(R.C>F)} (\pi_F S - \pi_F T))$$

where attribute F (belonging to S and T) is distinct from ID. The entity algebra does not provide facilities for projection, and difference can only be applied to entity sets including an ID attribute. Thus we cannot write a subexpression corresponding to $(\pi_F S - \pi_F T)$. Such an expression would not even be an entity set. Further, since $R \ltimes_\theta (S - T)$ is not, in general, equivalent to $(R \ltimes_\theta S) - (R \ltimes_\theta T)$, we cannot write this expression as the difference of expressions that include an ID attribute.

The lack of a projection operator means that all operations apply to entities "as a whole" and not to arbitrary subsets of attributes. This is a reasonable choice in our context, in which entities are the central concept, and manipulations of attributes without reference to their corresponding entities is unlikely to be common.

2.8   Virtual Classes

Consider Example 3, and suppose that we wish to insist that a pot must be classified as either small, medium, or large. If we could represent such information, then we should be able to infer that the expression

$$\sigma_{capacity=medium}(Pot)$$

has type M. Without the extra information, there may be a pot with medium capacity in class Pot (and not in its subclasses), meaning that the type of the expression above would be Pot rather than M.

The intuitive way to specify this extra information would be to formulate a sentence in the constraint language CL stating that any member of class Pot must be in $S \cup M \cup L$. Because such a constraint relates more than one class, it places additional requirements on CL beyond those we have assumed so far. Further, an explicit constraint relating Pot with $S \cup M \cup L$ is vulnerable to schema changes. If another category "extra-large pots" was to be added as a subclass of Pot, then the constraint on Pot would also need to be changed.

Rather than requiring an extended constraint language, we propose a simpler solution to represent the kind of constraint mentioned above. A non-leaf class may be declared as *virtual*, which means that it has no explicit members beyond those of its subclasses. In order to achieve the correct type for a query expression Q, we rewrite Q. A virtual class C mentioned in Q is replaced by the expression $C_1 \cup \ldots \cup C_k$, where the C_i are the subclasses of C. Subclasses that are themselves virtual are recursively rewritten. The resulting query Q' is equivalent to the original query Q on instances in which virtual classes contain no members beyond those of their subclasses. We then type Q' as described in Section 2.4.

Example 8. Consider the query Q given by

$$\sigma_{capacity=medium}(Pot)$$

on the schema of Example 3, but in which we declare class Pot as virtual. We rewrite Q as Q', i.e.,

$$\sigma_{capacity=medium}(S \cup M \cup L).$$

According to Algorithm 1, the type of Q' is M.

2.9   Presentation Layer

While writing queries using the entity algebra allows one to define entity sets in a compositional way, users may like to *display* an answer set using a more elaborate language. Entities should be viewed in ways appropriate to their types. For example, entities with image attributes could have those images displayed. Entities with foreign keys to other entities may have the referenced entity displayed as a component of the original entity. Entities belonging to multiple classes should have the individual displays concatenated in some meaningful way. Entities in an entity set may be heterogeneous; each entity in the set may be displayed differently.

In principle, the presentation language may be more expressive (and have higher complexity) than the entity algebra. We are willing to accept this dichotomy because (a) the presentation language does not have to be compositional, (b) the purpose of the presentation language is different from the query language, and (c) the fundamental constructs of the language may be different.

A familiar example of such separation is the "order by" clause in SQL, which can only be applied at the top-level of a query. A relation is fundamentally an unordered structure. Yet, for the purposes of presentation, users benefit from getting their answers in a particular order. Geographical Information Systems provide another example, where the rendering of the query results is (largely) independent of the definition of the query.

The presentation layer can be developed separately from the query language. Custom presentations of entity sets can be applied at each point in a sequence of intermediate queries, but they will not affect the outcome of subsequent query operations applied to these intermediate queries.

In Section 3 we describe an implementation that makes particular choices about how entities are presented. However, alternative presentation language designs are possible.

2.10   Related Work

Our work is orthogonal to work that looks at how to model domain hierarchies using XML, RDF [2], OWL [5], or some other standard interchange format. Entity identifiers could be URIs. In principle, our query system could use any kind of hierarchy or identifier representation, although it is likely to work best for a hierarchy representation that has an explicitly faceted organization, such as XFML [1].

In systems like Flamenco, there is no formal schema. Entities are tagged with metadata describing their attributes. After a partial search that results in some entity set S, each attribute mentioned by some entity in S is available for further querying. (When a user uses such an attribute, he or she is implicitly limiting the result set to entities having that attribute.) This kind of approach is typical of Information Retrieval applications in which one does not have control over the underlying data. It is also typical of semistructured data models and query languages, although see [17, 18] for ways to infer an approximate schema from semistructured data.

In contrast, we take an approach more typical of conventional structured databases, in which there is a formal schema, and the integrity of the data with respect to the schema can be ensured. For us, an attribute cannot be accessed unless we know that all entities in the underlying entity set possess the attribute. Advantages of our approach include: (a) The correctness of a query statement can be ensured at compile-time, without running intermediate queries. A single overall plan for the final query can be generated, rather than forcing a subexpression-by-subexpression evaluation. (b) The structure of the output of a query does not change in response to data updates. This is particularly important for the correctness of view definitions. (c) Schema conflicts can be resolved. For example, a schema-less system would have difficulty disambiguating metadata tags that happened to share the same attribute name.

Note that we could simulate the Flamenco-style approach by showing all attributes of all entities as part of the presentation language; to process a selection on an attribute A present in just some members of an entity set S, the system can first intersect S with the class defining attribute A.

Tzitzikas et al. describe techniques for identifying meaningful compound terms (i.e., intersections of classes) in a faceted taxonomy [19].

Object-oriented models [16] organize the data hierarchically, and make "objects" the central concept. Like our proposal, every object has a unique identifier. However, object-oriented models are usually extensions of object-oriented programming languages, in which an object has a single type. The only way to obtain objects with the characteristics of multiple types is to define new classes that inherit from multiple parent classes (multiple inheritance). In general, such an approach requires a combinatorial number of classes, corresponding to all semantically possible combinations of classes. More sophisticated approaches to multiple inheritance, such as mixins [11], could be used to simulate the entity algebra, but at the cost of significant conceptual complexity.

Our work can be viewed as an algebraic formulation of a limited description logic [9, 10, 12], with roles being representable by the constraint language. The algebraic formulation allows us to explicitly compare the entity algebra with the relational algebra, and to directly use database engines that implement relational operations. Our representation of hierarchies is similar to that of description logics and conventional semantic data models [14]. An interesting direction for future work is to clarify the expressive power of the entity algebra relative to various limited description logics.

3   Implementation

We now give a brief overview of our implementation to demonstrate how it supports the entity algebra. We have implemented two applications, one based on human anatomy and one based on an archeological excavation. For brevity, we describe just the archeology application, which is being used for a real archeological excavation [13].

Our system stores its underlying information in a special format using a commercial relational database system. A query engine interacts with the underlying database to implement the entity algebra operations. A lightweight client, implemented using Java Servlets, provides a user interface that interacts with the query engine over the Internet through a browser. Data cannot be directly updated; it may be periodically refreshed from the external source database(s).

The query engine takes a query formulated in the entity algebra, expands all subexpressions, and converts the entire query into an SQL query over the stored data. The results of the query are returned to the user interface. The current implementation uses a very simple constraint language: a basic constraint is an equality between an attribute value and a constant. Distinct constants are not equal. Basic constraints can be combined using conjunction and disjunction.

The user interface uses text to express query operations rather than explicitly presenting the algebra, so that users familiar with the application domain (but not with the algebra) can use the system effectively. The interface is de-

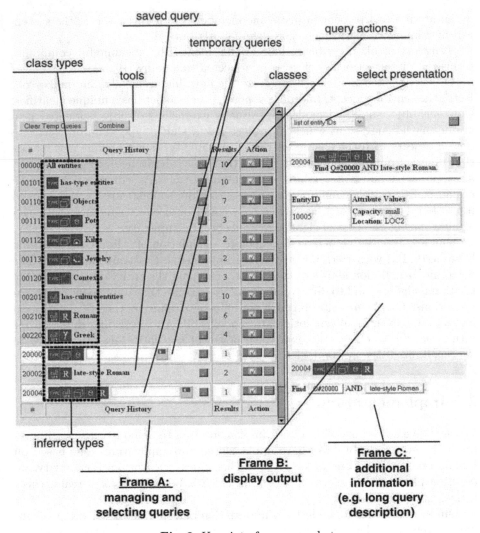

Fig. 2. User interface screenshot

signed so that complex queries can be assembled from simpler pieces, where each piece corresponds to a subexpression in an entity algebra query. Users have access to past query results when formulating subsequent queries. The user interface supports shortcuts, so that frequently accessed classes or subexpressions are pre-loaded into the list of past query results. Commonly used relationships are directly expressed. For example, if selecting objects based on the distance between the object's location and some other location is common, the distance function on points is made available for use within semijoin operations.

The presentation layer is implemented through code plug-ins. As the client application is implemented using Java servlets, the details and style of the presentation can include formatted text, images, audio, and video.

Figure 2 shows a screenshot of the client user interface for the query system. It is a Web-based interface that can be accessed from any conventional Web browser. There are three frames, A, B, and C. The query manipulation area (Frame A) lists the classes as well as the entity sets generated from the user interaction. The content of this frame depends on the number and type of entity sets, and on the stage of completion of a formulated query. The Tools bar contains the currently available actions. The entity sets listed in this frame can be: classes (dark grey background), temporary queries (light grey background), or saved queries (medium-level grey background). This frame is also used to specify operators and attributes while building a new query. For each class or individual entity set, the user interface provides type information in form of a sequence of visual icons. Each type is associated with a number of possible actions either for building a new query, or obtaining additional information.

After executing a query, the resulting entity set is displayed in the output frame (Frame B). This frame also provides tools to select the mode of presentation of the entity set. Any entity set can be viewed in this frame by clicking on the list action icon (▣) in Frame A or Frame B. Frame C contains a simple browser with which the user can navigate through the parts of the hierarchy that were used to arrive at a particular entity set.

3.1   Walk-Through Example

In this section, we will demonstrate the workings of the system by example. We use domain data based on the class hierarchy in Figure 1. We show how the user can find all *Kilns found near medium-sized Roman Pots*, i.e., Example 5. An operation *entity_set$_1$ near entity_set$_2$* is available for all Objects based on the location attribute and a distance parameter. Knowing this, we can find Kilns that are near some object in an entity set with a single query. But we must first build a query that will give us all *medium-sized Roman Pots*. Capacity is an attribute of Pots. We can either first find all *medium-sized Pots* then select only those that are also Roman, or first find all *Roman Pots* then select only those that are medium sized. For this demonstration, we choose the second option.

The interface would start in a state like that of Figure 2, except that only the first ten classes would appear in Frame A. We use the Combine tool (with the AND option) to effectively intersect the classes "Pots" and "Roman". The Combine tool allows ANDs and ORs of an arbitrary number of entity sets. The interface at this point is shown Figure 3.

As shown in Figure 3, Frame A now contains an additional entity set, and Frame B describes the set in terms of entity count, and a textual description of the query that built the set. The newly created entity set also demonstrates the automatic typing, which is evident from the icons in each entity set entry in Frame A. Each icon corresponds to one node in the type hierarchy, and the icons displayed are the union of all icons found on all paths from the entity set to the root of the type hierarchy. For example, the Object type is visualized with the icons ▦▱, the type Pots has icons ▦▱▤, and the Roman entity set contains

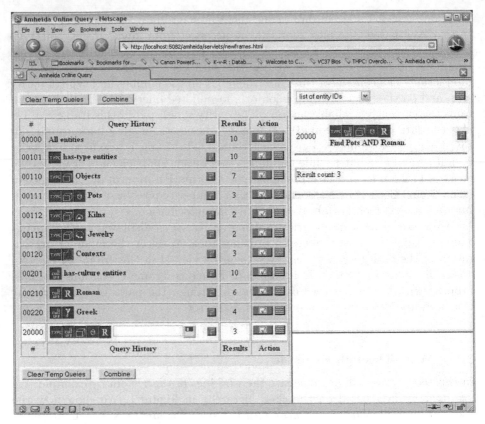

Fig. 3. Intermediate Query: Roman Pots

icons ![icon] ![R]. The new entity set is of type Pots AND Roman, and therefore is
represented by a collection of all icons for the two classes: ![icons].

We can select on the attributes of our intermediate entity set by clicking
on the find action button (![icon]) for the last row of Frame A in Figure 3. The
attributes displayed are precisely those corresponding to the composite type
of the entity set, and therefore include the capacity attribute. We choose the
condition "capacity=medium", which appends another entity set to Frame A
corresponding to medium-sized Roman Pots.

To complete the query, we click on the find action button (![icon]) for the Kiln
class. The options include "Find all Kilns in the same location as ...", which is
chosen. The system then displays all entity sets that could be used correctly to
complete this sentence, i.e., all entity sets having a location attribute. There are
six of these, including the entity set just constructed for medium-sized Roman
Pots, which we select. Figure 4 shows the final result after we have chosen to
save the query (so that it will appear in the user's subsequent sessions) using
the name "Kilns near medium-sized Roman Pots".

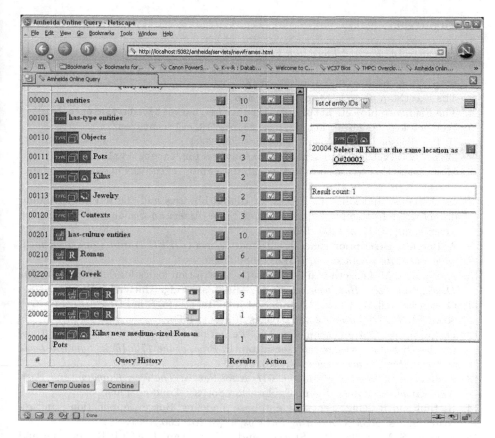

Fig. 4. Final Query Result: Kilns near medium-sized Roman Pots

Our system resolves types as discussed in Section 2.4. The intersection of "Pots OR Kilns" and "Pots OR Jewelry" is determined to have the attributes of Pot, based on a constraint that Pots, Kilns, and Jewelry are mutually exclusive.

4   Conclusions

We have described the entity algebra, a query language designed for posing queries over complex faceted hierarchies. We have examined its complexity and expressive power. It achieves linear space and quadratic time data complexity. Yet it retains most of the expressive power of the relational algebra for queries returning sets of entities; only projections and joins with cyclic hypergraphs are "excluded." An implementation of the language is described, with particular focus on an application in archeology.

References

1. eXchangeable Faceted Metadata Language. `http://www.xfml.org/`.
2. Resource description framework (rdf):concepts and abstract syntax. `http://www.w3.org/TR/rdf-concepts/`.
3. The FacetMap project. `http://facetmap.com`.
4. The Flamenco project. `http://bailando.sims.berkeley.edu/flamenco.html`.
5. Web ontology language. `http://www.w3.org/TR/owl-features/`.
6. H. P. Adkisson. Use of faceted classification, 2004. `http://www.webdesignpractices.com/navigation/facets.html`.
7. M. J. Bates. How to use controlled vocabularies more effectively in online searching. *Online*, 12(6):45–56, 1988.
8. M. J. Bates. Indexing and access for digital libraries and the internet: Human, database, and domain factors. *Journal of the American Society for Information Science*, 49(13):1185–1205, 1998.
9. A. Borgida. Description logics in data management. *IEEE Transactions on Knowledge and Data Engineering*, 7(5):671–682, 1995.
10. A. Borgida, M. Lenzerini, and R. Rosati. Description logics for databases. In *The Description Logic Handbook*, pages 472–494. Cambridge University Press, 2002.
11. G. Bracha and W. Cook. Mixin-based inheritance. In *Proc. OOPSLA/ECOOP, ACM SIGPLAN Notices 25(10)*, pages 303–311, 1990.
12. D. Calvanese, G. De Giacomo, and M. Lenzerini. Description logics: Foundations for class-based knowledge representation. In *Proc. of the 17th IEEE Sym. on Logic in Computer Science*, pages 359–370, 2002.
13. L. Giddy. *The Survey of Memphis II. Kom Rabi'a: The New Kingdom and Post-New Kingdom Objects*. Egypt Exploration Society, London, 1999.
14. R. Hull and R. King. Semantic database modeling: Survey, applications, and research issues. *ACM Computing Surveys*, 19(3):201–260, 1987.
15. J. Jaffar, S. Michaylov, P. J. Stuckey, and R. H. C. Yap. The CLP(R) language and system. *ACM Transactions on Programming Languages and Systems (TOPLAS)*, 14(3):339–395, 1992.
16. A. Kemper and G. Moerkotte. *Object-Oriented Database Management*. Prentice Hall, 1994.
17. S. Nestorov, S. Abiteboul, and R. Motwani. Infering structure in semistructured data. *SIGMOD Record*, 26(4):39–43, 1997.
18. S. Nestorov, S. Abiteboul, and R. Motwani. Extracting schema from semistructured data. In *Proceedings of the ACM SIGMOD conference*, pages 295–306, 1998.
19. Y. Tzitzikas, A. Analyti, N. Spyratos, and P. Constantopoulos. An algebraic approach for specifying compound terms in faceted taxonomies. In *13th European-Japanese Conference on Information Modelling and Knowledge Bases*, pages 67–87, 2003.
20. J. D. Ullman. *Principles of Database and Knowledge Base Systems*. Computer Science Press, Rockville, MD, 1989. (Two volumes).
21. B. S. Wynar. *Introduction to Cataloging and Classification*. Libraries Unlimited, Inc., 8th edition, 1992.
22. M. Yannakakis. Algorithms for acyclic database schemes. In *Proceedings of the VLDB conference*, pages 82–94, 1984.
23. K. P. Yee et al. Faceted metadata for image search and browsing. In *ACM CHI*, 2003.

Constructing and Querying Peer-to-Peer Warehouses of XML Resources

Serge Abiteboul[1], Ioana Manolescu[1], and Nicoleta Preda[1,2]

[1] INRIA Futurs & LRI, PCRI, France
firstname.lastname@inria.fr
[2] Université de Paris-Sud, France

Abstract. We present KADOP, a distributed infrastructure for ware-housing XML resources in a peer-to-peer framework. KADOP allows users to build a shared, distributed repository of resources such as XML documents, semantic information about such documents, Web services, and collections of such items. KADOP2P builds on distributed hash tables as a peer communication layer, and ActiveXML as a model for constructing and querying the resources in the peer network. We describe KADOP's data model, query language, and query processing paradigm.

1 Introduction

The increasing popularity of P2P architectures and Web services as a data exchange mechanism open up new possibilities for building very large-scale data management applications. We describe KADOP[12], a system for constructing and maintaining, in a decentralized, P2P style, a warehouse of *resources*. By resource, we mean: data items, such as XML or text documents, document fragments, Web services, or collections; semantic items, such as simple hierarchies of concepts; and relationships between the data and semantic items. KADOP allows a user to perform the following tasks:

- *publish* XML resources, making them available to all peers in the P2P network and in particular maintain indexing up to date;
- *search* for resources meeting certain criteria (based on content, structure as well as semantics of the data);
- *declaratively build thematic portals* from resources of the system.

KADOP leverages several existing technologies and models. First, it relies on a state-of-the art Distributed Hash Table (DHT) implementation [6] to keep the peer network connected. Second, it uses the power of ActiveXML (AXML) [1], which allows specifying parts of a document as *intensional* (obtainable by activating or finding service calls). In this context, Active XML is used (*i*) for

---

[1] KADOP stands for: *Knowledge and data on a P2P network*.
[2] This work is partially funded by the French government research grant ACI MDP2P.

C. Bussler et al. (Eds.): SWDB 2004, LNCS 3372, pp. 219–225, 2005.
© Springer-Verlag Berlin Heidelberg 2005

intensional indexing; and (*ii*) for supporting a tool to *declaratively specify a thematic portal*, which can be thought of as a partially materialized view over the XML resources of the P2P network. Finally, KADOP employs sophisticate XML indexing and optimization techniques [3] (not covered here).

This document is structured as follows. Section 2 describes the KADOP's data model, and Section 3 its query laguage. We present the system architecture in Section 4, and discuss related work and perspectives in Section 5.

2   KadoP Data Model for Distributed Data and Knowledge

KADOP's data model can be declined in two levels. The *internal* data model is generic, application-independent, and focused on simple resource types. The *application-level* data model can be built as a customized view on top of the internal data model, including e.g. more complex semantic relationships.

The Internal Data Model. The KADOP internal data model, depicted in Figure 1, supports the types of resources that can be published and searched for in our system. We distinguish two kinds of resources: *data items*, and *semantic items*. *Data items* (at left in Figure 1) correspond to various resource types:

- A *page* is an XML document. Pages may have associated *DTDs* or *XML schemas* describing their type; we treat DTDs as sources of semantic items (see further). Other formats such as PDF can be used; we ignore them here.
- We consider data with various granularities. A *page fragment* is a subtree of a page and a *collection* is a user-defined set of data items. Inside pages, we also consider element labels, attribute names, and (composed) words. We will ignore here issues such as stemming and detecting composed words.

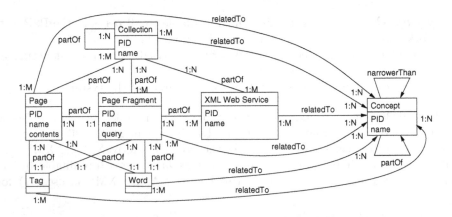

Fig. 1. E-R representation of the internal KADOP data model

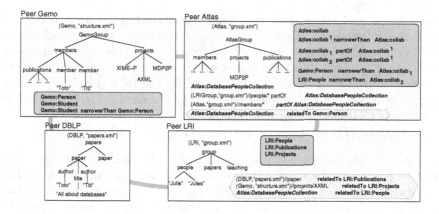

Fig. 2. Sample KADOP instance of the internal data model, over four peers

- Finally, a *web service* is a function taking as input types XML fragments, and returning a typed XML fragment.

Any data item is uniquely identified by an PID (peer ID) and a name. The PID provides the unique name (logical identifier) of the peer that has published the data item, and where the item resides; names allow distinguishing between data items within the peer. Data items are connected by *partOf* relationships, in the natural sense: thus, a word is part of a fragment, a fragment part of a page etc. Furthermore, any type of data items can be part of collections. A data item residing on one peer may be part of a collection defined on another peer.

Semantic items, depicted at right in Figure 1, consist of *concepts*, connected by two types of relationships: *partOf*, and *narrowerThan*. A graph of concepts, structured with *narrowerThan* links, is called a *(concept) hierarchy*. A graph of concepts connected through *partOf* edges is called a *(concept) schema*.

Particular knowledge items are derived by an *implicit conversion of DTDs* associated to pages. From each element type τ in the DTD, we create a concept c_τ; similarly, for every parent-child relationship between DTD types τ_1 and τ_2, we create a *partOf* relationship between c_{τ_1} and c_{τ_2}. This implicit conversion reflects the fact that DTD types may correspond to interesting concepts, and parent-child relationships in DTDs typically reflect complex object nesting.

A data item may be connected to a concept via an *relatedTo* relationship, reflecting the fact that the data item is pertinent to the concept. Such relationships may be produced in three ways. First, they may be specified by a user. Second, they may be inferred automatically between fragments matching a DTD type τ, and the corresponding concept c_τ. Third, they can be derived automatically e.g. by a document classifier, or using relevance functions: above a given threshold of relevance of a data item to a concept, a *relatedTo* relationship is created.We focus on the exploitation of *relatedTo* links.

Application-Level Data Model. For a specific application, it may be interesting to define semantically rich relationships between concepts. Let P_r:*rel* defined by peer P_r, be a specialized binary relationship between concepts. To record this relationship, KADOP creates a new concept $P_r{:}c_{rel}$. Each time an application defines an instance of $P_r{:}rel$ relationship, three new concepts are created: $P_r{:}c_{rel}^p$ which stands for that instance of $P_r{:}rel$ (p represents instance's identifier), and $P_r{:}c_{relk}$, $k \in 1, 2$, which stand for the roles (two in this case) of concepts involved in *rel*. To connect $P_1{:}c_1$ to $P_2{:}c_2$ under $P_r{:}c_{rel}$, KADOP creates the following relationships: $narrowerThan(P_r{:}c_{rel}, P_r{:}c_{rel}^p)$, $narrowerThan(P_k{:}c_k, P_r{:}c_{relk})$, $partOf(P_k{:}c_k, P_r{:}c_{rel}^p)$ where $k \in 1, 2$.

Example. Figure 2 shows a sample instance of the KADOP internal data model, over four peers corresponding to French database labs. A page is depicted as a tree; next to the root, we show the PID and the page name. Rounded boxes contain concepts and relationships between them, published on each peer. Collections, and collection memberships, are listed in italic font, and *relatedTo* statements appear in diamond-shaped boxes. Now assume on the Atlas peer we declare the binary relationship collaborates (*collab*). The instance *collaborates(Gemo:Person, LRI:People)* of this relationship yields the concepts shown in (Figure 2, Atlas peer).

3   KadoP Query Language

The KADOP query language allows retrieving *data items*, based on constraints on the data item and on their relationship with various concepts. A KADOP query Q is a tree pattern, whose nodes represent data items, and whose edges represent containment relationships among the nodes. Each node may be annotated with: (*i*) a data item name (tag, document, or collection name) n, or with a $*$ name; (*ii*) semantic constraints of the form *relatedTo c*, where c denotes a concept, using a name, and either a PID or a $*$; (*iii*) textual constraints of the form *contains w*, where w is a word. We distinguish a single *return node* N_R of Q.

Let G be the instance of the internal data model, consisting of data items, semantic items, and relationships from the whole KADOP network. A *embedding of Q in G* is a function ϕ from Q to G, under the following conditions. First, ϕ must preserve *partOf* relationships among data items: if q_1 is a child of q_2 in

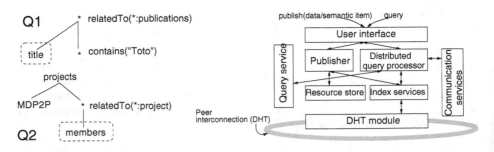

Fig. 3. KADOP queries (left); sketch of KADOP system architecture (right)

Q, then there is a chain of *partOf* relationships going from $\phi(q_1)$ to $\phi(q_2)$ in $\mathcal{G}$. Second, ϕ must preserve the node constraints specified by the query: for a query node q, $\phi(q)$ respects all the tag, text, or semantic constraints associated to q.

We now define the *exact* and *extended* semantics of Q. With exact semantics, for each embedding ϕ, Q returns the node obtained associated to N_R by ϕ. The *extended* semantics of Q is obtained by relaxing the definition of embeddings, to take into consideration also *narrowerThan* relationships. Let $q \in Q$ be a query node, annotated with the constraint *relatedTo c*. With extended semantics, ϕ can associate a node $n \in \mathcal{G}$ to q if n is an instance of a concept c', such that a chain of *narrowerThan* relationships connects c and c'.

Example. Figure 3 (left) shows sample KADOP queries; query nodes are labelled by their names, and the returned node is shown in a dashed-line box. Q_1 returns the title of all papers containing "Toto". Note that we refer to papers as instances of the concept "publications". On the configuration in Figure 2, this concept is defined on the LRI peer; thus, Q_1 returns the titles of DBLP papers containing "Toto", since they are instances of LRI:publications. Q_2 returns all project members, from labs that are members of MDP2P. In Figure 2, this denotes members of the AXML, MDP2P, and XIME-P projects of Gemo.

4   System Architecture and Functionalities

A KADOP peer consists of several modules, depicted at right in Figure 3.

The DHT is in charge of providing the indexing of resources at the physical level. This is achieved by supporting a hash table, in which key-value pairs can be registered using *put(k,v)*, while key lookup can be performed using *get(k)*, with guaranteed bounds on the number of messages exchanged.

Users' requests of publishing a resource are processed by the Publisher. First, the resource is serialized in a standard XML form and written in the local Resource Store. Resource *storage* remains thus under the control of the publishing peer. However, the *resource index* must be distributed over the DHT, to enable all peers to look up resources. To that purpose, the Publisher extracts from the resource a set of *key-value* pairs describing the resource and its location on the peer, and calls the *put* service of the DHT layer. The publisher is implemented as a set of AXML documents [1]; it maintains the P2P index up to date using periodic calls to the *put* service.

To answer a user query, search keys are extracted from the query, and a set of corresponding calls to the *get* DHT service are issued. The calls return locations of resources in the KADOP network, which may contribute to the query result. The Distributed Query Processor then calls the Communication Services, asking for the transfer of the relevant resources to the query peer, and combines them in the final query result. Every peer provides a Query Web Service, which takes as input a KADOP query, evaluates it as above, and returns its (XML-ized) result. A portal on a given topic can be easily built as an intensional AXML document: an XML document including calls to the Query Service [1].

Key-Value Indexing of Graph-Structured Resources. The crux of this architecture lies in the choice of the *key-value* pairs to be inserted in the DHT P2P index. The idea is that *search criteria* (such as category or tag names, precise words etc.) make up keys, while *resource location* (PID and precise location of a resource in the peer) make up the associated values. The complete instance $\mathcal{G}$ of the internal data model over all peers is a graph, with 7 types of nodes and 3 types of edges (corresponding to the entities, resp. relationships in Figure 1). Key-value pairs are extracted from $\mathcal{G}$ as follows:

- For each node $n \in \mathcal{G}$ identified by PID:name, we compute the key concat(nType,PID,name), where nType is a 3-bit prefix specifying the node type. This key can be used for a precise lookup, when both PID and name are known. We also compute the key concat(nType,*,name), to be used for lookups by name only. With both keys, we associate the value concat(PID,location).
- For each edge $e \in \mathcal{G}$, connecting the nodes n_1 (identified by PID_1: $name_1$) and n_2 (identified by PID_2: $name_2$), we compute the keys concat(eType, PID_1, $name_1$), and concat(eType, *, $name_1$), where eType is a 2-bit prefix specifying the edge type. To each of those keys we associate the value concat(PID_2, $location_2$); these key-value pairs allow to search for n_2, if n_1 is known (to traverse the relationship from n_1 to n_2). Finally, we create two symmetric key-value pairs, swapping the roles of n_1 and n_2.

Intensional Indexing. KADOP takes advantage of the intensional aspect of ActiveXML (parts of a document are specified by service calls) to intensionally index resources. The key of an intensional index entry is obtained just as above. However, the value associated to the key is not the location of a resource, but of a Web service that, when called, will return pertinent resources. Intensional indexing is much more concise: a single intensional index entry replaces several extensional (regular) entries, at the expense of one extra service call.

5   Related Works and Perspectives

We are currently implementing the system described here using Pastry [6] and AXML [1]. Our system is related to XML-based P2P frameworks [1,7,13] and semantic P2P networks [8,10]. KADOP improves over [1,13] by using a DHT layer allowing each peer to search for resources anywhere in the P2P network. Differently from [1,13,7], we set data and knowledge items on equal levels as first-class citizens. The SPIN project [12] addressed building a semantic warehouse of Web resources; in contrast, KADOP focuses on a decentralized P2P context. More motivations for the work presented here may be found in [2].

Semantic data management in P2P has been addressed in [5,8,10]; KADOP is different since it relies on a DHT symmetric network, providing each peer direct resource lookup. In contrast, the work described in [10] considers a two-layer hierarchical peer organization. Another difference is that KADOP's query language simultaneously exploits structure, contents, and semantic information.

The conceptual part of our internal data model can be seen as a subset of models such as RDF [11] or description logics [8]; many languages and platforms for querying such resources exist [4, 9]. More restricted in this aspect, our query language does not directly support e.g. navigation along customized semantic relationships (although our P2P index does). We plan to explore the tradeoff between P2P efficient evaluation, and semantic expressivity, in the near future.

References

1. ActiveXML home page. http://purl.org/net/axml.
2. S. Abiteboul. Managing an XML warehouse in a P2P context. In *Int'l Conference on Advanced Information Systems Engineering*, 2003.
3. Vincent Aguilera, Frédéric Boiscuvier, and Sophie Cluet. Pattern tree queries in Xyleme. Gemo report no. 200, osage.inria.fr/gemo/Gemo/PUBLI, 2001.
4. B. Amann, C. Beeri, I. Fundulaki, and M. Scholl. Querying XML sources using an ontology-based mediator. In *Proc. of CoopIS*, pages 429–448, 2002.
5. A. Crespo and H. Garcia-Molina. Routing indices for Peer-to-Peer systems. In *Int'l Conf. on Distributed Computing Systems*, pages 23–34, 2002.
6. The FreePastry system. www.cs.rice.edu/CS/Systems/Pastry/FreePastry/.
7. L. Galanis, Y. Wang, S. Jeffery, and D. DeWitt. Locating data sources in large distributed systems. In *Proc. of the VLDB Conf.*, 2003.
8. F. Goasdoué and M-C. Rousset. Answering queries using views: a KRDB perspective for the Semantic Web. *ACM TOIT*, 2003.
9. G. Karvounaraki, S. Alexaki, V. Christophides, D. Plexousakis, and M. Scholl. RQL: a declarative query language for RDF. In *Proc. of WWW Conf.*, 2002.
10. W. Nejdl, M. Wolpers, W. Siberski, C. Schmitz, M. Schlosser, I. Brunkhorst, and A. Loser. Super-peer-based routing and clustering strategies for RDF-based peer-to-peer networks. In *WWW Conference*, pages 536–543, 2003.
11. The resource description framework. www.w3.org/RDF.
12. B. Nguyen S. Abiteboul, G. Cobéna and A. Poggi. Construction of sets of pages of interest. In *Bases de Donnees Avancees*, Evry, 2002.
13. I. Tatarinov and A. Halevy. Efficient query reformulation in peer-data management systems. In *Proc. of the ACM SIGMOD Conf.*, 2004.

Author Index

Abiteboul, Serge   219
An, Yuan   84

Bamba, Bhuvan   185
Benatallah, Boualem   1
Borgida, Alexander   9, 84
Bowers, Shawn   57
Buczak, Anna L.   27

Calì, Andrea   167
Caragea, Doina   41
Czajkowski, Michael   27

De Bo, Jan   109

Hofmann, Martin O.   27
Honavar, Vasant G.   41

Janevski, Angel   199

Kotis, Konstantinos   155

Lin, Zuoquan   64
Liu, Shengping   64
Ludäscher, Bertram   57

Madnick, Stuart E.   127, 140
Manolescu, Ioana   219

Meersman, Robert   109
Mei, Jing   64
Mukherjea, Sougata   185
Mylopoulos, John   9, 84

Nezhad, H.R. Motahari   1

Padilla Alonso, Jerónimo   155
Pathak, Jyotishman   41
Preda, Nicoleta   219

Robertson, Edward L.   91
Ross, Kenneth A.   199

Siegel, Michael D.   127

Tan, Kian-Lee   140
Tan, Philip   140
Thau, David   57

Verheyden, Pieter   109
Vouros, George   155

Williams, Rich   57

Yue, Anbu   64

Zhu Hongwei   127

Lecture Notes in Computer Science

For information about Vols. 1–3296

please contact your bookseller or Springer

Vol. 3418: U. Brandes, T. Erlebach (Eds.), Network Analysis. XII, 471 pages. 2005.

Vol. 3412: X. Franch, D. Port (Eds.), COTS-Based Software Systems. XVI, 312 pages. 2005.

Vol. 3406: A. Gelbukh (Ed.), Computational Linguistics and Intelligent Text Processing. XVII, 829 pages. 2005.

Vol. 3404: V. Diekert, B. Durand (Eds.), STACS 2005. XVI, 706 pages. 2005.

Vol. 3403: B. Ganter, R. Godin (Eds.), Formal Concept Analysis. XI, 419 pages. 2005. (Subseries LNAI).

Vol. 3398: D.-K. Baik (Ed.), Systems Modeling and Simulation: Theory and Applications. XIV, 733 pages. 2005. (Subseries LNAI).

Vol. 3397: T.G. Kim (Ed.), Artificial Intelligence and Simulation. XV, 711 pages. 2005. (Subseries LNAI).

Vol. 3393: H.-J. Kreowski, U. Montanari, F. Orejas, G. Rozenberg, G. Taentzer (Eds.), Formal Methods in Software and Systems Modeling. XXVII, 413 pages. 2005.

Vol. 3391: C. Kim (Ed.), Information Networking. XVII, 936 pages. 2005.

Vol. 3388: J. Lagergren (Ed.), Comparative Genomics. VIII, 133 pages. 2005. (Subseries LNBI).

Vol. 3387: J. Cardoso, A. Sheth (Eds.), Semantic Web Services and Web Process Composition. VIII, 147 pages. 2005.

Vol. 3386: S. Vaudenay (Ed.), Public Key Cryptography - PKC 2005. IX, 436 pages. 2005.

Vol. 3385: R. Cousot (Ed.), Verification, Model Checking, and Abstract Interpretation. XII, 483 pages. 2005.

Vol. 3382: J. Odell, P. Giorgini, J.P. Müller (Eds.), Agent-Oriented Software Engineering V. X, 239 pages. 2005.

Vol. 3381: P. Vojtáš, M. Bieliková, B. Charron-Bost, O. Sýkora (Eds.), SOFSEM 2005: Theory and Practice of Computer Science. XV, 448 pages. 2005.

Vol. 3379: M. Hemmje, C. Niederee, T. Risse (Eds.), From Integrated Publication and Information Systems to Information and Knowledge Environments. XXIV, 321 pages. 2005.

Vol. 3378: J. Kilian (Ed.), Theory of Cryptography. XII, 621 pages. 2005.

Vol. 3376: A. Menezes (Ed.), Topics in Cryptology – CT-RSA 2005. X, 385 pages. 2004.

Vol. 3375: M.A. Marsan, G. Bianchi, M. Listanti, M. Meo (Eds.), Quality of Service in Multiservice IP Networks. XIII, 656 pages. 2005.

Vol. 3374: D. Weyns, H.V.D. Parunak, F. Michel (Eds.), Environments for Multi-Agent Systems. X, 279 pages. 2005. (Subseries LNAI).

Vol. 3372: C. Bussler, V. Tannen, I. Fundulaki (Eds.), Semantic Web and Databases. X, 227 pages. 2005.

Vol. 3368: L. Paletta, J.K. Tsotsos, E. Rome, G.W. Humphreys (Eds.), Attention and Performance in Computational Vision. VIII, 231 pages. 2005.

Vol. 3366: I. Rahwan, P. Moraitis, C. Reed (Eds.), Argumentation in Multi-Agent Systems. XII, 263 pages. 2005. (Subseries LNAI).

Vol. 3363: T. Eiter, L. Libkin (Eds.), Database Theory - ICDT 2005. XI, 413 pages. 2004.

Vol. 3362: G. Barthe, L. Burdy, M. Huisman, J.-L. Lanet, T. Muntean (Eds.), Construction and Analysis of Safe, Secure, and Interoperable Smart Devices. IX, 257 pages. 2005.

Vol. 3361: S. Bengio, H. Bourlard (Eds.), Machine Learning for Multimodal Interaction. XII, 362 pages. 2005.

Vol. 3360: S. Spaccapietra, E. Bertino, S. Jajodia, R. King, D. McLeod, M.E. Orlowska, L. Strous (Eds.), Journal on Data Semantics II. XI, 223 pages. 2004.

Vol. 3359: G. Grieser, Y. Tanaka (Eds.), Intuitive Human Interfaces for Organizing and Accessing Intellectual Assets. XIV, 257 pages. 2005. (Subseries LNAI).

Vol. 3358: J. Cao, L.T. Yang, M. Guo, F. Lau (Eds.), Parallel and Distributed Processing and Applications. XXIV, 1058 pages. 2004.

Vol. 3357: H. Handschuh, M.A. Hasan (Eds.), Selected Areas in Cryptography. XI, 354 pages. 2004.

Vol. 3356: G. Das, V.P. Gulati (Eds.), Intelligent Information Technology. XII, 428 pages. 2004.

Vol. 3355: R. Murray-Smith, R. Shorten (Eds.), Switching and Learning in Feedback Systems. X, 343 pages. 2005.

Vol. 3353: J. Hromkovič, M. Nagl, B. Westfechtel (Eds.), Graph-Theoretic Concepts in Computer Science. XI, 404 pages. 2004.

Vol. 3352: C. Blundo, S. Cimato (Eds.), Security in Communication Networks. XI, 381 pages. 2005.

Vol. 3350: M. Hermenegildo, D. Cabeza (Eds.), Practical Aspects of Declarative Languages. VIII, 269 pages. 2005.

Vol. 3349: B.M. Chapman (Ed.), Shared Memory Parallel Programming with Open MP. X, 149 pages. 2005.

Vol. 3348: A. Canteaut, K. Viswanathan (Eds.), Progress in Cryptology - INDOCRYPT 2004. XIV, 431 pages. 2004.

Vol. 3347: R.K. Ghosh, H. Mohanty (Eds.), Distributed Computing and Internet Technology. XX, 472 pages. 2004.

Vol. 3346: R.H. Bordini, M. Dastani, J. Dix, A.E.F. Seghrouchni (Eds.), Programming Multi-Agent Systems. XIV, 249 pages. 2005. (Subseries LNAI).

Vol. 3345: Y. Cai (Ed.), Ambient Intelligence for Scientific Discovery. XII, 311 pages. 2005. (Subseries LNAI).

Vol. 3344: J. Malenfant, B.M. Østvold (Eds.), Object-Oriented Technology. ECOOP 2004 Workshop Reader. VIII, 215 pages. 2005.

Vol. 3342: E. Şahin, W.M. Spears (Eds.), Swarm Robotics. IX, 175 pages. 2005.

Vol. 3341: R. Fleischer, G. Trippen (Eds.), Algorithms and Computation. XVII, 935 pages. 2004.

Vol. 3340: C.S. Calude, E. Calude, M.J. Dinneen (Eds.), Developments in Language Theory. XI, 431 pages. 2004.

Vol. 3339: G.I. Webb, X. Yu (Eds.), AI 2004: Advances in Artificial Intelligence. XXII, 1272 pages. 2004. (Subseries LNAI).

Vol. 3338: S.Z. Li, J. Lai, T. Tan, G. Feng, Y. Wang (Eds.), Advances in Biometric Person Authentication. XVIII, 699 pages. 2004.

Vol. 3337: J.M. Barreiro, F. Martin-Sanchez, V. Maojo, F. Sanz (Eds.), Biological and Medical Data Analysis. XI, 508 pages. 2004.

Vol. 3336: D. Karagiannis, U. Reimer (Eds.), Practical Aspects of Knowledge Management. X, 523 pages. 2004. (Subseries LNAI).

Vol. 3335: M. Malek, M. Reitenspieß, J. Kaiser (Eds.), Service Availability. X, 213 pages. 2005.

Vol. 3334: Z. Chen, H. Chen, Q. Miao, Y. Fu, E. Fox, E.-p. Lim (Eds.), Digital Libraries: International Collaboration and Cross-Fertilization. XX, 690 pages. 2004.

Vol. 3333: K. Aizawa, Y. Nakamura, S. Satoh (Eds.), Advances in Multimedia Information Processing - PCM 2004, Part III. XXXV, 785 pages. 2004.

Vol. 3332: K. Aizawa, Y. Nakamura, S. Satoh (Eds.), Advances in Multimedia Information Processing - PCM 2004, Part II. XXXVI, 1051 pages. 2004.

Vol. 3331: K. Aizawa, Y. Nakamura, S. Satoh (Eds.), Advances in Multimedia Information Processing - PCM 2004, Part I. XXXVI, 667 pages. 2004.

Vol. 3330: J. Akiyama, E.T. Baskoro, M. Kano (Eds.), Combinatorial Geometry and Graph Theory. VIII, 227 pages. 2005.

Vol. 3329: P.J. Lee (Ed.), Advances in Cryptology - ASIACRYPT 2004. XVI, 546 pages. 2004.

Vol. 3328: K. Lodaya, M. Mahajan (Eds.), FSTTCS 2004: Foundations of Software Technology and Theoretical Computer Science. XVI, 532 pages. 2004.

Vol. 3327: Y. Shi, W. Xu, Z. Chen (Eds.), Data Mining and Knowledge Management. XIII, 263 pages. 2005. (Subseries LNAI).

Vol. 3326: A. Sen, N. Das, S.K. Das, B.P. Sinha (Eds.), Distributed Computing - IWDC 2004. XIX, 546 pages. 2004.

Vol. 3325: C.H. Lim, M. Yung (Eds.), Information Security Applications. XI, 472 pages. 2005.

Vol. 3323: G. Antoniou, H. Boley (Eds.), Rules and Rule Markup Languages for the Semantic Web. X, 215 pages. 2004.

Vol. 3322: R. Klette, J. Žunić (Eds.), Combinatorial Image Analysis. XII, 760 pages. 2004.

Vol. 3321: M.J. Maher (Ed.), Advances in Computer Science - ASIAN 2004. XII, 510 pages. 2004.

Vol. 3320: K.-M. Liew, H. Shen, S. See, W. Cai (Eds.), Parallel and Distributed Computing: Applications and Technologies. XXIV, 891 pages. 2004.

Vol. 3319: D. Amyot, A.W. Williams (Eds.), Telecommunications and beyond: Modeling and Analysis of Reactive, Distributed, and Real-Time Systems. XII, 301 pages. 2005.

Vol. 3318: E. Eskin, C. Workman (Eds.), Regulatory Genomics. VIII, 115 pages. 2005. (Subseries LNBI).

Vol. 3317: M. Domaratzki, A. Okhotin, K. Salomaa, S. Yu (Eds.), Implementation and Application of Automata. XII, 336 pages. 2005.

Vol. 3316: N.R. Pal, N.K. Kasabov, R.K. Mudi, S. Pal, S.K. Parui (Eds.), Neural Information Processing. XXX, 1368 pages. 2004.

Vol. 3315: C. Lemaître, C.A. Reyes, J.A. González (Eds.), Advances in Artificial Intelligence – IBERAMIA 2004. XX, 987 pages. 2004. (Subseries LNAI).

Vol. 3314: J. Zhang, J.-H. He, Y. Fu (Eds.), Computational and Information Science. XXIV, 1259 pages. 2004.

Vol. 3313: C. Castelluccia, H. Hartenstein, C. Paar, D. Westhoff (Eds.), Security in Ad-hoc and Sensor Networks. VIII, 231 pages. 2005.

Vol. 3312: A.J. Hu, A.K. Martin (Eds.), Formal Methods in Computer-Aided Design. XI, 445 pages. 2004.

Vol. 3311: V. Roca, F. Rousseau (Eds.), Interactive Multimedia and Next Generation Networks. XIII, 287 pages. 2004.

Vol. 3310: U.K. Wiil (Ed.), Computer Music Modeling and Retrieval. XI, 371 pages. 2005.

Vol. 3309: C.-H. Chi, K.-Y. Lam (Eds.), Content Computing. XII, 510 pages. 2004.

Vol. 3308: J. Davies, W. Schulte, M. Barnett (Eds.), Formal Methods and Software Engineering. XIII, 500 pages. 2004.

Vol. 3307: C. Bussler, S.-k. Hong, W. Jun, R. Kaschek, D.. Kinshuk, S. Krishnaswamy, S.W. Loke, D. Oberle, D. Richards, A. Sharma, Y. Sure, B. Thalheim (Eds.), Web Information Systems – WISE 2004 Workshops. XV, 277 pages. 2004.

Vol. 3306: X. Zhou, S. Su, M.P. Papazoglou, M.E. Orlowska, K.G. Jeffery (Eds.), Web Information Systems – WISE 2004. XVII, 745 pages. 2004.

Vol. 3305: P.M.A. Sloot, B. Chopard, A.G. Hoekstra (Eds.), Cellular Automata. XV, 883 pages. 2004.

Vol. 3303: J.A. López, E. Benfenati, W. Dubitzky (Eds.), Knowledge Exploration in Life Science Informatics. X, 249 pages. 2004. (Subseries LNAI).

Vol. 3302: W.-N. Chin (Ed.), Programming Languages and Systems. XIII, 453 pages. 2004.

Vol. 3300: L. Bertossi, A. Hunter, T. Schaub (Eds.), Inconsistency Tolerance. VII, 295 pages. 2005.

Vol. 3299: F. Wang (Ed.), Automated Technology for Verification and Analysis. XII, 506 pages. 2004.

Vol. 3298: S.A. McIlraith, D. Plexousakis, F. van Harmelen (Eds.), The Semantic Web – ISWC 2004. XXI, 841 pages. 2004.